Virtual Music

Virtual Music

*Sound, Music, and Image
in the Digital Era*

Shara Rambarran

BLOOMSBURY ACADEMIC
NEW YORK • LONDON • OXFORD • NEW DELHI • SYDNEY

BLOOMSBURY ACADEMIC
Bloomsbury Publishing Inc
1385 Broadway, New York, NY 10018, USA
50 Bedford Square, London, WC1B 3DP, UK
29 Earlsfort Terrace, Dublin 2, Ireland

BLOOMSBURY, BLOOMSBURY ACADEMIC and the Diana logo are
trademarks of Bloomsbury Publishing Plc

First published in the United States of America 2021

Cover design by Alex Robbins
Cover photo by Claire Greenway/Getty Images

Library of Congress Cataloging-in-Publication Data

Names: Rambarran, Shara, author.
Title: Virtual music: sound, music, and image in the digital era / Shara Rambarran.
Description: New York City: Bloomsbury Academic, 2021. | Includes
bibliographical references and index. | Summary: "A survey of key areas related
to digital music and the internet with a focus on how technology impacts
the relationship between music and its listeners"– Provided by publisher.
Identifiers: LCCN 2020039614 | ISBN 9781501333606 (hardback) |
ISBN 9781501333613 (epub) | ISBN 9781501333620 (pdf)
Subjects: LCSH: Music and technology. | Music–Social aspects. | Music and
the Internet. | Virtual reality. | Mixed reality. | Sound recording industry.
Classification: LCC ML3916 .R36 2021 | DDC 780.285/65–dc23
LC record available at https://lccn.loc.gov/2020039614

ISBN: HB: 978-1-5013-3360-6
       PB: 978-1-5013-3637-9
       ePDF: 978-1-5013-3362-0
       eBook: 978-1-5013-3361-3

Typeset by Deanta Global Publishing Services, Chennai, India
Printed and bound in the United States of America

To find out more about our authors and books visit www.bloomsbury.com and
sign up for our newsletters.

This book is dedicated to Mum and Bobby.

CONTENTS

FIGURES

ACKNOWLEDGMENTS

To begin, I want to sincerely thank Bloomsbury, especially Leah Babb-Rosenfeld for her patience and support, and for the opportunity; Rachel Moore for her help; the production team; and the peer reviewers of my book and its original proposal. I am eternally grateful to the following who have genuinely supported my work for many years, and who would be very familiar with the discussions that are presented in this book: Derek B. Scott, Stan Hawkins, Benjamin Halligan, Eirik Askerøi, Andrew Blake, Mike Dines, Katia Isakoff, Alex Stevenson, Simon Zagorski-Thomas, and the Art of Record Production family. Special thanks to George McKay, Richard James Burgess, Gareth Palmer, Timothy Warner, Matt Grimes, Craig Hamilton, and Tom Attah. I am very grateful to David Sanjek, Jan Fairley, Nathan Wiseman-Trowse, Stuart Meads, and Sheila Whiteley—even though they are no longer here, I will never forget how much they supported my work. I would like to thank the following who knew about this book and who in their own way have supported me, whether it is assisting with my enquiries, reading draft chapters, or really encouraging me to "get this book done!": Hillegonda Rietveld, D Ferrett, Zoe Bond, Louise Jackson, Pogus Caesar, Johnny Hopkins, Justin Gagen, Chris Christodoulou, Russ Bestley, Paul Scott, Gareth Dylan Smith, Mark Whelan, and Paul Gilroy. In addition, I would like to thank Kris Maddigan, Paul Novotny, and Rob Toulson, for their wonderful conversations regarding this book, and StudioMDHR's Ryan Moldenhauer and Chad Moldenhauer for their help. I would also like to thank Bader International Study Centre (Queen's University), my students, and my friends. My heartfelt thanks to my following friends who supported me in the final preparation of this book: Jennifer Ringwood for image editing and for the naughty giggles, and Lucinda Hawksley for reading and editing my manuscript, and for always giving me words of encouragement. To my mum and my brother Bobby, thank you so much for your continuous support, patience, and love.

Introduction

The Future of Music Has Arrived

Connected, Broadcast, Ghetto Blast, Dig it All, Digital . . .
—FINLEY QUAYE[1]

Virtuality has entered and saturated our lives, making anything we desire, possible. If we choose to (and, indeed, are fortunate to have access to), we can indulge in running our everyday lives with digital technology, whether it is for communicating, online shopping, reading, studying, paying bills, assisting with our needs, or listening to music on the go—anything can be found online. This leads to the famous line sung by Gorillaz, that the "digital won't let [us] go"[2]—most of us cannot cope without digital technology. The concept and the interplay of digital and virtual, virtual and digital, digital virtual, digital, or virtual (etcetera) is complex to define and understand, but somehow we are perhaps all guilty of freely applying the terms in everyday conversation without justifying their usage. For now, a way of understanding these terms is to consider that our creative thoughts and imagination (i.e., the virtual) can be either transformed or *nearly* transformed into reality and actuality through digital means.

To apply this concept in music, the creation and arrangement of sounds have mostly been solely reliant on and manipulated with digital technology; this has transformed musical practices in culture and society. In the twenty-first century, traditional rules and conventions of music creation, consumption, distribution, and performance have been erased and substituted with exciting and unthinkable methods, where anybody— yes anybody, not just professional and amateur musicians—can explore, enjoy, and participate in creating and listening to music. Digital technology, including the internet, is rapidly evolving, and continues to make an impact on music creativity, industry, culture, and society.

We are also experiencing and witnessing a technoscape[3] where we can access, exchange, receive, or send information immediately, without having to think about restricted boundaries in distance, location, time, and space, as these previous barriers have now been annihilated,[4] thanks to digital technology. Provided we have access to such technologies, we do not have to overly plan or wait to acquire information. Furthermore, we are going through a digital era in which we can indulge in a virtual environment from our personal space. In other words, we are not restricted as to where we must be situated, as long we have a decent internet connection, and in the case of music, we can unite with, or witness musicians and audience/consumers interacting, uniting, and championing existing and new musical creations. It is no surprise then, that the musician and audience/consumer relationship is now rarely separated, as together they can participate at anytime and anywhere in virtual inventions and collaborations. This is aided by digital technology such as the use of musical instruments or machines, software, and apps. We can participate in a virtual jam or online recording projects where music is created or performed "live"—either simulated, or in real life/time in cyberspace.

We must not, however, forget that experimenting with music in the digital era is not only about what we hear but also about what we "see" and "feel." There is a fascination surrounding "live" virtual artists presented in virtual reality (VR), augmented reality (AR), or mixed reality (MR), where we gaze at digitally enhanced projections of cyborgs, such as Gorillaz or Hatsune Miku, yet at the same time, we are conversing or questioning the virtual artists' identities and their creators.[5] We are reminded of their playful personas that were previously presented by post/meta/ultra/super modern (delete as appropriate!) artists in human form, such as the late David Bowie, Grace Jones, Madonna, and Daft Punk, and question whether they are presenting their "real" or "unreal"[6] identities. Their human and virtual bodies carry fused identities that are coupled with experimental music, and, due to their artistry, they can leave a lasting impression on their audience. Such artists have received global attention and gained a mass audience, as well as earning respect for their musical creativity. This was demonstrated by the tragic demise of David Bowie in 2016, which saw his fans virtually grieving on social media and across the internet. While Bowie's demise was trending on Twitter, his visual-musical album, *Black Star* (2016), which he left as a parting gift to his fans, grabbed social media attention. The virtual exposure of the album enhanced the meaning of the term "virality": a music video from the album, "Lazarus," which was released three days before Bowie's death, went viral across online digital platforms and virtual environments. Thus the virtual collective of fans were able to celebrate Bowie's final musical release, while at the same time, grieve for him.

With digital technology, it has been possible to seek further ways to preserve the musical memories of a deceased artist. In the past, this was normally practiced through record collecting or participating in memorial events, such as tribute concerts, conventions, posthumous album releases, or cover version albums. Nowadays, however, sharing memories, images, and music of the deceased artist can be achieved and archived online through digital storytelling or virtual conversation. This successfully maintains the artist's legacy in reality and more significantly, in VR. Furthermore, fans and consumers can now witness a resurrection of an artist, where his or her nonexistent body can be digitally revived for "live" concerts: 2Pac and Whitney Houston are two examples of this phenomenon.

Today, living artists, including independent artists, are able to take control of their work in a way that has never been possible before, having the freedom to determine how they create, perform, and share their music with their fans. These changes are causing disruption of the traditional music industry, because this independence means record labels may miss out on securing the next big talent and that they may struggle with their lack of control in distributing music.

The industry needs to look at the threats which evolving digital music practices may pose to their businesses and learn how to react to these changes. If they no longer need to concern themselves with finding the next big talent, then the issues they have to face may, instead, involve copyright, piracy, or how to adapt to developments in technology. Take as an example the infamous Napster incident of the late 1990s: university students, Shawn Fanning and Sean Parker, had a P2P (peer-to-peer) network that facilitated a file-sharing service, where computer users could illegally and freely upload, share, and download music as MP3s.[7] With infringing copyright and piracy being major concerns in the music industry, in 2000, Fanning and Parker had their site shut down and were sued by most of the record labels belonging to the Recording Industry Association of America (RIAA).[8]

Another example of the music industry trying to introduce ways to prevent piracy was the Sony-BMG's rootkit scandal of 2005, a controversial attempt to prevent piracy of MP3s.[9] The label released around fifteen million copy-protected CDs in the United States. The copy-protected CD contained security vulnerabilities that would install hidden software called XCP (Extended Copy Protection)[10] inside a user's computer. While XCP allowed up to a maximum of three copies of an album to be made, it discreetly coded its own media player on the computer. There were two consequences that the users faced if they successfully uninstalled the XCP: they were liable to be prosecuted under the DMCA (Digital Millennium Copyright Act),[11] and their computer would be damaged by the XCP altering its registry. While this could have been one solution for reducing digital piracy on the internet, the concept failed because of the software's intrusion and intervention in consumers' personal property. There are other ways to combat digital piracy (and other incidents where intellectual property is compromised). Where appropriate, these protect the creator and consumer with laws such as Fair Use in the United States and Fair Dealing in the United Kingdom.[12]

Despite these technological disruptions, the music industry will always introduce ways of expanding its avenues and revenues in selling music, and determining how consumers can have "access" to hearing music in the digital virtual era. These include creating user-generated content on social media platforms (as a marketing tactic), and investing more in producing live and virtual concerts, to encourage fans and consumers to buy the music of artists/groups and to attend their shows. However, music streaming is now the most favored way to access and consume music.[13] Why are streaming services such as Spotify so successful? Mostly because they are not reliant on a physical format or download consumption—this means the music is more portable and accessible to anyone with access to the internet. Streaming is also successful because the consumer does not need to set aside time and effort to search for and purchase music—and for the music industry, it is a way to combat piracy.

While this type of digital music consumption has boosted the revenue of the music industry, there is, however, the consistent argument that artists, publishers, independent labels, and even creators of less known genres/styles may receive little profit from streaming.[14] This debate needs to be resolved, so the "real" creators of the music can rightfully earn their fair dues.[15] As the continuous digital revolution of creating, performing, distributing, and consuming music is incessantly growing, it could be argued that the music industry is now formed of micro industries, where major[16] and independent labels' business models and infrastructures are continuously changing, fragmenting, merging, and expanding to accommodate the developments of digital practices so that they can stay ahead in the game.

With creativity, music making in the digital era has enabled creators to experiment and present the unimaginable, unthinkable, and unexpected in music. Creations based on a fusion of previously incompatible genres and styles have been made into compatible music, thanks to digital technology. When creators pay references to older, often nostalgic music, through sampling or modifications, such as interpolation, they can transform the sounds into a new creation. Not only does this invite new listeners to hear older music, but it also opens opportunities for interested audiences to be inquisitive about the sounds they're hearing.

Another example of virtually presenting the unimaginable, unthinkable, and unexpected in music is in recording practices where creators, such as musicians and producers, are no longer physically confined to one recording studio. This means they can collaborate virtually in creating music using sound sources alone, such as samples,[17] or that they can record in various virtual spaces, places, and locations. This can be done either synchronously or asynchronously.[18] The increasing practice of asynchronous and collaborative online recording is intermundane, and can be beneficial for the creators if finances, technology, and time allow. However, we must not be misled into thinking that such a collective project was performed together, although when hearing the recording, it will give that illusion. This concept also raises the question: How is this any different to a group recording in a studio? In a studio, it is the norm to record tracks separately and then mix and blend them together, resulting in one piece of music. The idea of a collective interacting together in "real time," in an online situation, was disdained by Jason Stanyek and Benjamin Piekut: "These 'worlds' do not preexist their enrollment in contingent assemblages; it is in and through effectively—collaboration—that they take shape."[19] Putting aside constraints on time and patience, virtual music in the digital era allows for new and exciting forms of creativity.

Interacting and participating in music is not a new concept, it has always been foremost a creative, performing, and learning activity for musicians (regardless of ability),[20] but the way in which we engage, experience, involve, and follow music is very demanding in the digital era. This brings additional meaning to Christopher Small's concept of "musicking," where anybody could participate in music "in any capacity, in a musical performance, whether by performing, by listening, by rehearsing or practicing, by providing material for performance."[21] Here, we can also consider applying musicking in the following: by immersing virtually in a musical performance, such as a concert, video game, or music video; performing in a virtual world, such as Second Life or Fortnite; building online social networks; generating and sharing digital content, such as music podcasts, social media posts, and videos; and creating virtual collaborations. On a deeper and psychological level, the increasing opportunities in participating and luxuriating in music activities of any kind promote an experience in what Mihaly Csikszentmihalyi calls a state of "flow," where the person becomes so involved in an activity (regardless of difficulty level), it results in a fulfilling experience.[22] When pursuing the activity, the users are so immersed in the task that they become unattached to reality and their physical surroundings, and they lose a sense of timelessness and space (in that particular moment), but they do resolve challenges and gain new skills. The evolution of virtuality of music in the digital era has expanded and opened new opportunities for *all* to somehow participate, interact, and build a relationship with music, either as collaborators or individuals—and these insights will be visited throughout this book.

About the Book

Virtual Music: Sound, Music, and Image in the Digital Era is about how music has been shaped by virtuality and digital technology. This is not a rigorous scholarly book overloaded with critical and philosophical concepts; the aim of *Virtual Music: Sound, Music, and Image in the Digital Era* is to reach out to those who have a genuinely fond interest in virtual music and digital technology, and who want to gain an understanding of its relationship with sound, music, and image. This topic is vast, and developments are constantly evolving in music, virtuality, and digital technology, so this book is the exciting start to studying a creation that can change and evolve daily. This book is an invaluable supplementary book and a textbook where chapters and case studies are useful for teaching and studying purposes. *Virtual Music: Sound, Music, and Image in the Digital Era* will appeal to those studying and teaching the disciplines of music, popular music, the creative and music industries, digital humanities, media, cultural studies, sociology, performance, film, and communication studies. It is also especially for anyone with a personal interest in music, and a desire to undertake self-education.

About the Title of This Book

The original title for this book was *Rewind the Future: Exploring Digital Virtual Music*, because I have an obsession with how music draws in elements of past sounds. I am intrigued by, and want to explore why, when we hear and view music, there are aspects of the creation in which we are reminded of the past, in the present. For example, the music and performance may carry retro signifiers[23] of past genres, styles, history, politics, fashion or props. When these are blended with current trends and aided with digital technology, some of these musical creations enhance a futuristic experience for the consumer (listener/spectator). This may result in a dialogue between consumers and they may discuss, share, or critique their remarkable experience of music, wanting to know "how did they manage to create that?" By this, I mean *how* the creators managed to present the unimaginable, unthinkable, and unexpected—that is, the virtual—in their music? I explore this notion throughout the book.

The original second part of the title is the crunch—a wordplay of both digital and virtual. As previously hinted, I have (and I am sure you have, too) been guilty of freely applying the words into everyday conversation, sometimes without justification. However, there is no fixed rule for how to apply the words digital and virtual in conversation, as they can have multiple meanings. This particularly applies to the term "virtuality," something which results in various meanings and confusion. For the sake of this book, I use this term when discussing how musical ideas (the virtual) are transformed into reality or, indeed, a near reality, and actuality, mostly due to the use of digital technology. Mark Grimshaw rightfully asserts that "Virtuality is not the domain of one field study alone,"[24] and his thought can be stretched to creational practices and interdisciplinary topics, hence the reason that I am only focusing on specific areas in music. I must admit, however, that there are many occasions in the book where I interchange the words virtual and digital, and I continue to marry the terms digital and virtual together (e.g., digital virtual), when referring to the specific time frame or concept, and more importantly, when discussing the human's "virtual" relationship with "digital" machines/technology, in the digital virtual era.[25] While Chapter 2 offers a critical understanding of the term "virtuality," I must emphasize that, overall, I do not offer a strict definition of the term, but, rather, complement our way of understanding how music builds a relationship with both the digital and virtual, or the virtual and digital, in the digital virtual era.

The book's main ongoing theme is exposing and transforming the unimaginable, unthinkable, and unexpected ideas into reality. Take experimental music for example, where unrelated sounds, genres, and styles can be transformed into magnificent works, and the distinction of hierarchies, cultures, and social status are irrelevant, therefore allowing the listener to simply enjoy the music, and where necessary and by choice, attempt to understand the creator's intentions. Another example is audiovisuals, where the feature of dystopian themes are commonly depicted in video games and music videos and "offer a type of sublime transcendence that allows people to deal with horror, without 'actually' having to experience it"[26]— therefore giving the subject in question (the music artist, or character) and viewer a virtual sense of the ordeal, without actually and physically (and maybe emotionally, too) experiencing the effects in real life in that particular moment.[27] Themes of retro/nostalgia in virtual music are also common in the digital era, mainly through the use of sampling and other means of audio (including visual) references, enabling the listener to reminisce in familiar sounds or to discover music of the past sources to widen his or her musical knowledge and experience. And finally, the theme of the breakdown of the separation between the creator and the listener/consumer/audience/spectator/gazer/viewer, including technology, is a developing one. This is where interactivity brings new opportunities and visions in building a relationship with virtual music,[28] through the use of sound, music, and image in the digital era.

Approaches when Discussing Audiovisual Examples

I have aimed to include a diverse range of music for discussion. Because analyzing music is part of my vocation and passion, I have refrained from going too deep, or being too subject-focused, as I want to offer the reader a friendly musicological—and where possible jargon-free—approach to understanding the music we are familiar with and enjoy. Therefore, there is no set methodological tactic to apply in the analysis; instead, I offer a variety of case studies and methods, in which some examples are more musically focused, and some are extended descriptions of the subject in question.

For the context of this book, I use the term "creator" in various ways. I refer to the creator as the person responsible for creating the music—and that could be the composer, musician, producer, recording/sound engineer, DJ, songwriter, or artist—so please keep that in mind. Most of the music discussed in this book should be accessible on the internet through online music, app stores, and video platforms, which I hope you will check out and enjoy.

Overview of the Book

Chapter 1, "Blame it on the Machines": Historical Placings of Digital Virtual Music, documents most of the history of digital virtual music and its associated mediums and technology. While it has an extensive history, only significant developments in technology that have transformed recording, creativity, and consumption in music over the last two centuries are featured. The technology that is mentioned (such as music machines and audio devices) provides the foundation for discussions presented throughout the book (such as sampling and the internet). This is then followed by an insight on the theoretical thinking in understanding the concept of the digital virtual and how it is applied in music in Chapter 2, "Technology Gives You Everything Immediately . . .": A Brief Critical Discussion on the Digital Virtual. This chapter is aimed at those who want to be introduced to the theoretical concepts that resurface and are identifiable later in the book. The following areas are introduced: technology, virtuality, hyperreality, postmodernism, hauntology, and actor network theory (ANT), and they provide the basis of the critical thinking on how to perceive the digital virtual in music. These brief theoretical concepts encourage the reader to have a choice in gaining a critical sense of appreciation in digital virtual music and look at how it can be valuable in everyday lives, society, and culture.

Chapter 3, "We Are Musical Makers": The Experimental and Digital Virtual Trademarks of Genre and Style, focuses on experimental music and argues that most music created over the last two centuries (including the formation of significant genres and styles) would not exist without some form of technology. This chapter also deliberates on understanding the word "experimental," and I argue that it is a hybrid term and has become the inspiration for future digital virtual music. To support this, I select specific genres and styles such as Krautrock, psychedelic, dub, hip-hop, ambient, and electronica that fall under what I call the experimental "umbrella," as well as identifying its digital virtual trademarks by using the following creators as examples: Kraftwerk, Pierre Henry, King Tubby, Madvillain, Brian Eno, and Bomb the Bass.

In Chapter 4, "Give Life Back to Music": Remixing Music, I propose that most of the music we hear today is constantly being recycled, and reminds us of past sounds. I explore a particular digital music practice, remixing, and illustrate examples of transformations and imitations of retro/nostalgic music and other past sources. I use the works of Danger Mouse (Brian Burton) and his creations as examples: the infamous remix of Jay-Z's *Black Album* (2003) and the Beatles' *White Album* (1968), known as *The Grey Album* (2004); and his group Gnarls Barkley's "Crazy" (2006) that is a classic pop, soul, hip-hop, and gospel song that disguises its musical base of spaghetti western music samples—except for its timbre and emotion.

To continue the theme of music that "rewinds" to and revisits the musical past, I explore other retro/nostalgic compositional styles, other than remixing, in Chapter 5, "The Game Has Changed": Video Game Music. Here, I investigate three styles of music used as a video game soundtrack, and highlight how certain creators recreated retro and nostalgic sounds, and the virtual impact it has on the gamer. I refer to the following creators and video games: Chipzel's "Focus" in *Super Hexagon* (2012), whose music is based on 8-bit also known as chiptune; jazz music in *Cuphead* (2017), in which composer Kristofer Maddigan, and bassist Paul Novotny explain to me the process of creating and performing this remarkable, award-winning soundtrack; and Danger Mouse and his collaboration with film music composer Daniele Luppi, in which their song "Black" (2011) was presented as the first interactive music video designed for Google Chrome.

In Chapter 6, "Living in a Fantasy": Performers and Identity, I begin to focus on performers and how they present their artistry in the digital virtual era. I question the authenticity of specific performers who have successfully manipulated their identities. Referring to well-known artists who are known for teasing and experimenting with their artistry, including David Bowie and Madonna, I look at how performers who play with their identities use technology to enhance visual performances. To illustrate this, I examine the audiovisual works of Grace Jones and The Weeknd. When discussing Grace Jones, I remark on her incredible career, identity, and music. I also discuss her virtual performance in the dub/pop song and music video, "Love You to Life" (2010), and how she controls her artistry with digital lighting effects. I follow the discussion by exploring The Weeknd (Abel Tesfaye), and present him as a possible (and very likely) contender to be included in the same musical reign as David Bowie, Madonna, and Grace Jones. I argue that, as a creator, Tesfaye has a vision with his identity and dark-themed music, as demonstrated by the spectacular audiovisuals. I also explain how Tesfaye invites his audience to immerse themselves in his music by participating in his performances, especially "The Hills" (2015), which is presented as an interactive 360-degree spherical music video game with a dystopian theme, and "Blinding Lights" (2019), where he invites the audience to interact, giving them the illusion that they are in control of his performance.

Live musical performances, in particular virtual shows, are at the center of Chapter 7, "Showroom Dummies": Live and Simulated Performers,

Performances, and Audiences. Various types of performers and performances are observed as a simulated or live performance, thanks to digital technology. While I acknowledge that this is an exciting and ongoing development in the digital virtual era, I question how virtual performers and their performances impact and communicate with real-life audiences. Here I refer to Gorillaz, Hatsune Miku, and Miquela. There is also an insight into how an audience can watch and be immersed in "live" concerts without being physically present—achieved by watching live streams of performances, or by virtually placing themselves in the event via headsets (with the Fortnite video game and MelodyVR concert app as examples). I also consider the consequences it may have on physical live events and the music industry.

In Chapter 8, "Take Control": Creators, Fans, and the Internet, I look at how creators (including established artists) are gaining control of their creativities online by releasing and digitally distributing music through means such as albums, video games, and apps.[29] This chapter discusses how and why music and app creators—including David Bowie, Radiohead, Massive Attack, and variPlay app's creator Rob Toulson—used the internet as a platform for their music and to connect and interact with their fans online. I also explore how this also gives them the opportunity to have a chance to "control" their music and listening experience.

Finally, in Chapter 9, "Digital Witness": Online Communities, Networking, and Virality, I extend the concept that the digital virtual era erases the barrier between the artist, industry, and fan or consumer. I explore the fans' virtual place in current music and society, and argue that the divisions between a performer, the music industry, and the audience/consumer/fan are now blurred. The audience/consumer/fan can be considered to be virtually part of the "music industry"—for example, by involvement and engagement in social networking and crowdfunding, where they can support the artists through funding a music project or with free promotion, such as praising the music on social media.[30] Fans can also instantly unite with unknown virtual friends and openly share their feelings, views, gossip, news, blogs, vlogs, and music online. Here, I refer to David Bowie's death to illustrate this notion and look at the types of rapidly shared music and videos across social media and networks, otherwise known as "virality" and "memes." I refer to Drake's "Hotline Bling" (2015) music video, Baauer's "Harlem Shake" (2012), the "iMourning" of David Bowie, Kendrick Lamar's *Damn* (2017) album cover, and Lil Nas X's "Old Town Road" (2018) as examples. I conclude by emphasizing that an interesting development in online communities is how the fans (the digital witnesses) are now the "media" in the digital virtual era.

1

"Blame It on the Machines"

Historical Placings of Digital Virtual Music

Without electronic technology, popular music in the twenty-first century is unthinkable.

—PAUL THÉBERGE[1]

Experimenting in music making has not been tied only to the twenty-first century. The application of most technologies induces creativity and consumption in music, fostering a sense of emotional fulfillment, connection, and communication for the user and the listener. Paul Théberge's opening epigraph of this chapter has always resonated with me and I have endlessly applied it in my research and teaching. Readers may also want to think about exchanging the word "electronic" for "digital" and omitting the word "popular." However you read it, today's music will always be reliant on some kind of technology, whether in the form of "instruments, recording [,] . . . playback devices,"[2] machines, screens, or the internet. While this chapter visits the history of technology, it should be noted that such history has frequently been documented by respected academics and writers, whose work has helped me in my own research over the last twenty years. However, rather than repeating familiar information, or documenting every technology that exists, I want to concentrate on discussing the history of devices, instruments, and machines that is most relevant for this book. After all, as noted by David Tough (2016), such history is at least 135 years old.[3] While Tough refers mainly to "sound" (more on this later), this thought can be stretched to music, electronic, and, obviously slightly later, digital technologies. Visuals also have a vital role in digital virtual music, so I want to apply my own approach in exploring the relationship between technology and digital virtual music, without missing out on its key features that involve creativity and consumption. This concept ties in with Mark Katz's argument that technology is not for one type of usage only, and that we must consider "the relationship between the technology and its users that determines the impact of the recording."[4]

Undeniably, there is also the consumer market to consider as highlighted by Antoine Hennion (2015) who argues, "the attempt to make music into an object depends at every step on an entire social framework, ranging from the interpreters' rehearsals to the conventions that govern the interpretation of the traces of music, and to the techniques used in the cultural industry to turn music into a product that can be sold."[5] Therefore, the purpose of technology is not only for creation and reproduction purposes, but it is also to transform music into some type of tangible object, and then, to sell it. Therefore, this chapter will focus on the following areas: music technology, audio players (Figure 1.1), and digital virtual technology in communications and media.

Music Technology

Recording Technology and Vinyl

When we think about how we "hear" music, we need to think about how sound is captured, stored, and manipulated.[6] Richard James Burgess argues that "[t]here has been a fascination with the idea of capturing sound and early attempts included mechanical instruments and music notation."[7] In his book *The History of Music Production* (2014), Burgess offers a captivating insight into early technologies that acquired and released sound, with something simple, such as a tuning fork (1771), to somewhat more technical, such as the phonautograph in 1857 (the predecessor to the phonograph or if you prefer, its ancestor).[8] When researching or discovering how technology captures sound, the phonograph is commonly the best starting point to discuss, and even though it was based on the phonautograph model, this was a groundbreaking moment where such a device could record, store, and play sound. For the listeners, this was an essential moment, as they had the opportunity to experience virtually a musical performance in their own space, at any time, without the need to physically transport themselves to a live performance or event.

While the phonograph was a game changer in terms of music recording and consumption, the format of the device gradually transitioned into what we know as the "turntable." The phonograph was invented in 1877 by Thomas Edison,[9] with the original purpose of being a dictation device; however, it was known to record, reproduce, and play music too, with "Mary has a little lamb" being its first musical recording. The device itself consisted of a tinfoil sheet and a cylinder,[10] and became the basis for analog recording, where the soundwaves were fluctuated "in sound pressure through the air, [and much later] into electric signals."[11] These fluctuations are recorded directly into the cylinder, and much later on, on the surface of a record. Unfortunately, the sound quality of phonograph recordings was not considered to be "pleasing" to the ear for all involved— including the musician, producer, and listener—but this was the young, developmental stage of recording technology. Despite its inaudible features, the phonograph was a major step forward for the future of music and the music industry. Additionally, the device was portable and it became a fashionable home accessory for the consumer. Further adaptations and rival models of the phonograph led to a gradual improvement in sound quality, such as the Graphophone invented by Alexander Bell in 1886; but it was the Gramophone, in 1888, that proved the true successor to Edison's invention of the phonograph.

The Gramophone was invented by Emile Berliner, and it used discs instead of cylinders to produce and transmit sound. Its one-sided shellac record discs were significant in that they had etched grooves, from which the sound was reproduced by a stylus.[12] A further improvement in sound technology was made with the introduction of stereo in 1933. This audio feature was invented by the British engineer, Alan Blumlein, who had become frustrated with the mono (one-sided) sound delivered via one speaker.[13] His idea was to create a binaural (stereo) system, where a sound source is transmitted into two signals and speakers, promoting a more natural sonic and soundscape experience for the human ear—with mono, the sound comes across as bleak, dry, and one-directional. The invention of stereo was another breathtaking moment for the music, film, and radio industries, a major technological advancement in music[14] in terms of both creation and consumption. For the consumer, in particular, the virtual experience of a simulated music performance is further enhanced because of stereo. Here, we can draw in Evan Eisenberg's thoughts on this concept, as he argues that "Stereo . . . arrays the musicians before you in empty space. You can almost pinpoint them, but they're not there. Instead of projecting, they are projected—but invisible."[15] The additional feature of stereo then, enables the consumers (listeners) to create a virtual temporary place in their own space, and indulge in a simulated music performance while soaking up all the sounds in which they are immersed.

As recording technology developed, the Gramophone gradually became replaced by electric turntables. Pivotal events marked distinctive stages in the story of the record disc. Shellac was omitted and replaced with vinyl, sparking a rivalry between record labels, known as "battle of the speeds." Originally, a vinyl disc would groove at 78 rpm (revolutions per minute)[16] but as vinyl developed, so did the speed formats. In 1948, Columbia Records produced the 33 1/3 rpm (12" long play (LP) vinyl), and RCA Victor developed the 45 rpm (7" vinyl). The original intention of Columbia was to replace the 78 rpm with the 33 1/3 rpm, 12" disc. However, when RCA responded by developing the 45 rpm, 7" disc, it resulted in rivalry between the two labels.[17] By 1952, through government mediation, the battle of the speeds was resolved when the labels agreed to have separate purposes for the discs.[18] The 12" LP catered for albums, and the 7" vinyl accommodated singles (later this was followed by the 45 rpm 12" single).[19] Both disc formats carried different intentions in the industry, music creation, and consumer markets.

The LP was a convincing way for creators to showcase their work as an album, and, in turn, to serve as a collector's item for the consumer (a trend that continues today). The 7" disc had its own appeal: it was accessible, cheap, and portable. It was also a direct way to sell and promote songs as singles to consumers. As the 7" disc could accommodate only three to four minutes of music per side, it did not have the longevity of a 12" album. A single (and its B-side) was easily replaceable—or forgettable—by the masses. Those consumers who were not record collectors, or committed to a certain artist, had changeable tastes and were easily influenced or manipulated by the industry and the media. This meant that the 7" disc was often considered disposable and changeable, just like fashion.

Vinyl culture continued to develop from the mid-1960s onward, as the use of the turntable led to further opportunities. Other than consumer use, the turntable started to become more recognized as a musical instrument, with its visible features of the stylus (needle), tone arm, cartridge, platter, and motor.[20] The role of the DJ would explore these features (especially the stylus and platter) and became more prominent in terms of creativity and collaboration. This was especially true in the Jamaican sound system culture, disco, hip-hop, and dance.[21]

Today, there is still a demand for turntables, despite their inability to compete with digital formats such as streaming. Turntables have kept up in the digital virtual era by serving as digital models: the USB version makes it easier to transfer music from vinyl into digital files; and the Bluetooth version can stream music wirelessly to speakers, thus making both devices portable (albeit not as easily portable as a smartphone or laptop, due to their weight). The development of records and their devices has served the user in many ways: for the creator, to record sound and later produce music; and, for the consumer, to listen to and replay music at his/her own leisure, in the place or space of his/her choosing. The following quote by Thomas Edison sums up the significance of the record player, "The phonograph will undoubtedly be liberally devoted to music."[22] Even though Edison was writing only about his invention, his thoughts can be applied warmly to all future turntables and records, too.

Tape

After the emergence of vinyl, other formats of technology started to materialize, including the tape. There are different variations of the tape, which proved useful for the creator and consumer, based on their recording, production, audio, and portability needs. There have been different developmental stages of the tape and its respective devices: (1) recording sound, (2) playback of recorded sounds, and (3) portable use. The tape proved to be another innovative shift in recording music, yet with a difference. Notable developers and manufacturers were responsible for magnetic tape that led to an era of multitrack tape recorders (such as the German company AEG in 1935 and America's AMPEX in 1948).[23] This machine enables the recording of individual sounds, bouncing them together to finalize the music, rather than recording a group of sounds (e.g., a band) in one session. To this, the creator—musician, producer, or recording/sound engineer—can cut, splice, edit, and re-record sounds. To put this into perspective, researchers use the classic Les Paul example, where he recorded an electric guitar. The listener will hear multiple guitars in the recording, yet, in fact, only one guitar was used to create the music, on an AMPEX 200 recorder.[24] As multitrack recording advanced and expanded, it revolutionized the creation and production of music, particularly from the 1960s onward, with the works of the Beatles and Rolling Stones being prime examples, but, of course, there are many, many others as well.[25] Where possible, the magnetic tape was replaced by DAT (Digital Audio Tape) in the 1980s. DAT became a preferred recording medium for creators because of "the lack of signal degradation and miniaturized size . . ."[26] Despite its high sound quality, and the fact that it could accommodate a healthy amount of recordings, there were reservations about whether DAT could be archived and preserved for as long as the traditional magnetic tape (if you think about it in terms of a digital format, if the contents are erased or destroyed, once it's gone, it has gone forever).[27] Furthermore, the music industry also had reservations about whether to release it as a playback device for consumers. Due to the attractive sound and audio qualities of the recordings, there was a concern that this might encourage piracy activity (such as digital tape to tape recording), which would have the consequence of decreasing physical music sales.[28] It became transparent that, despite these concerns, DAT still continued to be a preferred recording format for the creator and that DAT, as a playback device, was not realistically affordable for the consumer. Consumers would later invest in much more affordable digital-based devices, such as the compact disc player (more on this later). This revolution in recording enabled creators to turn their virtual thoughts into reality through musical experimentation and manipulation, thanks to technology.[29]

As a form of consumption, the tape was a successful format. When the manufacturers, Philips, released the cassette tape in 1963, it had a maximum storage of forty-five minutes per side. The appeal of this format was that it had decent sound quality and it was portable. When treated with care, the tapes were durable, and economical[30] and the consumers were not tied to where they were able to listen to their music. They could take a cassette player with them to work or to a friend's home, or play a tape in their car cassette deck. The main disadvantage when compared to vinyl was that it was harder to skip or search for particular tracks and, in time, it was discovered that the sound quality degraded. The tape did have its advantages, however, and it became a major competitor in the album market (with vinyl as the rival), because it was easier to distribute.

With the introduction of blank tapes, consumers were able to compile their own selection of favorite songs, or record their own music, for mix tapes or to send out as demos. The accessibility of the cassette tape made it easier to market. For example, music magazines would give away free music on tape, and cassette singles, known as "cassingles," and sometimes even albums were often created with collectors' perks, such as bonus music, unique packaging, or gifts. It is also interesting to note that the cassette served as a virtual magazine in the early 1980s; this meant that the magazine was not produced on paper, only on tape, with *SFX Cassette* being an example.[31] This can be considered as an earlier form of a podcast (more on this later).[32]

A radical development that secured the success of tape consumption was the portable cassette player, famously known as the Sony Walkman, which debuted in 1979.[33] The concept of the portable tape player was devised by Sony's co-founder Masaru Ibuka, who wanted a device that would store music and that he could take on his business travels.[34] After his colleague Norio Ohga (Executive Deputy President) recreated Ibuka's vision, he convinced Sony to invest in the portable tape player with the following unique selling point: "Try this. Don't you think a stereo cassette player that you can listen to while walking around is a good idea?"[35] The chunky but compact device, with headphones, quickly took off in the consumer market. People were using the device while commuting and exercising, making the Walkman part of their daily activities. The popularity of this device motivated rival manufacturers, such as Panasonic and Toshiba, to make similar devices, all of which helped the cassette to overtake vinyl sales in 1983.[36] On a personal note, I have lost count of how many Walkmans I have owned and would safely say that cassettes continued to be very popular up to the end of the 1990s (at least). With that in mind, it could be argued that the Walkman was a significant part of culture, along with later portable and digital mediums that followed, such as the portable compact disc (CD) player, the iPod, MP3 players, and smartphones.[37] The Walkman also became more associated with the individual on a personal level, and it transformed how consumers not only "consumed" music but also "lived" in the music. As argued by Paul du Gay, Stuart Hall, Linda Jones, High Mackay, and Keith Negus (1997):

> [T]he Walkman is "cultural" because we have constituted it as a meaningful object. We can talk, think about and imagine it. It is also "cultural" because it connects with a distinct set of *social practices* (like listening to music while travelling on the train or the underground, for example), which are specific to our culture or way of life. It is cultural because it is associated with certain kinds of people (young people, for example, or music-lovers); with certain *places* (the city, the open air, walking around a museum)—because it has been given or acquired a social profile or *identity*.[38]

While the Walkman is perhaps not really in demand today (although I expect a nostalgic revival), this concept is still applicable to the later portable and digital mediums that followed, such as the iPod and smartphone, thereby making music consumption even more mobile in a personal environment especially in the current digital virtual era.

Player-Piano

Let's remind ourselves of Paul Théberge's argument that popular music and technology are inseparable,[39] and focus on how technology has played a vital role in music creation. To begin, let's focus on a rather unusual but compelling instrument, the player-piano, which dates back to the nineteenth century. The reason for its inclusion is that "[t]his early automatic instrument is an example of a programmable machine and thus anticipates in mechanical form the later software/hardware paradigm of the digital computer."[40] When we think about instruments, or machines that reproduce (virtual) sounds, readers may immediately think of a digital sampler, drum machine, or synthesizer, when, in fact, there have been previous attempts to experiment with instruments, and reproduce their sounds.

Better known as the Pianola, the player-piano was invented by American engineer, E. S Votey, in 1897, and reached popularity in 1914. The instrument/machine is "fitted with a self-playing mechanism normally pneumatic, capable of playing from a perforated paper music roll (piano roll)."[41] The process of recording was done separately: the music required a pianist to perform a piece of music on a recording piano. As they played, the sounds from the piano were marked mechanically onto the roll, which was then cut by an operator.[42] The playback of the recording was "played" on the player-piano via the roll. The player-piano could be found in cafes, restaurants, and hotels as coin-operated devices,[43] but, overall, the player-piano was directly aimed at consumers who could afford it. Like the phonograph, and later the Gramophone, the player-piano was a fashionable home accessory and form of home entertainment, rather than an instrument itself. Furthermore, the consumers could buy piano rolls—the equivalent of sheet music—with their favorite tunes and simply let the player-piano do the work. Interestingly, however, because of its novelty factor, consumers who were not actual pianists could give the illusion that they were playing the piano when, in reality, they were operating it with their foot!

To play music on a player-piano, the user turns into the operator and pushes the piano pedals with his or her foot. This process can lead to another illusion, that the consumer-turned-user is both the operator and controller of the player-piano, when in reality, as Lisa Gitelman argues, he/she is actually the "displaced" user, where he/she hears and watches invisible pianists depress the keys with *virtual* fingers and hands.[44] For such a fancy, novel, and somewhat simplified machine, this is a very persuasive concept as the consumers can offer various experiences as the player-piano-players: they can appear to be the user, by imagining that they are the pianist and thus simulating a performance to entertain their peers; and they are both displaced users and controllers enabling the machine to self-play the music, virtually.[45]

Theremin

Another remarkable and very fascinating instrument is the Theremin. The "touchless,"[46] electronic, and monophonic instrument, consists of a box and two antennae. Originally intended to replace the string sections in an orchestra, it became more widely used in future experimental music. It was invented by Leon Theremin (real name Lev Sergeyevich Termen) in 1920 and later adapted by the synthesizer inventor Robert A. Moog. It was known for its unusual timbre (an eerie wailing sound) and performance technique, achieved by moving hands through the antennae's invisible electromagnetic fields. Through the conduction of the hands, the movements can control the dynamics and timbre, which are picked up virtually by the antennae, which then transmit sounds. The instrument has since gone through various developments, and has been used in recordings and performances, such as The Beach Boys' "Good Vibrations" in 1966.

Synthesizers

An electronic keyboard instrument known as the synthesizer has existed in both analog and digital forms. All types of synthesizers produce oscillators (sound-generating modules), filters (sound-shaping modules), and time-shaping modules (voltage-controlled amplifiers), operated through either hardware (analog) or software (digital), with its operation controlled by the creator.

Robert Moog started a trend in making synthesizers from the 1960s.[47] The "Moog" synthesizer was first restricted to educational and audio-related purposes. In the 1970s, the "Minimoog" model series became more accessible, more portable, and most importantly, more affordable for creators. It was monophonic, meaning that only one note could be played at a time, with three oscillators, where the sound of the pitch was manipulated to various waveforms and opulent harmonics, and filters to shape timbres. Where possible, this became a staple in recording studio furniture, and has been used and praised by creators of various genres and styles, including Herbie Hancock, Gary Numan, Pink Floyd, Tangerine Dream, Kraftwerk, Depeche Mode, and Sun Ra.

Rival models of the synthesizer followed, manufactured by the likes of ARP, Korg, Roland, Oberheim, Buchla, Sequential Circuits, and Yamaha. The Yamaha, in particular, started a trend for the digital synthesizer, most notably the DX7 (invented in 1983). The DX7 and subsequent synthesizers, manufactured by the likes of Korg and Roland, served as a combination of machine and keyboard that allowed more opportunity to experiment with sound, to simulate "real" instruments (including piano, trumpet, violin, and so on), and to program and customize the tones and timbres with provided interfaces. It also included Musical Instrument Digital Interface (MIDI), which changed the way music could be created and became a popular instrument during the 1980s.[48]

Drum and Bass Machines

If we rewind slightly to the mid-1970s, there was a significant moment in the advancement of technology involving the digital reproduction of sounds in instruments and machines. Digital technology was important in that it provided innovative ways of creating music and exploring sounds. Digital technology recording involves "converting the fluctuating analog electrical signal into binary data."[49] This can be transferred onto and stored in a variety of formats. Furthermore, where possible, it opens up opportunities for nonmusic creators to become music creators through the application of digital technology.[50]

Other significant instruments and machines that were developed include the digital drum machine, bass machine, MIDI, and digital sampler. The drum machine, for example, was particularly popular in the 1980s and could be heard in hip-hop, synth-pop, and pop.[51] As opposed to playing an actual drum kit, these machines featured drum samples, enabling the creators (musicians/operators) to either compose or punch their own drum patterns, or to add an underlying backbeat (a click or guided rhythm) to the music. Significant early models included LinnDrum and the Roland TR series (e.g., TR808, TR909, and TR606). Another significant machine, developed around 1982, was a bass (analog) machine, which was supposed to simulate bass sounds to replace an expensive session bassist in the recording studio. Famously known as the Roland TB-303 Bassline,[52] it was like a mini synthesizer, allowing the operator to set the tones and tempo. However, as DJ Pierre (real name Nathaniel Pierre Jones) of Phuture[53] puts it, "it did a crappy job,"[54] and Roland discontinued the product. Because so many of the machines could be found in secondhand shops for an affordable price, they became very much part of dance music, in particular acid house, where creators (DJs and producers, including DJ Pierre) experimented with the filters and oscillators, and transformed the "crappy" bass into thumping squelching sonics, which created a futuristic effect in music.

MIDI

MIDI was another major contribution to digital technology after 1983.[55] The interface was designed for instruments and computers to connect and communicate with each other. An early setup would consist of a synthesizer, drum machine, and computer. As MIDI developed during the 1980s and early 1990s, the interface would also connect samplers, guitars, and multitrack recorders, and would become a common recording practice, not only in a professional studio but also in any personal (recording) space.

The purpose of MIDI is to enable the creator to record different musical parts of a composition separately—similar to a standard and physical multitrack machine, but on a computer. As MIDI developed, it would integrate with audio plug-in computer software, better known as VST (Virtual Studio Technology)[56] to simulate a recording studio in hardware. Just like a standard multitrack recorder, the creator could edit and mix the parts afterwards on the computer.[57] Although at first the equipment was expensive to purchase, it became more affordable in the 1990s and was favored as a cheaper option to record from one's personal space, such as one's bedroom, rather than hiring an expensive professional recording studio. Currently, it is DAW (Digital Audio Workstation) that has enhanced MIDI. DAW is a very popular form of recording technology that usually consists of the following: computer, digital audio software, and digital audio interface. The digital audio software (which is really a virtual recording studio) is installed in the computer. Like MIDI, the creator can record directly to the computer, then edit, and mix the sounds. To connect instruments to the computer, a digital audio interface is needed so that the sound can travel in and out of the computer, and be manipulated in the software.

Another feature of DAW is a plug-in, a recording software application that provides extra features, such as compressors and effects, but more exclusively, virtual instruments such as synthesizers and samplers[58]—which is particularly useful for the creator if he/she does not have access to the physical instruments and devices. Popular DAW software includes Pro Tools, Maschine, and Ableton Live.

Digital Sampler

The digital sampler is either a stand-alone digital machine, integrated computer software, or a synthesizer that allows a limited number of sounds to be sampled and stored in RAM (Random Access Memory). These are then edited or manipulated—with features that allow for altering sound including time-stretching, pitch-shifting, transposing, tempo alteration, rhythm construction, sliced, chopped, looped, and reversed—and transformed into new music. The first digital sampler from the late 1970s was the "The Fairlight Computer Musical Instrument," which was combined with a synthesizer and sampler workstation.[59] This was followed by the E-mu Emulator sampler in 1981.[60] The Emulator was mainly used in hip-hop to sample drum beats from funk and soul records, which was accidently discovered by DJ and producer Marley Marl, who fondly recalls: "I wanted to sample a voice from off this song with an Emulator and, accidentally, a snare went through. . . . I was like 'that's the wrong thing' but the snare was sounding good. I kept running the track back and hitting the Emulator. Then I looked at the engineer and said 'You know what this means?!'"[61]

Sampling can be a key feature in other styles of music, particularly when creators sample to disguise the absence of a live instrument[62] or to experiment with sound. So, for example, if a producer wants a particular sound of an instrument but cannot afford to hire a session musician, he/she can sample the sound, manipulate, and blend it with the music so that it sounds natural. Therefore a sampler should be considered as a cherished compositional tool and instrument because it can digitally and virtually simulate, and generate, sounds.

Laptop

At the time of writing, nontraditional musical instruments based on digital technology are constantly being developed that allow musicians and wannabe musicians to explore and experiment with music at their own pace. A major development that became popular from the 2000s was making music on a stand-alone computer, such as a laptop. While we were already aware that the computer is a major contributor to music technology (to run VST and DAW software—see earlier), now it can actually serve as a digital musical instrument itself. Andrew Hugill persuasively regards the computer as a software instrument "which will do all the things (and more) that can be done by a physical instrument . . . [the] concept of the virtual instrument is already well established in commercial software."[63]

As well as serving as an instrument, the computer has multiple uses for the creator and consumer. Nick Prior justifies that the laptop in particular has successfully been used as a digital instrument through the following combinations: "the functions of composition (including online access to histories of recorded sounds and samples) with dissemination (uploading, distribution and marketing songs) and consumption (listening to, streaming and downloading songs)."[64] In addition, the creation of music on the laptop has enhanced digital virtual collaboration between creators to make music together on the internet.[65] In what Théberge (2004) calls the "network studio,"[66] the nonphysical collaboration between collaborators brings in creativity and connectivity to exchange and record music without being tied to time, physical place, and space (e.g., a recording studio), and where possible, save costs.

Even though its original purpose was for entirely different forms of work and communication, the laptop has been observed as disruptive technology (and this term can be applied to myriad other computers as well).[67] I like to use the term "disruptive" in a positive tone, for example, in this instance, a laptop allows users—regardless of their musical ability—to create music. As a result, the use of laptop music has enhanced the creative industries, by bringing together music creators, labels, software designers, and manufacturers.[68] The laptop can, arguably, be compared to traditional musical instruments, by being a mobile instrument, with its own musical setup (alongside the inclusion of other digital devices, such as controllers). The most popular musical software used in laptops includes Ableton Live and Native Instruments.

Touch Sensitive Digital Virtual Instruments

There are also other unmentioned instruments, machines, and devices in existence. While some are successful, others never materialize, yet for the creator there always remains that hope that eventually their "unsuccessful" instrument will be discovered as a "disruptive" instrument, allowing for a new concept to be launched.[69] As digital technology makes future inventions of instruments possible, we need to value history, in order to understand how both analog and digital sound develop, capture, and perform, through different mediums. While we can argue that, thanks to the never-ending development of technology, there has been a surge of synthetic and digital synthesis of sound, as featured in most modern music, we cannot forget that their predecessors in storing, recording, and creating music laid the framework and bodywork for new musical trends, apparent in creating and performing music today. Newer instruments and machines, in particular, are becoming more accessible to the creator (that is the potential operator, or performer), allowing him/her to explore the device and experiment in creating synthetic and digital synthesis of sound at his/her own pace. Here are some examples:

Nomis

Nomis is a musical instrument created by Jonathan Sparks. The setup has two light towers (where the MIDI sounds are represented by color) and an octagonal interface. To generate sounds, the hand presses the octagonal interface in which MIDI processes sounds into light. Guided by the hand, sounds can also be looped, sequenced, amended, and stored, and this process can be viewed through interaction of the tower lights. This suits a live audiovisual performance where the creator makes music, and its sounds and melodies are illuminated in the tower.[70]

Optron

Optron has been described as a "multi-sensory electronic music controller and visualizer," and was invented by Chet Udell. First impressions of this device and how it is structured may come across as a combination of air guitar and light saber, but it is, in fact, a tube underlined with a silicone sensor pad, allowing the creator to use his/her fingers to create sounds. It also has IR (infrared) sensors so that it can detect hand movements that virtually activate sounds and colored lights. This digital virtual instrument allows the creator to control and to interact with sounds and lights through his/her hand movements (e.g., by virtually strumming), or how he/she moves the instrument, such as tilting or shaking, in his/her audiovisual performance.[71]

Du-touch

The Du-touch is a small, multiuse instrument invented by Jules Hotrique. Although it may resemble a futuristic accordion, it is a combination of a synthesizer (without the traditional keyboard), sampler, and MIDI controller. The backlit keyboard (which is reminiscent of the famous hexagonal grid board on the nostalgic British TV game show, Blockbuster) allows the creator to select sounds (synth, percussion, effects), make loops, and record music. As with the Nomis and Optron, the operation and navigation of the Du-touch corresponds with the lights[72] on the keyboard, which creates an audiovisual experience for the creator and the viewer.[73]

Skoog

The Skoog is a musical instrument invented by David Skulina and Ben Schögler. It was initially designed as assistive music technology, but is beneficial to anybody wanting to learn, play, and create music. It is formed of a cube, with spongy foam on each side and serves as a tactile controller, which is connected to an app (which has soundbanks and effects). Once the app is activated, the user manipulates the sensitive sponges (they can push, twist, and squish) and the cube itself (they can roll and shake) to create and control sounds. It can also be used as a sampler and has a MIDI controller.[74]

MI.MU

MI.MU gloves are an innovative wearable musical instrument, where the sounds are created from upper-body movements. Endorsed by acclaimed musician Imogen Heap, MI.MU gloves have wireless sensors allowing the hands, wrists, and arms to create music, to explore sound through movement, and to interact with music software (such as Ableton Live and Logic Pro). There are many advantages in using this instrument: it gives the user the opportunity to create music regardless of music-playing ability and it frees the user from physically using an instrument, meaning that he/she can liberally create music and be more expressive with sound. In a live setting, the gloves allow musicians greater connection with their fans and enhanced control of their performances.[75]

Audio Players

Radio

The radio was invented by Guglielmo Marconi in 1896 in Britain,[76] and was a form of wireless telegraphy used for communication. Ever since its invention, the radio has been highly significant in the music industry and for the consumer. Major developments that led on from Marconi's invention included radio stations, such as the British Broadcasting Company (BBC) in 1922 (the name changed in 1927 to the British Broadcasting Corporation); the introduction of FM (Frequency Modulation) radio in 1933, which had stereo sound; the invention of the portable transistor radio in 1954; the rise of pirate radio from the 1960s; and the advent of digital radio (otherwise known as DAB—Digital Audio Broadcasting) in 1995.[77] Radios give the consumer the choice of how and when they want to listen to music; as Simon Frith argues, "it is rare nowadays to find someone who only listens to the radio, or who only listens to records."[78] Radio, alongside television, newspapers, and the digital press (including music magazines, websites, blogs), remains an essential way for the consumer to discover new music. In addition, the radio serves as a leisurely distraction or virtual companion to the listener—for example, the listener who listens to music to accompany him/her to work or when driving.

FIGURE 1.1 *A selection of audio players. Credit: BEHROUZ MEHRI/AFP via Getty Images.*

In general, radio broadcasts are divided into "commercial" and "public service" programs. Commercial radio is more audience-targeted with specifically curated programs and types of music (and makes profit by airing advertisements), whereas public service radio caters for the masses who are exposed to a variety of music.[79] As the digital revolution quickly evolved and led to greater music consumption for the listener, DAB radio expanded too. DAB has the advantage of scanning and saving radio stations (rather than the consumer manually searching for it with a dial), with the addition of displaying the name of the artist and title of the song on the radio itself. With the addition of the internet (in particular, streaming), the consumer has access to a variety of global digital radio stations, with many offering a limited backlog of shows in case he/she wants to "catch up" and listen to it in his/her own time.

In addition to digital radio, the podcast appears to have changed the consumer's approach to listening to the radio. Podcasts are audio programs that are transmitted on the internet.[80] The name "podcast" is a wordplay based on Apple's device, the "iPod," and the word "broadcast," and the original podcast was intended as an app for the Apple iPod in 2004, where a consumer could pay and download shows from iTunes and listen to it in his/her own time.[81] At first, the podcast was considered as a form of amateur radio.[82] However, the concept of the podcast gradually took off on its own, where anybody could set up his or her own show with affordable software. The appeal of the podcast is its content, such as interviews, music chats, documentaries, reviews, and storytelling, and it simulates a live radio experience. Kris Markman highlights this notion: "recreating a live experience in an asynchronous platform is a reflection of podcasting's deep roots in the tradition of live broadcast radio."[83] Nowadays, the podcast is successfully evolving and becoming more mainstream, as public service broadcasts (such as the BBC) and streaming platforms (such as Spotify) now offer their services. In what could be argued as the new wave of the "radio," what makes the podcast appealing is its accessibility and mobility. The consumers/listeners no longer need to wait for a particular show; instead, they can download, store, and listen to podcasts at their own leisure— anytime, and anywhere.

Compact Disc

The CD was a digital audio format that arrived in the 1980s. The CD was initially designed to be a technological advancement in digital consumption, and to rival the tape and vinyl. The buzz of the CD was that it was a small, delicate, plastic, and shiny silver 5" disc, which could store up to eighty minutes of music. The CD did not rely on a needle (as vinyl did) or a magnet (as tape did) to pick up and transfer sounds. Instead, the sounds were digitally read by a laser beam and transmitted with high audio qualities. Another feature in playing the CD was that one could easily "skip" to a desired track, rather than having to search with the stylus/tone arm (vinyl) or the fast-forward push button (tape player).

The CD was released to the consumer market by Sony and Philips in Japan in 1982, and Europe and North America in 1983.[84] From personal experience, as a child in the 1980s, I was fascinated with the CD and its packaging (usually in a plastic jewel case along with an eye-catching CD booklet filled with images, lyrics, and credits), but if I recall right, it was not very affordable at the time. The CD took time to be recognized as a competitive format against vinyl and tape. A decade later, in the early 1990s, a CD album would be around £14, and as that was not affordable to me, I stayed with buying vinyl and cassettes. It was not until the mid-1990s that CDs finally became more affordable, in addition to which there was the rise of the cheap CD single (which carried similar novelty features to the cassingle), meaning it gradually succeeded vinyl and cassettes. The CD led the market until around 2008,[85] when consumers began buying (legal) MP3s, and later subscribing to streaming services.[86]

MiniDisc

Regrettably, not a very popular music consumption device but a "must have" for music creators was the MiniDisc. Invented by Sony in 1992, this device was meant to rival both the cassette and CD, in terms of durability and audio quality. The format of the MiniDisc was a magneto-optical disc that could store up to seventy-four minutes of music (or 320 minutes in long play mode). It had an audio compression and coding system known as ATRAC (Adaptive Transform Acoustic Coding) that allowed the user to make digital copies of recordings in high audio quality.[87] I was a big fan of the MiniDisc when I was a music student. It was an affordable way for me to record my own music, and to record sounds anywhere. It was also a favorable device among my peers, as we would copy and share albums with each other—and we could also name the tracks to make it more personal. Most important of all, however, is that we were amazed by the decent audio quality—but what we would not do was actually buy MiniDisc albums, because they were very expensive. Instead, we would invest in a portable player, which was also expensive but worth it at the time as it became a staple for home recording. Despite Sony's $30 million marketing campaign in the 1990s, the MiniDisc did not sell well. The majority of music consumers were not interested because of the expense: the starting price of a MiniDisc portable player was £150.[88] Despite the MiniDisc's struggle to remain in the consumer market, it rapidly declined when MP3 and its storage digital players, including the iPod, arrived, leading Sony to produce the last batch of the portable players in 2011.

MP3

The MP3, also known as ISO-MPEG Audio Layer-3 or MPEG1,[89] was developed by the German Frauenhofer Institute in 1993. The format was developed to compress audio while maintaining decent sound quality. Although the MP3 became the next digital virtual format in music consumption and the first to be exclusively accessible on the internet, in addition to storing the downloaded tracks on an attractive compact, light, and portable device (more notably the iPod), at first it was more associated with music piracy. What was significant about the MP3 was its invisible (virtual) format totally reliant on digital data (sound) and technology (internet) for it to be accessible. Another distinctive and obvious facet of the MP3 was the omission of fancy packaging. Although later files would include digital virtual visuals—such as album covers, images, text, and credits—initially, it was an exciting invisible format for the consumer. With the MP3, the listening practices or rituals of the consumer were also altered, as consumers were lured into investing in a compact portable device and a new sonic experience. The main physical feature that was erased was, of course, the recorded material in tangible form. Instead, the music was accessed from the internet, downloaded, and collated on a computer. This marked exciting changes in music consumption in the digital virtual era.

The first song to be used as an MP3 was Suzanne Vega's 1987 track, "Tom's Diner." The German Frauenhofer team used the track as a template for finding a way to compress the song, while maintaining its original sound quality for the format. Because Vega's track helped to "crack" the invention of the digital virtual format, she has been nicknamed the "Mother of MP3s."[90] There are conflicting reports about when the first digital single was officially released, but it was considered to be either David Bowie's "Telling Lies" (1996)[91] or Duran Duran's "Electric Barbarella" (1997).[92]

The first MP3 portable player "Diamond Multimedia Systems Rio PMP300" was made available in 1998.[93] It was however Apple's iPod that sealed the success of the MP3 and its generation of digital portable players. While the concept was devised by Tony Fadell and designed by Ben Knauss, it was the CEO of Apple, the late Steve Jobs, who invested in the product.[94] Indeed, while there are other famous brands of MP3 portable players (e.g., Sony MP3 Walkman), the iPod (and its respective models, such as the Nano, Touch, iPhone, iPad) carried unique qualities that made it a high-profile product that was much in demand and intensified the digital virtual listening experience for the consumer. As argued by Michael Bull (2006), the iPod offers the consumer more freedom and more choices, because of its device's features such as generous storage, shuffle (where the device randomly selects tracks), and playlists (where the user can create a list of songs/albums to suit a mood or event).[95] To access the music, the users need to install software (formerly known as iTunes), after which they can upload their existing music collection or buy MP3s and transfer them to the iPod. What differentiated the iPod from earlier devices, such as the iconic Sony Walkman, is that the iPod was a small and light device able to digitally store up to 10,000 songs. Where, in the past, the consumers may have needed to be choosy about what selection of tapes or CDs to take with them when traveling, the iPod meant that users could digitally store their entire music collection and "carry" their music everywhere. Think of it like this: the consumer had become his/her own mobile music library.[96]

Streaming

At the time of writing, consumers now have the choice to partake in the streaming era, which is a rapidly growing, digital virtual form of gaining access to music. Streaming is accessible only via the internet, and consumers can listen to music (in addition to watching videos and films) in real time. Streaming media does not consist of digital files; instead, it is based on data/bits and bytes (a tactic to prevent piracy), and it can be played on most devices, for example, any smartphone, Apple device, or computer. The advantage is that the consumers can listen to music anytime without having to think about their storage—although there is the consideration that listening on a smartphone can eat up the phone's data limit and can result in the users paying additional 3G/4G/5G charges for their music. When handled correctly, streaming can be affordable, mainly through subscription-based services. Depending on the bit rate of the stream and internet connection, however, the audio quality can, at times, be sketchy. There are a wide variety of streaming services, such as subscription-based, on-demand, video-sharing platforms, and internet radio—and these are increasing all the time.

While there is a variety of music-streaming sites on offer, such as Tidal, SoundCloud, BBC iPlayer, YouTube, and Apple Music, Spotify[97] is arguably the most successful subscription-based service. With different packages on offer (based on a monthly subscription), the consumer has access to a wide variety of songs. Spotify also uses algorithms to monitor the consumer's music tastes and automatically recommends a playlist,[98] making the "Spotify" experience personalized and unique.

While this can be viewed as a promotional tactic, it can also be approached as an exciting way to discover new music. Furthermore, Spotify serves as a social tool, because it can connect with social media platforms, such as Facebook and Instagram, and invites the consumers to share their musical tastes (and playlists) with their friends. In addition, Spotify allows the consumers to customize their listening experience. They can create playlists, connect with social media, personalize the look and feel of the interface, listen to music offline, read mini-biographies of artists, create a virtual radio station on the Spotify's radio app, and add friends (whose music tastes or recommendations they can check out). The main disadvantage with music streaming, however, is that the consumer cannot "keep" or "own" a copy of the music.[99] This may not go down well with music-lovers and collectors, but may suit people who are casual listeners, not concerned with storing or "owning" music.

In the digital virtual era, music consumption practices have altered, that is, many consumers now have to *access* the music,[100] rather than *owning* a copy of the song. This brings in choices for the consumers and may question their decision about whether they choose to access or "own" the music. Is accessing the music for casual listening a way of not being judged by one's musical tastes? Or does the consumer who prefers to maintain tradition in buying and owning the music see it as a format for emotional connection and nostalgia (including better sound quality)? We are in a position to have many choices on how we buy, access, hear, and "own" music, and those choices are still evolving, thanks to the digital virtual era. As Frith neatly said, music is "open to appropriation for personal use in a way that other popular cultural forms . . . are not."[101]

Digital Virtual Technology— Communications and Media

We all have different experiences of digital virtual technology and its evolution over our own life spans. When we look at the developments of communication (better known as ICT—Information Communication Technology), it becomes apparent that it was not only music technology that sparked radical and exciting changes in culture and society. What music technology has in common with any other kind of technology is that it has made a personal impact on our everyday lives, whether in terms of work, leisure, or independence—so it is significant to gain an overview of how we got here.

1940s to the 1950s

During the 1940s and 1950s, computers were for military and governmental use only. In 1947, the first transmitter was invented by John Bardeen, Walter Brattain, and William Shockley at Bell Laboratories in New Jersey, United States. It consisted of a semiconductor device to amplify and switch electronic signals.[102] In 1951, the first computer was used for arithmetic and data handling (mainly for census purposes). It was known as UNIVAC (the Universal Automatic Computer) and was designed by J. Presper Eckert and John W. Mauchly.[103] The machine was described by the *New York Times* as an "eight-foot-tall mathematical genius [that could] classify an average citizen as to sex, marital status, education, residence, age group, birthplace, employment, income and a dozen other applications."[104] The machine was huge and heavy, needing a great deal of floor space. The year 1957 saw the invention of the Sensorama Simulator, which was considered to be an early form of VR (virtual reality) technology.[105] Created by Morton Helig, the Sensorama consisted of a 3D video machine that enabled the user to virtually drive or fly a form of transport (e.g., motorbike or helicopter) while experiencing the "real-life" surroundings (scenery) and senses (smells, sounds, vibrations, or wind).

1960s to the 1970s

In 1963, Ivan Sutherland developed the first interactive graphics program, "The Sketchpad." This interactive program enabled the user to create designs on a screen by using a light pen, which could be stored and retrieved.[106] The year 1965 saw an early form of CGI (Computer Generated Imagery) with a computer-generated ballet created by A. Michael Noll of Bell Laboratories. It was created by using small figures and made an impression of the figures "rushing around" on the stage.[107] This was considered to be groundbreaking as it also involved living animals, not merely objects or geometric shapes in virtual form.[108] In 1968, the film *Hummingbird* was the first to be represented as a computer-generated animation, created by Charles Csuri. In 1969, the ARPANET (Advanced Research Projects Agency Network), a precursor to the internet, was created by Lawrence Roberts. ARPANET's purpose was to connect computers over Pentagon's research organizations via telephone lines.[109] In 1971, Ray Tomlinson created the "email" for ARPANET users so that they could send messages electronically. Email was further developed by Larry Roberts in the following year when he created the following functions when using this type of electronic communication: "list" (inbox), "select" (choose message), "forward" (to send the email to another user), and "respond" (reply to the message).[110]

The first video game console was created by Nolan Bushnell with Atari, and it debuted in 1972; this was followed by Atari's successful "Pong" home console version in 1975.[111] Also in the same year, a pioneering moment saw the first computer-generated hand (better known as "The Computer Animated Hand").[112] This was created by scientists Ed Catmull[113] and Fred Parke, who transformed Catmull's hand into a sequence of polygons, which were then digitalized into a hand shape. The fascination surrounding this computer graphic was that the digital virtual hand could move, like a normal hand.

1980s

From the 1980s, computers became smaller, desktop size, and commercially available to the public. Computers back then were marketed as PCs (Personal Computers) and manufactured by the likes of IBM, Commodore, and Amstrad. Computer design in digital video media was flourishing too. For example, in 1981, a 3D-simulated performance animation, titled *Adam Powers, The Juggler*, was created by scientists and film producers Gary Demos and John Whitney Jr. The creators placed the juggler Ken Rosenthal in a motion capture suit and filmed him juggling and doing backflips.[114] Returning to the commercial computer, that same year saw the advent of the portable laptop computer. Created by Adam Osborne, the laptop computer "Osborne 1" could be stored inside a suitcase and was designed for both work and home situations, and, as suggested by its name, it could rest on "top" of the "lap." It featured a 5" monitor, weighed 23.5 pounds, stored up to 64k of memory, and contained two disk drives.[115] In 1983, the first mobile phone, designed for commercial use, was launched in the United States, invented by Martin Cooper for Motorola. Two years later, in 1985, the UK's first model was the Transportable Vodafone VT1. Famously known as the "brick" phone, it weighed around five kilograms and, depending on the model, the price was around $4,000 in the United States and £1,400–1,600 in the UK.[116] The phone was aimed at users who were always "on the go" and working long hours. A disadvantage (other than the size of the device) was that a ten-hour battery-charged phone meant only thirty minutes of usage. From the 1980s, mobile phone technology has been majorly revolutionized and has continued to evolve at a breathtakingly rapid rate ever since! Fast forwarding to 1989, the World Wide Web (WWW) was created by Tim Berners-Lee at CERN.[117] Similar to ARPANET, the WWW was to enforce a global information system by merging digital virtual data networks on the internet and hypertext (e.g., web pages/website) via computers. This proved to be a radical advancement in digital virtual technology with the WWW becoming vital for communication, for everything from emails and social networking, to banking and security, and, of course, sharing music. A world without the WWW now seems unimaginable.

1990s

During the 1990s, computers and laptops were becoming increasingly popular at home, in schools and colleges, and in the workplace. In 1992, the internet became commercial to the public as a dial-up service;[118] this meant it had to be connected via a phone line in order for the user to have access to the internet. Memories of those days are colored by the sounds of its screeching tone and very slow connection rates. In 1994, the first smartphone was introduced, designed by IBM and Bellsouth. "Simon," the name of the smartphone, was almost like a mini-computer. It did not have a web browser at this time, but the user could send emails, faxes, and, of course, make phone calls. Apps were unknown back then, but "Simon" had digital virtual features that resembled applications. The features represented a Filofax (a personal organizer) as it consisted of an address book, calculator, calendar, note pad, and clock.[119] "Simon" was a very expensive device, meaning it did not do well in the consumer market.

In 1997, SixDegrees.com was the first (but short-lived) social media site to be created. This site allowed users to post profiles of themselves and connect with friends.[120] Social media features we take for granted now were nonexistent then, the site allowed solely the function of sending direct messages to friends. Then, in 1998, the world witnessed the advent of Google, a free web search engine developed by two university students, Larry Page and Sergey Brin.[121] Google has successfully (but at times controversially) developed exponentially over the last twenty years, offering internet services such as social networking, shopping, blogging, emailing, saving and writing documents online, navigating directions in real time via Google Maps, saving files in the cloud (on its virtual drive), and providing its own web browser (Chrome) and app platform (Google Play). Google also owns many other companies, including apps, digital platforms such as YouTube, and the smartphone operating system, Android. In 1999, Bluetooth was launched: it was a form of wireless technology designed for users of phones, computers, and digital cameras which allowed the transfer of digital files/data over a short distance, without needing the internet.[122]

2000s

From 2000 onward, digital virtual technology began to evolve rapidly and became more affordable. In 2000, Broadband came into effect in the UK, promising a much faster internet connection.[123] Over time, the internet speed of Broadband increased and attracted many consumers with its mega-quick download time, the ability to instantly share files, to stream audiovisual media in real time, and to participate in online activities such as shopping, learning, conferences, and gaming. New communication platforms included Skype, a digital virtual video service, which debuted in 2003,[124] making it easier for users to converse with friends, colleagues, and "watch" them—or simply speak to them, like in an old-fashioned phone call, in real time, from anywhere in the world, to anywhere in the world (as long as the users had access to an internet connection). This revolutionized how we communicate with each other, allowing the impression that users were talking to and seeing each other face to face in VR.

In 2003, the game Second Life was launched by Linden Research Inc. This 3D virtual world game allowed people to experience their ideal life as a digital embodiment otherwise known as an avatar (which is created with the software provided).[125] In this digital virtual environment, avatars live a "normal" second life, in which they can build and live in their ideal home, work at their dream job, go shopping—while spending the local Linden currency—study a course, go on holiday, buy land, form relationships, socialize, and get married.[126] Crucially, avatars can also create and perform music in Second Life.[127]

Further inventions came through the increased development of social media, with the likes of MySpace in 2003 (see Chapter 9) and the more successful but also increasingly controversial Facebook (founded by Mark Zuckerberg in 2004). Facebook allows users to share all kinds of information about themselves including images, and can be a convenient way of keeping in touch with family, old school friends, and colleagues. Furthermore, users are invited to post their thoughts, easily connect with acquaintances, engage in activities, and share media, such as their favorite music. Facebook can also serve as a promotional platform for musicians, making it easier for them to showcase their material and connect with fans.

In 2005, the video-sharing platform YouTube was launched,[128] enabling viewers to watch or upload visual material, such as music, videos, documentaries, and vlogs. It is also another great promotional tactic, especially given the viral opportunities for music labels to upload their artists'/bands' videos. The more the video is watched and shared, the more success it garners for the uploader and his/her associates in terms of popularity and some financial gain.[129]

Another major breakthrough in technology was the 2007 release of the iPhone. Apple's CEO, Steve Jobs, confidently predicted it would "reinvent" the telecommunications market[130] by being a handheld and mobile computer. The iPhone sparked a wave of rival smartphones (notably from Samsung). The smartphone has come a long way since the "Simon," as most smartphones have multiple uses and functions including making videos, using Wi-Fi, conferencing, checking social media, and sending data/music.[131] Apple followed up the success of the iPhone in 2010 with the introduction of the iPad, a computable touchscreen tablet where one can "hold the whole web in your hands."[132] While considered by some as merely a bigger version of the iPhone (it carries very similar features), the iPad was the most compact computer to date (along with newer generations of models and obviously rival branded tablets), due to its light weight and lack of keyboard (it's all digital).

Another revolution happened in 2011, with the arrival of the popular digital/crypto currency: the Bitcoin. Created by a programming collective, known as Satoshi Nakamoto, Bitcoin users could trade digital currency for physical money or for goods or services.[133] Then, in 2016, the tech revolution continued into the progression of human interaction with VR, AR (Augmented Reality) and MR (Mixed Reality), which all started to take shape in the digital virtual world.[134] VR technology, for example, allows the users to "virtually" immerse and travel anywhere, or participate in activities (such as sports or concerts) in real time, without even having to leave their homes, yet at the same time, they are situated in a virtual environment. To use this feature, users would need a VR headset such as Oculus Rift, Google Cardboard, Samsung Gear VR, or a gaming console such as PlayStation VR. This VR experience is popular with video games and YouTube 360-degree videos.

AR, is very similar to VR, but is mixed with actual reality. To clarify, the user can interact in reality with the digital virtual through a smartphone's app. The difference with VR is that in VR the user is "placed" in a virtual world (thanks to the appropriate headset), whereas AR enhances your actual environment with virtual objects.[135] A classic example of AR would be the Pokémon Go game where users would search for virtual creatures (objects) in their own (actual) environment (for example, at work, in a park, or on their own street).[136] There is also MR, where VR and AR are merged together and the users can interact with digital virtual objects in a virtual space, which coincides with their own actual/physical environment/space.[137]

Currently, we are living in the digital virtual era, or the information age, in which we are becoming completely dependent on technology. Digital virtual technology has an impact not only on music and media, it has also stretched into everyday life. The excitement of digital virtual technology, however, has not always been positive. There is a dark side to this where users can take their liberation and freedom of speech for granted, in order to spread hate or to blackmail, cyberbully, cyberstalk, or spark heated political debates. They can roll out fake news, spread digital viruses, compromise cyber security, use fraud, troll strangers, and breach copyright-protected works. Policing the internet, distributing sanctions, or practicing censorship can minimize these issues, but it is a stark reminder that digital virtual technology users (depending on the country) have the freedom to use the internet and their devices as they please—regardless of their ethics and morals. On a positive note, the digital virtual era is continuing to grow fast, and if we choose or are fortunate to have the opportunity to have access to it, it can *transform* our lives, in the way we communicate, learn, create, collaborate, consume, and, to survive.

2

"Technology Gives You Everything Immediately . . ."[1]

A Brief Critical Discussion on the Digital Virtual

It is necessary to draw some critical thinking on the concept of how we indulge in digital virtual music and technology, and to encourage a critical sense of appreciation of digital virtual music and why it is valuable not only in music but also in wider society and culture.

Technology

When researching the critical thinking on technology, Martin Heidegger's 1954 essay "The Question Concerning Technology" is a useful starting point, as he provokes questions on how we perceive technology. Heidegger argues that technology is "a way of revealing."[2] He explains that the ancient Greek term "techne" (technology) is defined as something coming into existence through technique and art. To elaborate, we may think of that definition of transforming something (based on an idea or imagination, i.e., the virtual) into some kind of reality and actuality through technology, but with added intention. It is, however, "modern technology" that Heidegger is more anxious about, as it may not carry the original intentions and meanings. Modern technology is more of a convenience for the consumer where technology is used as a digestible resource, and this is of concern to Heidegger because it may bring unexpected consequences for the user. We may want to apply this thinking to digital technology, computer-generated environments, and even ICTs (for example, smartphones), where the users may become too involved or dependent on their virtual world or on their devices without realizing it, which may result in isolation. As an example, when we engage on the internet we briefly forget our physical surroundings. In the previous chapter, we looked at how technology has transformed music creation and consumption and, more significantly, built an aesthetic relationship with the devices. Today, we are exposed to all types of technology, and perhaps without us realizing it, we depend on them or replace them too frequently. For example have you ever had that moment when the Wi-Fi connection is lost and you need to reply to an urgent email? Or how about the disposable technology (such as cars, smartphones) that we no longer need, or consider outdated, therefore we discard them, leading to waste that damages the environment, humans, and animals? While Heidegger's essay brings critical debate, if we choose to, we can apply some of his thoughts to challenge our thinking on how and why we perceive technology and what it actually means to us.

We can develop this concept further by perceiving what it means for the user to use the application in its fixed technology. Take sound, for example. Playing a "copy" of the music, such as on the record player, simulates a live performance in the user's space. This motivates the user (creator or consumer) to virtually place himself or herself *in* the performance, or to reminisce about a past event. While the music and the user are brought together, the sounds transferred from the device may give the illusion that the user is the holder of the music, especially in the way he or she is emotionally absorbing the sonics and music which personalizes his or her listening experience. But back in reality, the user is only the holder of a "copy" of the music rather than owning the original music. The user was not present in the actual performance or the recording process, therefore he or she does not have the unique (master) recording. Does this change the perception of how the users perceive music or their listening experience? Should it change it? In *The Work of Art in the Age of Mechanical Reproduction* (originally written in 1936), Walter Benjamin argues that any art form, such as a painting or photograph (or, indeed, a recording), can be reproduced into a copy but this copy cannot convey its "aura" and its unique and original intention.[3] Benjamin did, however, argue that the copy, that is, the representation of the original, may or may not carry the original intentions of the format to the consumers, but that they can use the copy to generate a new meaning of their experience. In addition, the reproduction of the original source may "place the copy of the original in situations beyond the reach of the original itself."[4] With this in mind, we can now focus specifically on the creator who applies preexisting recordings, or sounds, in his or her music, where such uses (e.g., sampling) are intertextual,[5] and may extend the original meaning of its origin or bring out a new context to support the subject of the song.[6] Furthermore, in a creative context, using preexisting recordings or sounds to digitally enhance music in particular, should be considered as "postproduction."[7]

Nicolas Bourriaud argues that the position of the preexisting work is significant as "[i]t is caught in a chain, and its meaning depends in part on its position in the chain,"[8] confirming the enhanced intentions of the music from its original to the copy. While a copy of any source (other than music) could never really fulfill a complete likeness of the original, it does provoke questions on whether a likeness (or copy) of something, or a desire made possible by technology, can achieve an intention. To explore this concept further we can now direct our thoughts to virtuality.

Virtuality

Defining the "virtual" is complex as there is no static or concrete meaning of the term. For example, when the term is traced back to its word origins, in Middle English, it means "efficacious" and "potential," and in Latin (known as *virtus*) is defined as "strength" and "virtue."[9] I am more persuaded by its definition meaning "potential," although I can virtually view how virtue can also be considered. There again, the definitions can draw out further meanings that extend the complexity in understanding the term, such as illusion, fake, fiction, incomplete, not real, almost real, fantasy, or sense of presence. It is no wonder then, that we have multiple ways of using the word in everyday conversation, yet at the same time, perhaps we can agree that our understanding of the "virtual" is potentially representing something that is real, almost real, or realness in actuality, or real life. While I could forever apply additional assumptions to this word, Charles Peirce attempts an understanding of the virtual by defining it as "A virtual X (where X is a common noun) is something, not an X, which has the efficiency (virtus) of an X."[10] While at first glance, Peirce's definition appears to have explained its meaning (and I like his definition a lot), upon reading it again—and slowly—it does bring out further challenges in understanding the term! However we may read it, the virtual does appear to be directing toward the "potential" or "representing," some kind of, or even an impression of, reality. This leads to the work of Rob Shields, who offers one of many ways of understanding the term, such as "the virtual captures the nature of activities and objects which exist but are not tangible, not 'concrete.'"[11] He uses his now-famous analogy as an example, by referring to the Roman Catholic practice where church attendees believe they receive the body and blood of Christ in the form of bread and wine during communion—thus giving the impression that Christ is actually present, when in reality, he is virtually present.[12] Shields also leads to an insight on how we perceive the virtual in our own internal space, or own personal world, where we momentarily forget about our surroundings (the external world) and, instead, are immersed in some kind of virtual environment. We can describe this occasion as being in a virtual reality where technology, in particular digital technology, can create environments and people.[13]

There are various claims as to when the term "virtual reality" was coined but there are two main contenders. In 1936, Antonin Artaud used the term "virtual reality" in his essay[14] to argue how creators, actors, stage, props, lights, objects, images, and audience result in performing and creating a "purely fictitious and illusionary world"[15] in the theater. In the late 1980s, Jaron Lanier popularized, rather than coining, the term. Lanier, a computer scientist, writer, and musician, owned VPL Research (Virtual Programming Languages), a VR company, that was the first to sell and invent VR-related products such as headsets and motion sensing gloves. Lanier describes virtual reality as

A technology that uses computerized clothing to synthesize shared reality. It recreates our relationship with the physical world in a new plane, no more, no less. It doesn't affect the subjective world; it doesn't have anything to do directly with what's going on inside your brain. It only has to do with what your sense organs perceive. The physical world, the thing on the other side of your sense organs, is received through these five holes, the eyes, and the ears, and the nose, and the mouth, and the skin.[16]

Lanier emphasizes that, in a virtual reality, it is about experiencing the sensations with the body rather than just witnessing it and questioning its realness (or un-realness) and absorbing the experience in that particular moment. Before virtual reality became more popular in music, it had already built a lasting relationship with film, most notably in science fiction, with *Bladerunner* (1982), *The Lawnmower Man* (1992), and *The Matrix* (1999) as commonly cited examples, as well as in video games, where the creativity of worlds, lifestyle, and changing of people's identities are limitless, and permit users to escape from reality to experience another "reality," albeit temporarily. In addition, postmodern bodies in virtual reality can be presented as a mixture of machine and human, known as cyborg (cybernetic organism), something commonly featured in films, including *Robocop* (1987), *The Terminator* (1984), and *Avatar* (2009).

Overall, virtuality (that is the virtual and virtual reality) can potentially be the representation of something wonderful, or dare I say distasteful or even fearful (see my earlier comment on dystopia), but as Brian Massumi insists, for it to accomplish itself, "it must recede from being apace with its becoming."[17] It must be highlighted, however, that, due to the advances of digital technology, there are moments when the division between the real and virtual appear to be blurred, or the user chooses to be oblivious of the distinction as argued by Jean Baudrillard and his concept of hyperreality.

Hyperreality

We can delve deeper into the relationship between the user and technology, and the real and the virtual, and how meanings are generated and experienced in the digital virtual era. As we are already aware, technology is becoming increasingly prominent in our lives and serves as an "extension" of ourselves as well as being reliant on it (as predicted by Marshall McCluhan)[18]—especially now in the digital virtual era, where the virtual can "duplicate reality,"[19] in addition to "slowly replacing reality,"[20] and making the unpresentable, presentable.[21] Jean Baudrillard makes a persuasive claim that reality can no longer exist as we are constantly surrounded by simulations of signs that represent the desirable, imaginable, and/or the original. He famously demonstrated that there are three stages of the representation known as the Orders of the Simulacra (1976).[22] To apply this in a musical context, the first order, the counterfeit, would represent a direct copy of music. While the word suggests fakeness, this could be perceived as piracy (with the intention of illegally distributing copyright material), or just having a flavor of preserving a copy of the music, even though it is not the original work. The second order, the production, would imply multiple copies of music (CD, tape, record), devices, and instruments. These are simply copies of the "original" recording or artifact, which lets the user have a taste of experiencing, consuming, and owning, for example, a record, even though he or she has no direct contact or connection with the original source (the product, idea, or process). The third order, the simulation, is the most discussed theory, as it ties with dialogues concerning technology, digital, virtuality, and culture. This order obliterates the divide between the real and imaginable, or the real and unreal. Examples would include a creator remixing a record (with existing recordings), or inserting samples (from an existing recording) in a composition making it unnoticeable or undetectable to the listener; a performer (or band) simulating a live performance by miming, yet offering a very convincing (but discerning) impression that it is real;[23] and, listening to a digital format (CD, MP3) or music streams, which allow the listeners to hear a simulated performance in their virtual environment. Another, but pertinent, example to include is when the consumers engage in the hyperreal—to witness a performance where the simulation is very appealing, one that totally, but temporarily and virtually, removes them from their surroundings.

To apply another perspective, but in a nonmusical approach, we can turn to the author Umberto Eco, who observed hyperreality in Las Vegas. Eco illustrated Las Vegas as a hyperreal city designed for entertainment (mainly gambling).[24] He asserted that the hyperreal city includes a simulation of well-known features, such as the Eiffel Tower and Egyptian pyramids, situated in an "actual" city but giving the illusion of loss of space, place, location, and time, whereas, in reality, it is the city of Las Vegas designed to make a profit.

A similar opinion was offered by Baudrillard who described Las Vegas as a "desert . . . bathed in phosphorescent lights" and for gambling,[25] making the whole experience of being exposed to the floating signs, such as the bright lights and attractive buildings, appear "more real than real," when in reality, what lies behind this illusion, in this particular context, is capitalism and crushing consumerism (for the consumers spending and perhaps losing their money in gambling, for example).[26]

Returning to music hyperreality, we can reintroduce the notion of technology that invites the consumers to have a VR, AR, or MR experience by participating in digital virtual performance and video game music. It should also be added that they can simply indulge in hyperreality by witnessing the performances on their screens (such as Gorillaz, Hatsune Miku, or a virtual collaboration of a choir or orchestra). However, if the consumers/creators choose to actually engage inside the hyperreal, it permits them to place their desires or to experience the unknown in reality on a temporary basis. In general, however we choose to engage in digital virtual technology regardless of time frame, we cannot deny that it shapes our imagination and cultural awareness, and while this notion overlaps with the topics discussed so far, the relationship between technology, virtuality, hyperreality, and the creator/consumer/audience draws in elements of postmodernism.

Postmodernism

The word "postmodernism" is a dated and debatable term[27] and the theory surrounding it is capable of causing a divide among academics: they will either champion it (like myself) or detest it. There's a vast amount of work on this subject, but the topic can still create an unsettling dialogue. Even to define the term creates issues, as postmodernism resists a fixed definition, and its historical origins are not fixed either.[28] One of my favorite definitions, which sums up the term neatly, was offered by Walter T. Anderson (1995):

> The word "postmodernism" is floating around rather freely these days, and it means different things to different people. To some, it means funny architecture; to others, French intellectuals you can't understand; to others, anything weird, campy, trendy or high-tech. Some people equate it with the idea that all values and beliefs are equal.[29]

It is true to think that the term tends to be openly used "these days," especially in the media. However, in the creative practices of music alone, postmodern elements are evident with the aid of technology where broken musical rules and conventions, nonexistence of musical hierarchies, "confusions over time and space,"[30] genre/style blending, and past and present fusion (see hauntology), are apparent in the music. Recognizing postmodern practices in music is likely to raise questions about authenticity, authorship, and identity of the creator and performer.

Hauntology

Originally devised by Jacques Derrida, hauntology can exist in creations where the past can unintentionally be in the present. However, Derrida argues that "to haunt does not mean to be present, and it is necessary to introduce haunting into the very construction of a concept,"[31] like a specter virtually existing without possible reason, yet at the same time, trying to find its purpose of existence. Hauntology is effectively heard in music, especially in remixes (Chapter 4) and video games (Chapter 5), which makes users of any kind (creators or consumers) relive their past without taking into account the fact that they are virtually revisiting or simulating elements of the "past" (the specter) in the present. Examples include seeing a sentimental photograph, or watching emotional videos and choosing to implement them in their works, activities, or everyday lives, thereby refusing to let go of that moment—as Colin Davis argues, "replacing the priority of being and presence with the figure of the ghost as that which is neither present, nor absent, neither dead nor alive."[32] With this in mind and due to the never-ending exciting developments of technology, questions are raised about how we can possibly think about moving forward, if we choose to be so fixated on the past? Applying this specifically to music, Mark Fisher makes a persuasive claim that the "futuristic" sound in music was halted toward the turn of the twenty-first century. He argues, "By 2005 or so, it was becoming clear that electronic music could no longer deliver sounds that were 'futuristic' . . . practically anything produced in the 2000s could have been recorded in the 1990s."[33] So where does this leave the futuristic sounds which "now connoted a settled set of concepts, affects, and associations"?[34] Fisher argues that we are experiencing the "after the future" where, in this context, music has reached a point where unique innovations are pretty much nonexistent because we cannot avoid acknowledging the music's past, especially in the digital virtual era. This postmodern treatment, where simulating, imitating, and recycling its past are dominantly evident in works, will evoke a sense of retro-ness and nostalgia, replacing the nonexistent future for the creator and consumer. Critics have not taken this move lightly, such as Simon Reynolds who argues that pop culture is addicted to its own past.[35] In a musical sense, the hint of the haunting, specter, and past used in the present should be celebrated as a form of renaissance. While the nonexistent futuristic sounds concept is certainly debatable, music creation in particular should be viewed as an opportunity for creators to experiment with previous sounds in an attempt to erase the division of the past and present, by making the unimaginable imaginable, and to bring life back to music.

Actor Network Theory (ANT)

Finally, in the digital virtual era, we must consider that our relationship with technology has strengthened, whether we are creators, controllers, operators, or consumers, or even perform all of these roles. We have relied on technology for everyday situations and technology has relied on us to make the concept meaningful. While it is likely that some will view technology as the "other" and will not consider its relevance in our lives, we do eventually have to accept that we cannot live without it. Like a traditional classical musician eventually accepting other forms of contemporary music, especially when technology is involved (mainly electronic and digital), he or she may eventually incorporate new methods into his or her music, in order to keep himself/herself relevant in his/her profession.

We realize most fully that technology is an intrinsic part of our lives when we lose that Wi-Fi connection, or our smartphone, or worst of all, when our computer crashes resulting in a loss of communication and important information. Technology is becoming increasingly significant, especially when we rely on it for our everyday needs. To critically evaluate this concept we can apply actor network theory (ANT) where the actor (the participant) does not act alone and needs other means, whether it is people or technology (or both), to make "action" happen. The theory was devised in 1980 by sociologists Brian Latour, John Law, and Michel Callon, who examined how actors and actons (nonhumans, e.g., technology) interact and build relationships (or "network") with each other. As Latour argues, "To use the word 'actor' means that it is never clear who and what is acting. . . . Does the audience's reaction count? What about the lighting? What is the backstage crew doing? . . . Action is borrowed, distributed, suggested, influenced, dominated, betrayed, translated."[36] Naturally, this concept can be applied in any situation and subject, including music.

Simon Zagorski-Thomas recognizes that there are two features when facilitating ANT in music: "the first arises from describing the participants, their environment and their relationship with each other; the second arises from elucidating the nature of their influence upon each other."[37] While that particular context is applied to record production, that notion could be extended further to how we perceive music and its relationship with creators, controllers/operators, consumers/audience, and technology.

3

"We Are Musical Makers"

The Experimental and Digital Virtual Trademarks of Genre and Style

Modern music creation is very reliant on various types of technology, making any virtual musical ideas possible, almost immediately. Rewind to the musical past, and we know it was a slow but ongoing development process, from analog, to electric, to digital (see Chapter 1). While studying or reviewing music, it is beneficial to examine the context of musical genres and styles,[1] and when the research is underway, it is reasonable to state that technology has shaped certainly many, if not all, musical genres and styles. Certain musical genres/styles would simply not exist without technology. However, in technology's shaping of genres and styles, experimentation is always involved, and it is no surprise when we hear music today, that we can often identify genre/style crossovers in a composition or song. How can the term "experimental" be understood and applied to specific genres and styles? There is a risk that, depending on the type of music we like listening to (or creating), individual perceptions of "experimental" music can be hotly contested. However, when formally studying "experimental" music (at university, for example), it can be considered as a compositional practice on its own (based on my personal experience). Therefore, we're going to look at ways in understanding experimental music, focusing on the genres/styles of Krautrock, psychedelic, dub, hip-hop, ambient, and electronica—all genres/styles that arguably fall under what I call the experimental "umbrella."[2]

Understanding Experimental Music

Experimental music is fascinating to explore because any genre or style can belong to it, and it can have multiple definitions—as a result, this often leads to confusion or debate. Some careful and persuasive definitions of "experimental" include "a position—of openness, of inquiry, of uncertainty, of discovery,"[3] and where the musical outcome is "not known in advance."[4] These impressions of the experimental being unpredictable but discoverable in the compositional process recall Brian Eno's concept of "variety,"[5] where so-called organized sound translates to "anything goes"—there are no concrete music rules to obey.

Common impressions when detecting experimental music include unconventional methods of creation, free form (that is no set form or structure), and, the application of everyday and nonmusical sounds ("found sounds" or unusual sounds). It is what the word "experimental" suggests, and that is, to "experiment." Experimental music does not, however, suit all listeners' musical palate, and for some, the word "marmite" comes to mind, in which the listener would either "love it" or "hate it."[6] The music may be easily digestible for the listener, or it may take more time to appreciate. All kinds of music include some degree of experimentation in creating (i.e., implementing and producing the musical idea). As we are already aware, experimental music invokes different meanings and musical experiences for the individual. When listening to all kinds of experimental music, I detect a lot of dedication and creation, and it is up to the individual listener whether to speculate as to the musical intentions, to appreciate the effort that was implemented in the music, or merely to enjoy it.

Tracing the history of experimental music can be quite daunting, because it can be as long as researching the history of technology. Experimental music always involves technology, whether it is using a traditional instrument, and/or digital machines.

On the History of Experimental Music

A good starting point would be the American composer John Cage's use of the "Prepared Piano" in 1940. He is highly regarded as an influential experimental composer,[7] although more on the avant-garde side of Western art music, and he is known to have dabbled in jazz and electronic music. Cage would "prepare" the piano by placing objects—such as screws, paper clips, or cutlery—between the piano's strings and hammers; this would then alter pitch and/or timbre when the piano was played. His technique developed the piano as an instrument, making it become more than an ordinary piano. The "prepared piano" created new percussive sounds and effects, yet all sourced from one instrument. Cage also created a prepared piano series with compositions including "Bacchanale" (1940) and "Sonata X" (1948).

Around the same time, *Musique concrète* was developing in France. The term was coined by Pierre Schaeffer in 1948,[8] and consisted of experimental music based on recorded sounds. The trademark of this style was the deconstruction and reconstruction of the collected sounds manipulated by technology and machines, such as turntables, tape recorders, microphones, mixers, and filters. Do not expect a well-structured, pretty, melodic piece! Schaeffer would collect, record, collate, splice, create, mix, and edit sounds into a composition on record or tape. Before experimenting with magnetic tape, he would manipulate the sounds of records by mixing, or making certain segments of sounds repetitive by placing them in a locked groove. Schaeffer's *Etude aux chemins der fer* (1948) was an experiment based on the sounds of trains. He recorded various train sounds and used those samples to manipulate and create a composition.[9] The music may give the listener the impression that there is only one train arriving at a station, when in fact it is based on an assortment of train sounds. For the attentive listener, he/she will hear not only the train sounds but also the signifiers presented in the rhythms and timbre based on the composer's original vision. In other words, the purpose is to "experiment" with existing sounds by deferring attention away from the sounds' original source and intentions (in this case a mode of transportation), and by deconstructing and reconstructing the edited, recorded segments (or samples) into a new assemblage of sounds.

Schaeffer also collaborated with fellow experimental composer Pierre Henry on *Symphonie pour un homme seul* between 1949 and 1950. The theme of the symphony was based on a man torn between his everyday life and technology. It was originally intended to be based on human sounds and the body alone where

> The lone man had to find his symphony within himself, not by simply thinking up music in the abstract but by being his own instrument . . . where [he] shouts, he whistles, he walks, he punches, he laughs, he groans. His heart beats, his breathing accelerates, he pronounces words, [he] calls out.[10]

However, the composers organized and threw more sounds into the mix, including prepared piano, banging of doors, creaking of stairs, anxious ascending and descending piano and violin runs, frantic rhythms, industrial sounds, and recorded them on multiple turntables.[11] Hearing the symphony with twenty-two movements may be a surreal experience for the listeners, due to what could be argued as "nonmusical" aspects of the piece, but it encourages them to identify the sounds, and envisage a story. This concept complies with Schaeffer's intentions that this symphony is "an opera for blind people, a performance without argument, a poem made of noises, bursts of texts, spoken or musical."[12] This could also be considered as a form of "virtual symphony," where the "ideal performances take place in the minds, and between the ears, of individual listeners."[13] Further versions of *Symphonie pour un homme seul* followed, such as a ballet adaptation in 1955,[14] and a stereo remix by Pierre Henry in 1966.[15]

The German composer, Karlheinz Stockhausen, was another influential experimental composer and part of the *Musique concrète* brigade. In the 1950s, his celebrated composition *Gesang de Jünglinge*[16] signified the beginning of the end of the first wave of tape composition as it was considered to have outdone other tape-recorded experimental compositions,[17] because of the way in which he combined electronically generated and acoustic sounds. The intention of this *Musique concrète* work was to recreate a youth choir reciting the biblical text, *The Book of Daniel*. Rather than hiring an actual youth choir, Stockhausen got a twelve-year-old choir boy (Josef Protschka) to sing all the instructed melodies. He recorded the vocal sessions, then edited, spliced, deconstructed, and transformed all the vocals (all sung by Protschka) into a fused multitude of innocent and cacophonic fragmented voices with electronically enhanced timbres and sonics making it sound (at times) nonhuman and hauntingly futuristic.

Gesang de Jünglinge was originally commissioned for a religious mass, but electronic equipment, especially loudspeakers, were not permitted in church,[18] despite the piece being based on Christian scripture. Therefore, Stockhausen debuted the piece in an auditorium, instead. This debut was significant to Stockhausen who asserted that "nobody in the world will have the opportunity to listen to this piece again as it should really sound . . . you have to imagine that the sounds really fly through space, turn, oscillate from side to side."[19] To turn his virtual dream into reality, Stockhausen used five groups of loudspeakers surrounding the audience in the auditorium. This unique simulation of a live performance transformed the audience's listening experience as they were soaked in 360° sound. This composition and "performance" are considered groundbreaking in experimental music, where *Musique concrète*, electronics (e.g., sine waves, pulses, filters, white noise), and acoustics are connected musically. While Stockhausen has influenced future experimental and electronic composers, his creations are also referenced in popular music. For example, *Gesang de Jünglinge* has been sampled in Arrigo Barnabé's rock song "Clara Crocodilo" (1980) and in the hip-hop track "Tenfold" by Thundercat (2013). Well-known musicians inspired by Stockhausen include Miles Davis, Frank Zappa, and Paul McCartney. Other highly influential and experimental composers who would play around with *Musique concrète* and anything involving analog/digital synthesis include Delia Derbyshire of the BBC Radiophonic Workshop,[20] Louis and Bebe Barron, Suzanne Ciani, Wendy Carlos, and Pauline Oliveros.

The Experimental Umbrella

Krautrock

Early experimental music provided the foundations for much future music. The works of Stockhausen, in particular *Kontakte* (1960) and *Hymnen* (1967), inspired German music from the late 1960s and throughout the 1970s. "Krautrock" (a questionable term coined by British journalists but widely and memorably marketed as such), otherwise known as *Kosmische Musik* (translated to Cosmic music) in Germany, blended various styles, and in true experimental form, identifying musical trademarks of groups such as Can, Faust, Tangerine Dream, and Neu! are infinite. In a postmodern sense, Krautrock makes unpresentable music presentable, and in some cases extremely surreal.

As with much experimental music, it may not appeal to a wide audience, but the timing of Krautrock is significant. During the 1960s, while mainstream popular music was dominated by US and UK acts, West Germany[21] needed a new identity and a scene of its own. In the past, German composers had dominated Western art music with names such as Bach, Beethoven, and Wagner, but that popularity evaporated while the nation recovered from the Second World War. Artists discovering Stockhausen, *Musique concrète*, and electronic and popular music styles, such as rock (especially psychedelic and progressive), saw a chance to escape the country's devastation and think toward a brighter future through musical creativity. These musicians spearheaded a German musical renaissance, starting with Krautrock, which is known for its grippingly experimental, postmodern, surreal, and sometimes hypnotic music based on a combination of rock, electronic music, *Musique concrète*, jazz, avant-garde, and minimalism. The musical elements are infinite, so expect to hear instruments, machines, or effects based on synthesizers, electric guitars, electronic pulses, and industrial sounds, fused with a chaotic play of timbre, tempo, textures, dynamics, and pitches. In a brief sociocultural context, Krautrock provided a way for young musicians to rebel against society and express their artistic freedom and identities.[22] While the 1960s is known as a decade of protest and resistance, Krautrock music worked as a nondirect way of rebelling, escaping from reality, and virtually voyaging into the future.

Kraftwerk—"Ruckzuck"

A group that originated in the Krautrock scene and "bridged the gap between rock and electronic dance music" is Kraftwerk.[23] The group formed in Düsseldorf in 1968. Founding members Ralf Hütter and Florian Schneider (Figure 3.1) met at a music college and later teamed up with other musicians, including Michael Rother and Klaus Dinger (both of whom later

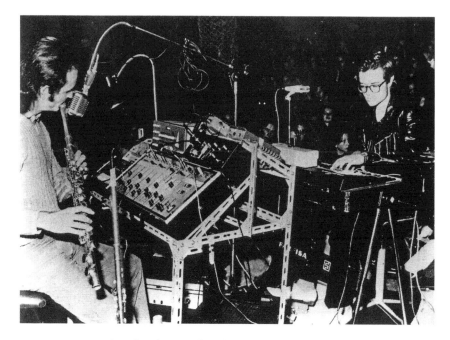

FIGURE 3.1 *Kraftwerk's Florian Schneider and Ralf Hütter. Credit: Gems/Redferns.*

left Kraftwerk to form another famous Krautrock group, Neu!). The group was known visually for their smart-formal-scientist look, and during their live concerts for the robotic aesthetics where they were seen "operating" the synthesizers and machines. Kraftwerk were passionate about participating in creating a new German music scene, as Ralf Hütter highlights: "it was more of a problem to make music in West Germany after the war, as everyday music had gone, it was wiped out. And our generation had to start again."[24] Even though Kraftwerk came from a classical music background (instrumental expertise included flute, violin, piano, and guitar), they became obsessed with playing synthesizers and machines, and breaking conventions of traditional recording practices, such as recording in a laboratory rather than a recording studio.[25] They created progressive electronic tracks and gained in popularity with their 1974 album *Autobahn*. While there are many noteworthy tracks from that album and others, such as the critically acclaimed 1977 album, *Trans Europe Express* or 1978's *Man Machine*, I am going to focus on "Ruckzuck" from their 1970 debut album, *Kraftwerk*, as it neatly depicts a typical Krautrock song.

"Ruckzuck"' is a blend of psychedelic, progressive, avant-garde, *Musique concrète*, and minimalist music.[26] The seven-minute track first comes across as psychedelic music with the "groovy" flute arrangement, hypnotic drums, organ, Moog synthesizer, bass, and sound effects. The music carries components of minimalism led by the multitrack flutes, with its almost lavish opening, followed by a semi-swarm of flute melodic cells.[27] The flute cells are contrapuntal with more flute parts added gradually, supported by a hypnotic rhythm section (which gradually subtracts drum parts) and bass (serving as one pedal note which discretely syncs out of time). While the first two minutes of satisfying and hypnotic sounds draw in the listeners, their enjoyment and psychedelic experience of the music is suddenly interrupted by an acceleration of the rhythm, supported by electronic sonics. These features take over the piece for at least three minutes and exhibit an advanced *Musique concrète* fragment with random sonics, including filtered, oscillated, and atonal sounds, creating a dizzying and disorienting experience for the listener (bearing in mind that one possible intent here was to simulate a drug-induced hallucinatory state). Barely detectable are the quick, random drum fills that gradually transform into a futuristic drum solo, technically manipulated with effects. The peak of the drum solo is suddenly traded for a spaced-out splurge of electronic bleeps, pulses, and sine waves followed by the return of the now fast-paced, minimalist-psychedelic "groovy" music, bringing the listener back to consciousness. Admirers of psychedelic and progressive rock may be reminded of Can, Jethro Tull, and King Crimson when they hear this piece, and may be surprised to learn that it is by Kraftwerk. While Kraftwerk may not always revisit their early music catalog (such as this track) in concerts, they graduated from Krautrock to pure electronic music that later influenced genres such as hip-hop, techno, synth-pop, and house. Many artists have sampled, and been influenced by, their work.[28] As acknowledged by the artist Moby, "None of us would've got involved in electronic music, if we hadn't heard Kraftwerk."[29]

Psychedelic

Famously embodied by much rock music of the 1960s and early 1970s, the term "psychedelic" is associated with recreational drug consumption. The *Merriam-Webster* dictionary defines psychedelic as "drugs (such as LSD) capable of producing abnormal psychic effects (such as hallucinations) and sometimes psychotic states."[30] Drug culture—the consumption of nonprescription drugs including LSD, acid, or marijuana—was popular among hippies and in youth culture, and this was organically reflected in rock music, particularly psychedelic rock, sometimes regarded as the precursor to progressive rock.[31]

Like Krautrock, musicians in psychedelic rock bands experimented with other genres and styles, such as jazz, folk, classical, R 'n' B, and avant-garde. They took advantage of the emerging studio-recording technology and instrumental devices by experimenting with multitracks, sound effects, and mixers.[32] Groups including the Beatles were also fans of *Musique concrète* and implemented it along with psychedelic music in their later works. This enabled creators to produce a simulation of a drug experience and alter the state of human consciousness by experimenting with technology and sound.

For listeners, Sheila Whiteley describes the psychedelic musical experience as a "move against reality . . . and as such there is a fusion with the psychedelic, the unpredictability of hallucinogenic search, the juxtaposition of unknown colors with chaos."[33] While the music may doubly enhance the sensory and hallucinogenic experiences of drug users (through hearing, vision, taste, and smell), nonusers experience the effects of drugs *virtually*, with psychedelic music.[34]

Pierre Henry—"Psyché Rock"

The most obvious people to mention here would be the Beatles, Jimi Hendrix, and Pink Floyd, but as they are so frequently discussed, I want to revisit Pierre Henry from the *Musique concrète* era and analyze his 1968 track, "Psyché Rock." Henry collaborated with French film composer Michel Colombier, and they were both commissioned to compose a dance suite, titled *Messe pour le temps present*, for chorographer Maurice Béjart. "Psyché Rock" was the popular track from the album due to its experimentation with psychedelic rock. It was also the time when Henry became fixated on the Moog synthesizer.[35]

At the beginning of the track, a subtle eruption of electronic buzzes creates a sci-fi atmosphere, which is followed by the main signifier of the music, "Psyché Rock." Here, Henry interpolates the famous vocal hook from Richard Berry and the Pharaohs' R 'n' B track, "Louie Louie" (1957), which is played by various guitars (one rhythmically playing the hook, the other as a fuzz lead), and this catchy melodic feature directs the music. Signs of minimalism are present, with mini melodic cells of double-tracked flutes and brass, and along with the steady drumbeat and bass groove, it serves as a rhythmic accompaniment. Randomly, the electronic (and distorted) bleeps, buzzes, squeals, and whirs freely sync in and out with the rhythm accompaniment, and the bells intriguingly attempt to be a main melody and improvised solo. For the listeners, while they are entranced by the 1960s grooves of the jangly and fuzz guitars, bass, flute trills, and brass, they will also be seized forcefully by the piercing electronic sounds that may alter their consciousness. This experience could either be terrifying (especially with the random loud ruptures of electronic sounds), or indeed, "trippy." While this is perhaps not a favorable example of psychedelic rock (see earlier), this is a great illustration of how this style is not always about the "rock" genre, but about its sensory experience, made possible through journeying in virtual reality, thanks to technology.

Like rock music, "Psyché Rock" has acquired musical longevity—as demonstrated in a tribute album in 2000[36]—and has inspired digital music creators. Timothy D. Taylor persuasively suggests that Henry's musical followers "focus on Henry's music because they can hear that it was never strictly about formal issues."[37] Creators who have sampled or imitated "Psyché Rock" in their music include Fatboy Slim, Stereolab, William Orbit, and Christopher Tyng, who famously revived and recreated the track for the popular animated series, *Futurama*.

Dub

Dub music, which derived from reggae, originated in the mid-1960s in Jamaica, and inspired the development of remixing and, later, British electronica. As best described by David Toop, "Dubbing, at its very best, takes each bit and fills it with new life, turning the rational order of musical sequences into an ocean of sensation."[38] While creators (musicians, producers, recording/sound engineers) were experimenting with technology and effects in popular music in North America and the UK, the trend also caught on in Jamaica, but more in the postproduction stage of studio recording. Sadly, on a socioeconomic level, the island was not as technologically advanced as North America and the UK, therefore the creator, at first, had to make do with the less sophisticated equipment to which they had access, such as a four-track recorder,[39] and ended up (re)creating incredible musical works. The genres and styles discussed so far clearly involved musical instruments and machines, but dub relied solely on recordings and on using any available studio equipment for experimentation.

The creators of dub were mostly recording/sound engineers and producers. Electrician turned recording/sound engineer and producer King Tubby (real name Osbourne Ruddock)[40] made use of recording technology, such as tape delay machines, mixers, and effects, and would experiment with studio recordings by remixing the vocals, drum and bass, and manipulating the timbre and texture with equalizers and filters.[41] The drum and bass (the "riddim" or rhythm) are the most important musical features of dub, and are embellished with excerpts of recorded (and later live)[42] vocals, talk-over, toasting (chatting or chanting), vocal dubs, and effects. From a sociocultural perspective, dub is musically influenced by its core genre, reggae, which mostly displays awareness of Jamaican history and politics.[43] While there are sparse lyrics and vocals in the recordings, Jamaican political and historical signifiers are virtually presented, heard, and felt in the common effects used in dub such as echo, reverb, spring reverb, flanger, thunderclaps, and delay.[44]

Dub originally featured as the "B-side" of a 45 rpm single and was better known as "version" —that is the instrumental or remix version of the song. Even though the instrumental parts are modified, it still retains the musical feel of the original. Dub creators such as King Tubby would press the mixes onto acetate and vinyl records so that DJs and toasters could instantly access the medium to play and perform "live" on sound systems, which quickly became popular.[45] As highlighted by Michael E. Veal, "[w]hat made dub unique in the context of pop music both in Jamaica and worldwide was the creative and unconventional use recording engineers made of their equipment . . . [t]his enabled them to fashion a new musical language that relied on texture, timbre, and soundspace."[46] As part of the musical language, engineers would scale back the vocals to bring the focus on the main lyrical themes of the song, such as the excerpts of the chorus, so the track "opens up an echoic space for the listener to inhabit with a sense of involvement and belonging."[47] Likewise, the sound in dub "is never static; it is only ever an effect, always transitory and ephemeral,"[48] thereby creating and recreating a unique and unified auditory experience for the listener.

As with experimental, Krautrock, and psychedelic music, dub invites the listener on a journey into sound, to experience a musical voyage, virtually. The manipulators or, indeed, the creators (recording/sound engineers, producers) were formally recognized as composers and musicians when dub became successful, such as Lee "Scratch" Perry, Bunny "Striker" Lee, Augustus Pablo, King Jammy, Mad Professor, Dennis Bovell, Adrian Sherwood, and, of course, King Tubby.

King Tubby's "Waterhouse Rock"

King Tubby's "Waterhouse Rock" is based on Mikey Brooks' "Money is not all" (1978). The original version is a roots reggae song but can easily be mistaken for dub due to its electronic features. When one hears this original version, the drowned-out melodica serves as a memorable hook, supported by typical roots reggae sounds such as the reggae rockers drum beat[49] (although it staggers now and then) decorated with pulsing fills, faint organ parts, deep groove bass, rhythm guitar, and additional (clean effect) guitar fills. The dub signifiers are evident in the drums, but become more exposed toward the end of the song. Here, the third beat of the rockers' drum style has the bass drum and snare's cross stick[50] intensified with delay and flanger effects triggering in a hammering sound. Toward the end of the track, the beats whir as they cross the rockers and steppers[51] with added phaser and delay, which generates a mild scattering effect. King Tubby's remix of "Money is not all" was known as either the "version" or "Money Dub" on the "B" side, but admirers of the "Godfather of Dub" (King Tubby) will know it more as "Waterhouse Rock."[52] Here, King Tubby deconstructed and reconstructed the original version. The bass is intact but carries a memorable and dynamic presence with its weighty militant feel that leads the music. The melodica still serves as a memorable hook with added reverb delay, but rather than reoccurring at regular times, it is neatly disseminated by fading in and out throughout the track. The rhythmic guitar and organ riffs irregularly fade in and out, and their role is to support the vocals that appear randomly. The guitar fills from the original version are more noticeable and dazzle in various parts of the track, supported by a hint of a piano riff that helps to push the music forward. Excerpts of the vocals are inserted with the main word, "Money," enhanced by echo and flanger, thereby maintaining the socio-theme of the song along with the frantic drum and bass. The drums are almost similar as in the original version, but this time, the cross stick and kick visit various effects: flanger, delay, reverse delay, and spring reverb. The stepper and non-accent scattering rhythms are filtered and randomly inserted throughout the track. Overall, King Tubby's "Waterhouse Rock" traps the listener's awareness of the futuristic sonics, drum, and bass from all directions in the dub chamber, putting their auditory experience in a transfixed state and creating a sense of timelessness. Dub has been influential in electronica and hip-hop genres, with a major focus on bass music culture, including, jungle/drum and bass, trip-hop, grime, dubstep, drill, and many more.

Hip-Hop

Hip-hop originated between the mid-to-late 1970s. A global culture of its own, hip-hop incorporates street art (graffiti), language, fashion, dancing (break dancing) and music. Although it was conceived in the Bronx borough of New York City and carries historical elements of various African American musical genres, part of its musical roots are also traced to Jamaica, as explained by Rodney Smith (aka Roots Manuva): "rap [and] hip-hop is definitively an American innovation but it kinda started at level in Jamaica with the toasters and DJs."[53] Take the vocals (rap), for example, where it has associations with "toaster" that is, the MC (Master of Ceremonies). The MC toasts (ad-libs or talks over) records played by the "selector" (of the records) and/or DJ, and would be heard along with the music on sound systems.[54]

A Jamaican DJ, Kool Herc (real name Clive Campbell), was one of the founders of hip-hop. After failing to impress his neighbors by playing reggae music on sound systems in 1973, he won their attention by playing funk and soul, and would "talk over" the records. Herc's musical setup would consist of two turntables, mixer, microphone, sound system, and vinyl records—this musical setup became a recognized form of instrumentation and creation, known as turntablism.[55] Herc was credited with developing new musical techniques with the turntable[56] such as the "break" (or breakbeat). This technique involves the DJ searching for a short rhythmic section to loop and perform the break by swapping between two copies of the same record to maintain the continuity of the breakbeat.[57] Other techniques include "cutting" (created by Joseph Saddler, also known as Grandmaster Flash), which involves removing sounds and cutting from the record. An example would be to cut out a stab, lick, or riff from one of the two turntables' records and "punch phase" the sound over the other (with a crossfader mixer).[58] Record "scratching" proved to be a popular technique created by DJ Grand Wizzard Theodore (real name Theodore Livingston) in 1977, which involves sliding a record back and forth in which the stylus needle creates a "scratching" sound.[59] These turntable techniques of breakbeats, cutting, and record-scratching can be seen as extensions of *Musique concrète* as they involve music composed by using excerpts of recorded sounds—similar to sampling—but not digitalized, yet. At the time, Kool Herc, Grandmaster Flash, and Grand Wizzard Theodore were branded as "human samplers" as they physically manipulated the recorded sounds themselves.[60]

The digital sampler proved to be a major contribution to hip-hop music (see Chapter 1 for more details). Common samples include breakbeats (mostly borrowed from funk, jazz, and soul records); vinyl sonics (such as scratches, glitches, and pops); guitar riffs, bass grooves, vocal hooks; and nonmusical sounds (such as gunshots, police sirens, or glass breaking).[61] Digital sampling, however, has a long controversial history involving intellectual property, mainly copyright, which has resulted in court cases.[62] Like the turntable, the digital sampler should be regarded as an instrument, as echoed by Chuck D of Public Enemy: "we thought sampling was just another way of arranging sounds. Just like a musician would take the sounds of an instrument and arrange them in a particular way."[63]

The notation of digital samplers are based on symbols (binary numbers: 1s and 0s), and the device plays a representation (aura, copy, simulation) of that sound including its captured sonic features. How the samples are used can generate signifiers in music, from the origins of the sample (when and where it was recorded and its original intentions)[64] to the present and current context (as discussed later).

Madvillain's "Curls"

Madvillain are a hip-hop collaboration project consisting of producer Madlib (Otis Jackson Jr.) and rapper/producer MF Doom (Daniel Dumile). Their take on hip-hop experiments mainly with jazz samples and freestyle; as a collaboration, they are known for their short songs and enigmatic lyrics. Their 2004 album, *Madvillainy*, contained twenty-two tracks, most of which were recorded in São Paulo, Brazil, after Madlib went "crate digging"[65] for local Brazilian music.

Madlib recorded most of the music in his hotel room on his portable turntable, Boss SP—303 portable Dr. Sample (portable sampler), and a tape machine; then he sent the recordings to MF Doom to add the vocals.[66] One track worth exploring is "Curls," in which the samples are borrowed from the music of Brazilian pianist and composer, Waldir Calmon. The 1970 track "Airport Love Theme"[67] serves as an airy and moderate-paced bossa nova—funk, supported with catchy hooks and chilled melodies ranging from the guitar to the bass, and from the Wurlitzer organ[68] (that changes timbre throughout) to the light brass and vocals. The Wurlitzer organ changes to a light airy solo with vibrato to accentuate the "bon voyage" theme of the track, thus creating a sense of a light-hearted escapade for the listener. Madlib samples excerpts of the track (guitar riff, bass, organ) and overlays it with a static breakbeat. He overturns the airy and funky bossy nova track by transforming it with a melancholic musical twist. Not to be deceived by the uplifting jangly guitar riff and bass groove in the introduction, but as soon as MF Doom starts reciting the mood of the music, it immediately swaps to an edgy-sounding timbre led by a Wurlitzer extract and bass, to match his storytelling—a narrative of two teenagers (one possibly himself) involving crime, drugs, and money. As the story turns for the worse (from the line "when he first started going raw . . ."), the looped pipe Wurlitzer hook presents an eerie timbre (which bears a resemblance to a church service setting, say a funeral) suggesting that this is not a smooth and dreamy narrative, but a reflection of realism. The music tenses as the story develops (from the line "Why are you so still? You need to smoke more brethren") with the sampled vibrato Wurlitzer arranged to sound like the classic film soundtrack of *Jaws*. Here, the alternating two note *Jaws*-like hook teasingly builds up suspense but is restrained when the edgy sound timbre returns. This is supported by MF Doom's setting the scene for another scenario (where the friend appears to become overconfident at school), but quickly switches when the misleading (uplifting) introduction returns (the jangly guitar riff), which signifies the story is about to conclude—or does it really? As MF Doom rounds off the story by saying he and his mate are running away from their criminal adventure, the somber organ part returns to imperfectly resolve the song. There is no resolution. The organ sample continues to loop as if to suggest the story is to be continued. By using only a small number of samples, Madlib presents the unimaginable, by recreating the sample sources of the serene airport lounge music (or Muzak) into a dark trip, while maintaining the themes of the nostalgic past.

Astonishingly, MF Doom and Madlib present the listener with various thematic and musical scenarios led by a retro bossa nova turned experimental hip-hop within one minute and thirty-five seconds. Hip-hop's reputation for incorporating the musical and social past into the present, and making it sound ahead of its time thanks to technology, has influenced and fostered crossovers with genres and styles such as pop and metal, and been inspirational to future music such as grime and reggaeton.

Ambient

In the late 1970s, another strand of experimental music developed: Ambient. Coined by experimental creator Brian Eno (notable for his work with the Scratch Orchestra, David Bowie, U2, Damon Albarn, Lee "Scratch" Perry, and many other artists), it is defined by him as "an atmosphere, or a surrounding influence: a tint . . . [that] is intended to induce calm and a space to think."[69] In retrospect, John T. Lysaker anticipates that ambient "is not designed to fully absorb the attention of those who hear it, but to interact with them nevertheless."[70] With ambient, it is more about listening to the music alone, and, ideally, the listeners should take into account both musical sonics and the sounds of their own surroundings. Even though he has always been an experimental creator, Eno became even more acquainted with nonmusical/everyday sonics while recovering from an accident. This became a "happy" accident as he was trying to listen to a record, but could not physically access the record player, leaving him frustrated at not being able to adjust the volume. While the record was more or less inaudible for Eno, he decided to detail the "real-life" surroundings of the music, that is the outside rain and daylight (the "tints") and this transitioned his listening into a relaxing and calming experience. As with the other experimental genres/ styles mentioned so far, timbre, texture, and tone are vital musical elements of ambient. The sounds are mostly electronically produced—and reproduced if samples are involved—and decorated with sound effects. In the past, there were minimal drum patterns or none at all, and as ambient developed as a genre, more instruments and sounds were added. The tempo is typically very moderate, to calm the listener, and as with other experimental music, it can be in free form.

Brian Eno—"Another Green World"

Brian Eno's 1975 album *Another Green World* used chance and oblique strategies to create the music.[71] The track "Another Green World" is a short tranquil and meditative soundscape. It begins by fading-in delicate white noise, giving one the impression of being in the open air. At first, the white noise is led by short piano cells and organ, but then gets overtaken by the prominent melodic guitar. The minimal texture of the musical layers is controlled by the dynamics (e.g., it sounds thicker when the volume gets louder, and vice versa), and the timbre is saturated with echo, delay, reverb, and distortion, which virtually transports the listeners and their own sonic surroundings to "another green world," where they can experience serenity. As the music gradually fades out, it may leave the listeners switched off or, more ideally, feeling refreshed from their brief meditative listening experience. This track and the album resulted in further ambient music (notably *Music for Airports*, 1978), and Eno has been respectfully recognized as the pioneer of this genre. Ambient has evolved into various related styles, including dark ambient, ambient house, ambient dub, and illbient, and has partially contributed to electronic dance and electronica. Eno has inspired many artists to create ambient music, including Aphex Twin, The KLF, The Orb, and Moby.

Electronica

Electronica started to become popular in the cities around the UK—including London, Birmingham, and Bristol—from the 1990s. Due to the rapid development of affordable music technology, electronica houses many genres and styles.[72] While there are too many of them to mention, I am most attracted to the UK evolution of electronica as it implements other experimental music. The term "electronica," and, indeed, the term "experimental," bring out different understandings and debates. Electronica has been used to differentiate "dance" (or electronic dance such as house, acid house, techno, and subsequent styles), commonly due to its upbeat tempo. Dance's musical origins arguably lie within disco music, which has minimal interaction with electronica. Dance music is specifically intended for night clubs, whereas electronica, as Will Straw describes, "is designed for quiet contemplation or concert-like performances."[73] Electronica, then, is more suited for personal listening, or for absorbing in underground events or small clubs (although arguably it has gained its popularity in music festivals). The main musical trademarks to listen out for are the drum and bass (mostly inspired by dub), upbeat tempo (based on dance music), and breakbeat (borrowed from hip-hop). A typical and original performance set would normally involve a digital sampler (usually any Akai model), drum machine, effects device, computer, and synthesizer, overlaid with sampled or live vocals. As electronica evolved and branched out to other styles, it was usual for creators to experiment more by bringing in live instruments. Popular styles include jungle, drum and bass, trip-hop, big beat, downtempo, and dubstep (and so much more).

As with dub and hip-hop, electronica also has a habit of musically blending the past with the present. Take, for example, jungle, which is known for its inclusion of reggae samples and everyday sonics blended with the low-frequency *tenuto* (a sustained note) rolling bass line, and sampled breakbeats/programmed drum patterns (set at least at 150 bpm). While the main features are the drum and bass including its tempo and timbre, its musical influences originated from dub and reggae. Also, a breakbeat sample was doing the rounds among early creators, and its source was a drum solo from the funk and soul group, The Winstons' "Amen Brother" (1968), aka "The Amen Break." This became a staple sample and was sped up and invitingly tortured in various jungle tracks.[74] While the musical layers are minimal, the sounds that are produced may carry a bulky texture, supported by a mixture of dark, frantic, and transcendent timbres.[75] Another example with an emphasis on the drum and bass, tempo, and the breakbeat, is trip-hop. Originating in Bristol, trip-hop also has strong links with dub and hip-hop (with a splash of ambient music). The tempo of trip-hop is slower, with the breakbeat time-stretched and matched with a bass groove. The samples can be based on melodic riffs from styles such as jazz and funk, and are overlaid with dark sonics. The minimal instrumentation carries somber and mystic timbres, overlaid with luscious or distressed vocals and / or rap. Famous examples include Portishead's "Glory Box" (1994) (with its main sample from Isaac Hayes' "Ike's Rap II" (1971)) and music from the Mo'Wax label.

Bomb the Bass—"Clear Cut"

The musical collective Bomb the Bass is a prime example of electronica. It's led by Tim Simenon, a perfect example of a modern experimental creator who is obsessed with technology.[76] Originally from Brixton, London, Simenon became known for his sampling mélange in British hip-hop (such as "Beat Dis" in 1988) and, later, in electronica. He is also known for his productions for Depeche Mode, Justin Warfield, Neneh Cherry, Sinead O'Connor, and Björk. In 2001, Bomb the Bass collaborated with German electronic group, Lali Puna. The collaboration on "Clear Cut" is an ultimate example of electronica, where all the experimental sounds of the genres/ styles mentioned in this chapter are unified. Starting with an ambient flavor of pattering raindrops soaked with reverb, the fading-in of the sonics lures the listener to immerse in the gentle taps of the raindrops before being directed to a one-note deep bass. Here, the bass is absorbed in double delay fluctuating between crescendo and decrescendo that is swiftly joined by whirs creating a halcyon timbre and psychedelic effect for the listener. The soundscape features ambient and psychedelic signifiers that build up when the alluring dub-style chords enter and are drenched with spring reverb and reverse-delay effects, before gradually driving toward the main track's genre, electronica. Here, a cycle of a fast-scattering breakbeat fuses with a sedating and modulating deep bass line that sweeps across the musical spectrum, and is blanketed with electronic sonics of whirs, bleeps, and pulses creating a futuristic tone.[77] This futuristic section is enriched with vocals provided by the lead singer of Lali Puna, Valerie Trebeljahr. As she toasts each phrase (e.g., "I change my mind," and "can't complain"), her voice is altered with a distorted speakerphone effect that distantly echoes in the ethereal. The music swiftly switches to a Trebeljahr solo, where she lusciously sings the chorus, and the listener is immediately drawn to her vocals. The immediate attraction of her voice is due to her multitracked vocals where each layer detects a combination of "real-life"/human and nonhuman (robotic/cyborg) voices that is utilized by a vocoder.

While this mesmerizing vocal arrangement overpowers the minimal spaced-out and ambient accompaniment (which consists of calming synth chords and whirs), Trebeljahr's vocals are an instant reminder of Laurie Anderson's famous 1981 track, "O Superman," where she exploited her recorded voices with technology.[78] In Trebeljahr's musical adaptation, her assortment of vocals (especially on the words "we've nearly lost it all . . .

I'm going with you") portrays optimism, catharsis, and looking forward. This tantalizing solace is quickly crushed when the upbeat music erases signs of optimism and Trebeljahr talks over the music seeking a resolution by emphasizing "we should sort it over," "misunderstood," and "clear cut." As before, her speech has been distorted, but this time there is a focus on the title of the song, "clear cut," supported by evaporating and hypnotic echoes, making sure these words are "clear" to hear. A final chorus follows, and is supported by droned synth chords that gradually get louder and more high pitched, increasing in intensity before the electronic sonics swarm to the music's conclusion, returning to and ending on the raindrops. "Clear Cut" invites the listener on a floating and virtual musical journey experiencing ambient, psychedelic, Krautrock, hip-hop, and dub, in electronica.

"Experimental" remains a hybrid term, making the most of how technology influences specific genres and styles crafted with their own trademarks. Technology continues to transform the unpresentable into the presentable, or, indeed, the unimaginable, unthinkable, and unexpected ideas into reality in the digital virtual era, thereby making experimental music infinite.[79]

4

"Give Life Back to Music"

Remixing Music

You know you've already got the references in your head once you hear certain kinds of music, and if you mix that with something else then maybe it will be something new or something different.

DANGER MOUSE, 2011.[1]

In the digital virtual era, we are constantly reminded of the past due to the recycled sounds that are presented in the music. As demonstrated in the previous chapter, music is constantly being experimented with, with sounds that are manipulated via technology and everyday sonics. However, we can also consider the use of sounds from past and existing sources being regenerated into new creations. To demonstrate some of the musical and postmodern features of remixing music, I consider how technology influences this phenomenal practice, and turn to the works of the creator, Danger Mouse (Brian Burton). I have been observing his musical trademarks for a very long time,[2] and while most of his earlier works have somehow disrupted technological practices of the music industry (for the better, in my opinion), he has always been on cue with specific developments of digital technology. As his music catalog developed over the last twenty years (and as the opening epigraph of this chapter suggests), it is clear that, either as an artist, collaborator, or producer, he carries an obsession of past music (mainly from the 1960s and 1970s), and this is evident in his creativities. His passion for music and for using vintage recording techniques and signs of hauntology, have shaped Burton as a prolific and respected music producer, despite his turbulent start in the music industry. *The Grey Album* illustrates how Burton dared to transform two mismatched works of the Beatles and Jay-Z—resulting in a mixed response from the music industry and audience. Burton then applied another method of remixing, by deconstructing samples from 1960s spaghetti western film music and transforming it into a perfect genre blend of pop, gospel, hip-hop and soul, making the song "Crazy" (sung by Cee-Lo Green) a classic record of the 2000s.

Remix

A remix illustrates the mixing of unthinkable sources into a creative and extraordinary feature. In Simon Reynolds's words, a "re-mix" is "disassembled and reassembled,"[3] or, as compellingly put by Kodwo Eshun, it "[is an] art of the drastic retrofit, the total remake, the remodel."[4] Thanks to the evolution of experimental music and technology, Jacques Attali convincingly states that "[t]oday, a new music is on the rise, one that can neither be expressed nor understood using the old tools, a music produced elsewhere and otherwise."[5] This ties in with my ongoing argument that existing creations and virtual ideas—such as remix, sampling, and genre/style blending—are too reliant on digital technology. With this in mind, Margie Borschke grippingly asks, "Is remix an apt metaphor for digital culture?"[6] which seems to highlight the concoction of existing and past sources presented in art, fashion, literature, and visual media, as well as music. The remix is a major feature in the digital virtual era, a view that Lawrence Lessig would support as he declares we are living in a "rip, mix and burn" culture.[7] Likewise, a remix could rightfully be considered as a culture on its own, which Eduardo Navas observes as "a global activity consisting of the creative and efficient exchange of information made possible by digital technologies."[8] While this statement is mostly true, there is no direct or single method in executing a remix, and more significantly, it is not tied to digital technology alone. In past music (dating back over a century), signs of the remix were presented as morphed interpolations (quotations) such as Charles Gounod's take on Bach's "Prelude in C Major" in "Ave Maria" (1892), and Luciano Berio's "Sinfonia," where he interpolated a wealth of composers' works, including Debussy, Brahms, Ravel, and Strauss,[9] and of course, we can refer to early experimental music too (see previous chapter).

Kembrew McLeod and Peter DiCola remark that remixing music became more achievable from the late twentieth century as a result of accessible and affordable technology, enabling "consumers—not elite engineers hired by a band or record company— [who] could now participate in reworking a song."[10] However tempting it may sound to mix music, or just to explore and experiment with sounds, creators of remixes have not always received respect for their art. Unauthorized use of recorded sounds has sometimes resulted in a backlash and legal threats from the music industry (including sound recording owners and publishers). It can also raise questions on authorship and the creative authenticity of the creator. The potential in creating a remix sounds enticing because the listener/consumer-turned-creator can refer to his/her existing musical knowledge, rewind and revisit sounds from the past, and reincarnate music into a new listening—and, where appropriate, new visual—experience.

Danger Mouse and *The Grey Album*

A momentous remix album that is frequently discussed and championed in popular culture is Burton's (Danger Mouse) *The Grey Album* (2004). Originally from New York, Burton spent most of his youth listening to rock and metal before discovering his love for hip-hop when he moved to Georgia. Aspiring to be a music creator, he moved to London in the early 2000s and became drawn to electronica music (especially trip-hop) as well as reliving the music of his favorite British groups, such as the Beatles. With a spot of DJ-ing and bedroom music-producing in London, he signed with British independent label, Lex Records (as well as joining US label Waxploitation). However, his music career did not materialize in the UK and he was running out of money, so he moved to California. By relocating to the United States, his creativity took a risky and drastic turn—this was a moment that he rarely discusses as it could have terminated his career in music, but which thankfully did not. Instead, the digital virtual success of *The Grey Album* led to the creation being appraised by fans, critics, and the music industry, and as I write this, Burton is much in demand as a music producer. So why should this album be regarded as a major innovation in the digital virtual era? My argument would be that the album unintentionally incorporated cultural elements impacted by digital practices.

The Development of The Grey Album

From the early 2000s, the popularity and development of MP3s and computer software, as well as internet usage, increased. Music-wise, digital technology encouraged new ways of creating and remixing music. Around 2003, a new offshoot of the remix was becoming trendy. Known as a mash-up (which originally consisted of two famous records mixed together with one song usually dominating the other), it was first associated with "Bastard Pop,"[11] a type of illegal music using unauthorized samples.[12] One possible trigger that led to the music industry warming up to the idea of the mash-up being creative and marketable music was perhaps the famous friction surrounding Burton's attempt in remixing two famous albums, Jay-Z's *Black Album* (2003) and the Beatles' *White Album* (1968), otherwise known as *The Grey Album*.[13]

In 2003, hip-hop and rap artist, Jay-Z, invited amateur and bedroom producers to remix the a capella version of the *Black Album* and this caught the attention of Burton. The unknown producer at the time wanted "to impress people who were really into sampling"[14] by remixing it with the Beatles' self-titled 1968 album (better known as the *White Album*). *The Grey Album* was distributed and downloaded through peer-to-peer file-sharing networks, and caught the attention of the press, such as *The New York Times* and *Rolling Stone*, in which its journalists praised the album.

The classic quote of Burton, where he confesses that "every, kick, snare, and chord is taken from the Beatles' *White Album* and is in their original recording somewhere,"[15] consequently landed him in trouble and he was immediately confronted with a "cease and desist" letter by EMI and Capitol Records in the United States.[16] The label argued that Burton had not obtained copyright permission for use of the Beatles' works, and ordered him and distributors to destroy all copies. Despite Burton obeying the instruction, while at the same time insisting that the remix was an artistic expression of his admiration of his favorite music, further conflict followed. It turned out that all downloaders of *The Grey Album* were also threatened by EMI. One reaction in opposing the censored remix was in the form of a one-day cyber protest, known as "Grey Tuesday,"[17] which was organized by an activist association, Downhill Battle. The association argued for fair use and creative freedom in art making, and to demonstrate "how the major record labels stifle creativity and try to manipulate the public's access to music." [18] As part of the protest, Downhill Battle encouraged activists and supporters to upload the album on websites and blogs. As Michael Ayers explains, blogs are a significant platform for posting activist information,[19] and in this case, visitors were encouraged to visit the blog, gain information on "Grey Tuesday," click on the hyperlink (the link to *The Grey Album*), download the album, upload it, and then share it on the internet.[20]

Further legal conflict followed, with participants in "Grey Tuesday" receiving "cease and desist" letters from EMI and Capitol Records, as well as DMCA's[21] "take down" notices from Sony Music and ATV Publishing.[22] Despite this, more than 100,000 people downloaded *The Grey Album* on "Grey Tuesday,"[23] "equivalent to more than one million digital tracks."[24]

Copyright

Copyright is always a complex and an expensive matter. In this case, there were many parties involved in *The Grey Album*, and it might have been less of a headache for Burton if he had applied interpolation of the music (or hired musicians to play the music), instead. In summary, Burton would have needed to approach the copyright holder of the master rights (sound recordings), and the owner of the publishing rights (compositions) of the following:

1) EMI and Capitol Records (owners of the sound recordings on the *White Album*),

2) Sony Music and ATV Publishing (owners of the compositions on the *White Album* and Lennon and McCartney's Northern Songs catalog),

3) The Beatles and Apple Corps Ltd. (which might involve other parties such as the estates of Harrison and Lennon),

4) Harrisongs and Wixen Music Publishing (owners of George Harrison's compositions),

5) Roc-A-Fella Records (owners of the *Black Album*), and

6) Owners of the compositions on the *Black Album*.

While it was later revealed that EMI and Capitol Records in the United States could not sue after all[25] because the *White Album* was not copyright-protected by US federal law,[26] the publishers of the *White Album* (Sony Music and ATV Publishing) tried to challenge Burton and his supporters by imposing the DMCA on them, but failed. *The Grey Album* gained recognition for all the wrong reasons because the focus was on intellectual property rather than the aesthetics of the remix. The subject of copyright still comes up almost whenever the album is mentioned, despite the record labels taking no further legal action in the United States.

Deconstruction

Before gaining a musical insight into *The Grey Album*, I want to look at why this particular remix received so much attention. What made *The Grey Album* so aesthetically appealing is the postmodern collage of two well-known records of different musical genres, timeframes, and hierarchies in popular music. In terms of hierarchy, I am referring to the Beatles' artistic status being recognized and absorbed by the high cultural establishments in England at the time of their success.[27]

From a critical viewpoint, to categorize *The Grey Album* as a mash-up is questionable. While the rise of the mash-up was due to the rapid increase in file sharing on peer-to-peer networks, such as the now defunct KaZaa and Limewire,[28] it received exposure on media platforms such as MTV (Music Television) and XFM radio. However, a mash-up can receive full attention only if the songs are immediately recognizable[29]—which is questionable with *The Grey Album*. To elaborate, the time frame of the works needs to be taken into account, as different artists and genres will, respectively, draw in different audiences and responses, making it possibly challenging to identify a Jay-Z or Beatles song (especially if the listener is unaware of the artist). Furthermore, identifying the Beatles music on *The Grey Album* might be problematic due to how Burton manipulated the samples, as Sasha Frere-Jones points out:

> *The Grey Album* is not a great example of a mash-up, because the musical bed is processed so radically that its source is sometimes not clear. One of the thrills of the mash-up is identifying two well-known artists unwittingly complementing each other's strengths and limitations.[30]

Therefore, the Beatles' tracks on *The Grey Album* are more suited to being a remix rather than being strictly labeled as a mash-up. Burton deconstructed, dissembled, and reconstructed the works into a new listening experience, and was perhaps unaware that he theoretically applied the Jacques Derrida's model of the deconstructionist method, where an opposition dominates the other. Derrida explains, "to deconstruct the opposition [. . .] is to overturn the hierarchy,"[31] and in the case of *The Grey Album*, Burton "overturned" the Beatles' hierarchical dominance musically by giving Jay-Z's vocals priority, which is an unusual but unique twist.

Authorship

Another critical approach to this particular remix is to consider the role of authorship. While it should be obvious that Burton is the "author" of *The Grey Album*, people may reject that status, especially if sampling and copyright issues are involved. Derek B. Scott argues that postmodern music, in particular the remix, questions its authorship when using music technology to execute "existing sounds to be recorded and reused or manipulated at will [and has] a major impact on ideas of originality, creativity and ownership."[32] For example, when you hear a remixed song, it may urge you to find more information on its creator. *The Grey Album* throws confusion to the possible contender of authorship: is it Jay-Z, as his vocals are evident from start to finish, the Beatles because of their (sampled) music, or Burton, because he creatively fused the two works together?[33] This has resonance with the work of Roland Barthes, who dejectedly announced the "death of the author," meaning that the creator cannot declare authorship as a work's intentions will be elucidated differently by other people.[34] His acquaintance Michel Foucault, however, insisted that any creation "in any given culture, must receive a certain status,"[35] thereby insinuating a sense of authorship. As such, Burton should be recognized as the author because through digital technology, he convincingly presented the unpresentable, merged the past into the present, and made the incompatible, compatible, by remixing two known works. Therefore, *The Grey Album* should grant Burton to be recognized as its author.

Musical Analysis of "99 Problems"[36]

An interesting track to discuss from *The Grey Album* is "99 Problems," which is a remix of Jay-Z's "99 Problems"[37] and the Beatles' "Helter Skelter."[38] *The Grey Album* was created on a computer with Sonic Foundry Acid Pro software, and Pro Tools for the final mix.[39] It took Burton two and a half weeks to create *The Grey Album* in his bedroom,[40] and as part of the creative process, he listened to the *White Album* four times searching for music he could use.[41] Burton actually found "99 Problems" to be a problem! To illustrate, Burton was careful about what to sample from "Helter Skelter" and how it would blend with Jay-Z's vocals. Five samples from "Helter Skelter" are evident: backing vocals, bass guitar, lead guitar, klaxon, and drums. Burton's beat matched both tracks and he decided to maintain Jay-Z's tempo (around 95 bpm), and increased the tempo of "Helter Skelter" (originally around 83 bpm), while retaining the original pitch. Burton explained his reason for using the tempo of Jay-Z's track, "It would have been easy to slap the vocals over music of the same tempo . . . but I wanted to match the feel of the tracks too."[42] It should be noted that with the tempo increase, the pitch of "Helter Skelter" was preserved thanks to Acid Pro software as it keeps the original key at any given tempo (known as time-stretching).

Unlike the other tracks on *The Grey Album*, Burton encountered a problem with the rhythm on "99 Problems," as the drums were challenging to sample. To overcome this, the bass line keeps "99 Problems" in time which is sampled from the first verse of "Helter Skelter." Burton manipulated the bass sample by boosting the low pass filter (to remove the treble effect on the bass and unwanted sonics), and added compression resulting in a dynamic groove. The bass repeatedly picks the note E, and accentuates the beat to keep "99 Problems" in time. The drum pattern is almost based on *Musique concrète* as Burton sampled and arranged a drum fill and five individual drum sounds (bass/kick, snare, tom-tom, hi-hat, crash cymbal) from "Helter Skelter," into a timbral breakbeat. He also applied the Beatles' harmonies as backing vocals. The "ahh" sample has been manipulated with compression and high pass filter (to drown out the bass and drums), to provide a bright and crispy effect to the vocals. A klaxon is sampled from the track and placed at the end of each chorus on "Helter Skelter." To maintain its rock element as in the original version, Burton sampled lead guitar fills from "Helter Skelter" and manipulated them with high pass filter to wash out the other instruments for a clearer sound.

The following analysis will describe some of the first verse only so that the reader can sense how the samples are used in the track. The introduction begins with the main vocal hook of "99 Problems," and is supported by the "ahh" sample (the "backing vocals" of the Beatles) on the words "99 Problems." The bass line sample enters and keeps the music in 4/4 time. A hint of the klaxon sample is heard on the word "dough," and gets louder in the following line "you can kiss my whole asshole." Toward the end of the first verse, the main hook of the song is supported by the samples "ahh" ("I got 99 problems . . .") and klaxon ("bitch ain't one . . .!"), which is followed by the lead guitar and drum fill, which leads to the chorus. The chorus includes the "ahh" sample and supports the words "99 Problems" which is musically responded to by the scaling lead guitar. The drum and bass supports the rest of the chorus ("If you're havin' girl problems . . . "), but vanishes when the "ahh" sample returns to support the main hook of the chorus. The layering of the samples is generally the same throughout the song, and may not sound musically challenging. However, certain segments such as the "ahh" sample make the hook stand out on "99 Problems." The klaxon sample tends to highlight specific words only (mainly derogatory terms). While the musical layers deceivingly sound minimal, the remixing of the samples and vocals were time consuming and challenging for Burton.

"The Grey Video"

In 2004, a mash-up video, created by "Ramon and Pedro,"[43] was released on the internet. As it was not affiliated to Burton, Ramon and Pedro clearly stated in the visuals that "The Grey Video" was an experiment and not intended for commercial use. The video is a digital collage of performances of both the Beatles and Jay-Z. The track used in the video is Burton's remix of Jay-Z's "Encore," with the Beatles' "Glass Onion" and "Savoy Truffle." In the black-and-white (or indeed, "grey") video, the Beatles' footage was sampled from their film *A Hard Day's Night* (1964).[44]

The video begins with the Beatles' crowd screaming in anticipation while waiting for their favorite "boy" band to perform.[45] In the sound and television gallery, the staff are monitoring all cameras and operators through their mixing desks and screens. The television director has difficulty communicating with one of the camera technicians but, with that aside, the Beatles start performing "Glass Onion." Suddenly, the monitor screens are visually hacked by Jay-Z, who is being transmitted on a big screen on the stage (behind the Beatles) and the television network. While Jay-Z is performing, the Beatles become the backing singers. There is a close-up of the Beatles' audience, which then focuses on a modern, hip-hop fan (recognizable by her attire), who phenomenally (and digitally) blends in with the 1960s crowd. The scene then focuses on the Beatles' drummer, Ringo Starr, whose drum kit transforms into a DJ set with the label "DJ Danger Mouse" on it. Starr's cymbals then turn into vinyl records, on which he scratches. John Lennon is performing to the crowd, but he is shot from behind—it is not him, but a double imitating him. When the Beatles' music changes to "Savoy Truffle," Paul McCartney and George Harrison are magically transformed to two women supposedly from the year 2004, and they all breakdance (yes, including the "real" John Lennon), while Jay-Z is rapping. While all this is happening, the fans are enjoying the performance and the control room personnel are left in shock. The music and video ends with John Lennon doing head spins and back flips, and then all the performers leave the stage.

This postmodern and hyperreal video displays genre-blending, a distortion of the past and present (in the visuals and music), and a sense of timelessness. At first, we are virtually rewinding to the 1960s to watch the Beatles' perform, yet are treated to the present images of Jay-Z, his audiences, and dancers. Also, Jay-Z appears in a screen (the big screen), within the screen (the main television network and the cameras), prompting questions on reality, virtuality, and hyperreality. Indeed, they are simulations of live performances, but both are intended to look "real" or, following Baudrillard (see Chapter 2), that the whole collaborative performance of the Beatles and Jay-Z is "hyperreal"—more real than real.

Overall, *The Grey Album* generated both positive and negative responses regarding copyright, technology, creativity, and authorship. It is debatable whether there are other reasons why EMI were not in favor of *The Grey Album*. Was it because Danger Mouse was an unknown producer at the time? After all, other groups, such as The Beastie Boys and Wu Tang Clan, were authorized to use the works of the Beatles.[46] Is it because it has been widely rumored that the Beatles refused permission for their sound recordings to be sampled, despite Sir Paul McCartney confirming his love for *The Grey Album*?[47] Arguably, it was likely to be a (failed) business tactic to serve the interests of EMI because at the time, they were one of the "big" major labels. EMI tried to hide their misjudgment by consolidating the rapid changes in music creativity and consumption in the digital era by releasing the first legal mash-up album in 2007.

In a legal sense, and perhaps out of courtesy, Burton should have enquired about gaining copyright permission—yet, knowing the likely outcome of such an application (despite knowing that EMI and Capitol Records in the United States could not sue after all), we might now be in the position of never having been able to hear the results, including his future music projects. Burton was demonstrating his creative skills in remixing two classic works he cherished. Furthermore, not only did it garner more recognition for Jay-Z and the Beatles, but it also made it possible to hear virtually incompatible music become compatible, thanks to technology. As described by *Rolling Stone* magazine, *The Grey Album* is "an ingenious hip-hop record that sounds oddly ahead of its time."[48]

Gnarls Barkley

Looking now at Burton's other projects, Gnarls Barkley demonstrates another approach of the remix. The song "Crazy" discretely carries an unusual relationship with spaghetti western film music. Burton transformed the samples behind "Crazy" and arranged them into what is now considered a classic pop song.[49]

In the fall of 2005, a British television advertisement promoted a music show for BBC Radio 1. The music show in question was presented by then BBC Radio DJ (and now globally renowned Apple Music/Beats 1 music curator) Zane Lowe. During his career at Radio 1, Lowe was known for exploring a wide range of musical genres and styles, such as electronica, hip-hop, and alternative rock. His musical expertise and enthusiastic championing of the records he played would contribute significantly to the success of the artists in question—with the aforementioned television promo as the perfect example of this.[50] When this advertisement for Lowe's show was aired, the audience demanded to know the identity of the artist and song. Lowe appeased his listeners by revealing that the artist was Gnarls Barkley, and that the song was called "Crazy."

In April 2006, when Downtown Records (a subsidiary record label of Warner Bros.) released "Crazy" in the UK,[51] it instantly hit the number one spot in the official charts—the first digital single to do. The identity of Gnarls Barkley was revealed to be Atlanta's Goodie Mob rapper/singer Cee-Lo Green (real name Thomas Callaway)[52] and Danger Mouse (Burton). What is interesting about "Crazy" is that, although it can be heard as a classic genre-blended song (based on soul, gospel, hip-hop, and pop), it is perhaps unknown to the average listener that the music is based on samples from the soundtrack of the 1968 spaghetti western[53] film *Preparati la Bara!* (*Prepare the Coffin!*).[54] One main reason Burton sampled excerpts from this particular soundtrack was that he studied film before becoming a musician. Burton was drawn to works of the incredible film music composer Ennio Morricone and his arrangement of the authentic choir sound sung by the amazing *I Cantori Moderni* di *Alessandroni* choir in spaghetti western films.[55]

Preparati la Bara!

The film *Preparati la Bara!* (1968)[56] is based on a titular, lone, and heartbroken cowboy called *Django*—who was known for carrying a machine gun in a coffin. The sources of the samples are based on the scene "*Nel cimitero di Tucson*" (In Tucson Cemetery) and the leitmotif for the main character Django. A leitmotif usually musically introduces the characters with a short and catchy melodic hook, and also builds a relationship between the character and the viewer—especially in emotional or heroic scenes of the film—where the viewer may feel a sense of compassion for the character.[57] In the case of Django, his allocated leitmotif portrays some kind of sorrow, pain, and loneliness.[58]

The leitmotif of Django as shown in Figure 4.1 is in the key of B-flat minor and consists of three notes: D-flat, F, and B-flat. This musical shape displays signs of lament in a *grave* manner, with the leading note of D-flat

FIGURE 4.1 *Django's leitmotif (provisional part transcribed by the author).*

gently leaping upward to an F that holds for six beats before moving downward to D-flat and then B-flat (which also last for six beats) before passing back through D-flat to end on F. This short melodic statement serves as the cowboy theme and is subconsciously introduced to the viewer, who will be reminded of this tune throughout the film, especially its "epic" version as heard in the main scene, "*Nel cimitero di Tucson.*"

To set the scene, Django faces a vengeful standoff with his enemy and eventually kills him. The musical accompaniment for the scene begins with the Baritone guitar playing, led by the *El Degüello* trumpet melody[59] (a distinctive feature in spaghetti western music), and is supported by a Morricone-inspired three-part choir reciting the leitmotif as "oohs."[60] This choir features in "Crazy" and serves as one of the main musical layers in the song. Just before Django executes his enemy, the strings play the leitmotif in a powerful manner which is supported by the choir but sung an octave higher, which doubles the intensity of the music (this section is also sampled and used in the chorus of "Crazy").

"Crazy"

The leitmotif of Django as a sample suits the song "Crazy," but is in no way "cowboy" music. "Crazy" contains three samples based on "*Nel cimiteri di Tucson*": the introduction (the Baritone guitar and choir), the string section, and the choir part. However, Burton omits the trumpet, which is significant because the spaghetti western style is lifted entirely—except for the mood of the music—as the song still presents signs of loneliness, grief, and pain.

Callaway (Cee-Lo Green) instantly attracts the listener by singing the first line of the verse "I remember when I lost my mind." Here, Callaway is freely reminiscing with emotion, making his intentions in the song sincere. In the chorus, Callaway sings the question: "Does that make me crazy?" in a falsetto soul. This vocal technique (falsetto soul) can either express joy, or in this situation, demand and grief, while singing, sighing, and shrieking.[61] Callaway sings and stretches (and sometimes shrieks) the two syllables in "Crazy" to make the title, word, and subject of the song striking. Callaway passionately repeats the question two times in the form of internalization as if he is confused and asking himself and the audience if he is "crazy." He answers the question himself by softly singing (with melisma and vibrato) on the word "possibly." Overall, in "Crazy," it is Callaway's voice that carries the emotional delivery and perhaps could be equivalently heard as the *El Degüello*.

In the music of "Crazy," Burton helps to complete the transformation of spaghetti western music into gospel, pop, hip-hop,[62] and soul by transposing and time-stretching the sample (leitmotif) up by one tone (from B-flat minor to C minor), and increasing the tempo to offer an upbeat feel. In spaghetti western music (especially when referring to the works of Morricone), the vocals consist of sounds or nonwords.[63] Here, the choir are continuously singing "oohs" and "ahhs" in "Crazy" as they are simply providing the accompaniment and "acting" as gospel backing singers. The Baritone guitar sample, in particular, has a different musical role in "Crazy." Unlike in the original recording, where the guitar has a distinctive sound, the sample in "Crazy" simply acts as a bass line and is directing and carrying the music. This guitar sample (based on four notes) is technically manipulated to not sound too dominating, and is balanced equally with the rest of the musical accompaniment.

In the chorus, the choir sample (the backing vocals) is transposed an octave higher to help the chorus/main hook stand out, and with added compression, it dynamically increases the tension and power of the song. However, it may at first sound misleading to the listener—as it now sounds as if there are females singing (alto and soprano), when in reality they are male voices. The convincing virtual "feminine" sounds of "oohs" and "ahhs" enhance the gospel feeling in "Crazy." The presence of Django's leitmotif is heard in the chorus where the strings help the chorus to stand out by harmonizing with the choir and by acting as a countermelody. Overall, the chorus holds a thick texture because of the strings' *forte* (loud) dynamics. The emotional timbre of the chorus maintains the force and tension by helping the vocals to dominate the song.

Overall, other than the added (main) vocal line, drumbeat, and sound effects, the major part of the music in "Crazy" is based on samples. It is arguable that the clever manipulation, deconstruction, transformation, and arrangement of the samples display a fresh and revived take on the genre, spaghetti western, where it has been remixed into a gospel, soul, hip-hop, and pop record. It is likely that when the listeners hear the famous Django/"Crazy" leitmotif today, many people will be unaware of the spaghetti western film but, instead, may recognize Gnarls Barkley. However, Burton does leave a very faint trace of spaghetti western in the music—to tease the listener of the "Crazy's" musical origins—by placing gunshot samples at the end of each chorus.[64] "Crazy" is an emotionally attached and memorable song with all of its musical layers (words, vocals, and, more importantly, samples) "that will break your heart a little bit."[65]

Burton has established a successful career since *The Grey Album* and it has not always involved remixing. He is now a music producer who is much in demand and who has collaborated and produced music for Gorillaz, Broken Bells, MF Doom, Red Hot Chili Peppers, Run the Jewels,

Beck, Michael Kiwanuka, and Adele. He continues to disrupt and enhance practices in the music industry with digital technology. Putting aside *The Grey Album* and "Crazy," Burton was drawn into yet another legal dispute with EMI in 2009. The record label refused to release *Dark Night of the Soul*, a collaboration with film director David Lynch and Sparklehorse's Mark Linkous. So Burton released the album himself as a limited edition CD package (which included a photograph book and a blank CD). The purpose of the blank CD was for the user to "illegally" download the tracks and burn them onto the CD. After Linkous's death in 2010, EMI agreed to release the album. In 2011, Danger Mouse's song "Black" (a collaboration with Daniele Luppi) was the first to be featured as a WebGL video (see next chapter). In 2019, he collaborated with Karen O (of Yeah Yeah Yeahs) on the album *Lux Prima*. As part of their project, they included an interactive multisensory art installation in exhibitions, titled "An Encounter with *Lux Prima*." The audience was immersed in the album along with its binaural sound and light effects, transmitted through the irregular shaped monolith. Overall, Brian Burton has excelled in his music career in the digital virtual era. More significantly, he experiments with elements of past music and successfully transforms it into *"something new or something different."*[66] The next chapter continues to discuss the fusion of past and present sounds, but this time in video game music.

5

"The Game Has Changed"

Video Game Music

It is future, it is retro, it is creative.

CHIPZEL, 2020[1]

A common feature in video game music is how certain themes and soundtracks recreate and revive past sounds, such as, retro, nostalgia, and retro-nostalgia—which this chapter discusses. It will discuss chiptune is a retro-signifier of 1980s Nintendo video games and a style of popular music, as demonstrated in the work of Chipzel, in which she maintained the classic Nintendo sound for the video game *Super Hexagon* (2012). Nostalgia in video game music visits historic popular culture and musical eras that may come across as sentimental—yet, at the same time, misleading for the gamer, as time and space are certainly distorted. For example, *Cuphead* (2017) is a simulation of classic 1930s animation presented as a video game, and is unexpectedly supported by jazz music. Returning to the work of Danger Mouse, he employed both retro and nostalgia in the song "Black" (2011), and the visuals (titled "Three Dreams of Black") are particularly fascinating as it was the first music video game designed for Google Chrome.

Video Game Music

Video game music is an important staple in music and media. Easily—if incorrectly—aligned with film music, video game music can also serve as an accompaniment to, and enhancement of, the visual. Yet, video game music tends to be overlooked in popular culture and music, because, historically, the music used to be almost nonexistent since the audio featured in video games comprised of very limited sound effects. Mark Austin highlights that "the seriousness of music is often overshadowed by its ludic nature,"[2] and, arguably so—music has an important role other than simply being background pleasure for the video gamer. Tim Summers convincingly expresses that "music is not a redundant echo of other aspects of the game, but is a central part of the audio-visual experience of interacting with video game."[3] Video gamers are becoming more acquainted and interactive with the music in a virtual sense, which coincides with William Cheng's thinking that "[m]any games grant opportunities to interact with audio phenomena in manners that may not be prudent, practical, or possible in the physical world."[4] Music in this form brings another kind of audio and visual experience for the gamer, in the way he/she engages and, where possible, communicates with game and sound.

Karen Collins, a leading scholar in this area, notes: "Unlike the consumption of many other forms of media in which the audience is a more passive 'receiver' of a sound signal, game players play an active role in the triggering of sound events in the game (including dialogue, ambient sounds, sound effects, and even musical events)."[5] Today, however the video game is presented—on a console, smartphone, online platform, or website—the gamers interact with video sounds, and in most cases, they can control the sounds they trigger with its interface, such as gun shots, jumps, crashes, points, awards, and alerts.

What other fascinations surround video game music? Like music, video game consists of various styles and, where relevant, has its own type of music, including chiptune/8-bit/ bitpop, classical, jazz, electro-pop/ synthwave, techno, industrial, metal, rock, glitch, and dubstep. Furthermore, video games have expanded into other digital virtual mediums such as music videos[6] and interactive websites.[7] There are also video *music* games to consider, in which the game focuses primarily on the music and allows the gamers to be even more interactive, where they can virtually place themselves as the musician. Mark Austin notes that there are four types of interactive video music games: matching, making, mixing, and metonymy.[8] "Matching" may involve rhythm or pitch, otherwise known as "rhythm" and "pitch" matching games. Rhythm matching (also known as "beat matching") requires gamers to perform in time to a set rhythm, and they are scored for their activity. To monitor their activity, the gamers press buttons/devices. Pitch matching is the same as rhythm matching but gamers are monitored for their vocal talent.[9] Overall, Kiri Miller describes "Matching" games as "sound reproduction technology, amateur musicianship and, commercial popular music [that] sets the stage"[10] for wannabe musicians, or, indeed, the gamers, giving them the illusion that they are rock stars. Examples of matching games include *Simon* (1978), *Beat Mania* (1997), *SingStar* (2004), and *Guitar Hero* (2005). "Making" is a way to engage in music making regardless of one's musical ability, such as *The Legend of Zelda (Ocarina of*

Time)[11] (1998), *Mario Paint* (2007), and *Nickelodeon Music Maker Music Game*. "Mixing" is similar to making games, but usually the gamers play with prearranged sounds/samples, allowing them to drag, drop, and mix the music; examples include *Incredibox* (2009) and *Fuser* (2020). "Metonymy," a figure of speech relating to a concept or person, can be applied in games, where the gamer creates a "feel" of the characters and set-space (e.g., a concert or work) within the game; examples include *Michael Jackson—The Experience* (2010)[12] and "Music Inc." (made by UK Music, 2014).[13]

There are vast areas of video game music to consider, but I am drawn to the retro/nostalgic-ness of the sounds presented in video game music. As with experimental music (Chapter 3) or remix (Chapter 4), retro/nostalgic video game music employs signifiers of the musical past and present, and sometimes hauntology, enhancing the user's digital virtual experience of the medium. Video game music is so popular today that musicians recreate the recorded music in concerts, such as the London Symphony Orchestra revisioning the *Final Fantasy* soundtrack composed by Nobuo Uematsu at the Barbican Hall in London, in 2016. Likewise, established artists may be invited to create a "theme" for a video game, such as Paul Oakenfold and Cee-Lo Green's "Falling" for *The Bourne Conspiracy* video game soundtrack in 2013.

While video game music has resulted in, or contributed to, various musical styles, it comes as no surprise that even beginner gamers may know the music better than the game itself; therefore, it might be the music that encourages them to play the video game. Hillegonda Rietveld and Marco Benoît Carbone remark that video game "music not only functions as a reminder of games played but it is also used to promote games. By becoming a defining part of the gaming franchises, game music can become a successful product in itself. In this sense one literally hears the music, and next plays the game."[14] This gives the potential gamers the opportunity to immerse themselves more in the music while exploring its place, space, and functions in an interactive way and enjoying the music in a (virtual) setting inside the video game. The purpose of music as heard in *Super Hexagon, Cuphead,* and "Three Dreams of Black" is to pull in the listeners, making them interact virtually with the video game as well as supplementing it by controlling the sounds, actions, and goals. I declare that each video game carries a sense of the past in the twenty-first century: "Retro" in chiptune—(reviving previous trends), "Nostalgia" in jazz (reminiscing or emotionally attaching to a previous era), and "Retro-nostalgia" in popular music (a combination of reviving previous trends as well as showing admiration for past styles).

Chiptune

Chiptune, also known as "Chip" and 8-bit music,[15] is a common, satisfying, dated musical feature heard in games, which references early 1980s video game music.[16] Chiptune, when heard, brings a sense of retro-ness to the familiar listener and gamer, thanks to the use of sound processors, and their immediate association with 1980s popular culture and music (e.g., electro/synth-pop). These sound processors, otherwise known as PSGs (Programmable Sound Generators), originally derived from 8-bit microchip hardware in which each chip could accommodate limited sonics such as bleeps, synthesized sounds, and sound effects. In the past, the video soundtrack's music creators were computer programmers rather than composers. The sounds of 8-bit were employed in video game consoles, notably Atari 2600, ZX Spectrum, and Commodore 64. Kenneth B. McAlpine notes that 8-bit music could not integrate musical expression and could offer little polyphonic experimentation.[17] Nevertheless, it still proved to be challenging for its creators, as Andrew Schartmann highlights: as 8-bit music developed, it became more obvious that limited melodic progression or, to be precise, "less is more," was a major feature in the composition.[18] The music has to sound simple, catchy, snappy, and keep the gamer engaged. To get an idea of the "less is more" approach and the early characteristics of 8-bit music, expect a noncomplicated form and structure—it was basically a very repetitive track that consisted of catchy hooks (usually up to three mini melodic phrases), almost mistakably heard as jingles. The tempo was significant, as it had to match the energetic pace of the video game, so it was usual to hear a musical rush set at 160 bpm. Tonality-wise, the soundtrack was usually set in a minor key, to synchronize with the action and suspense presented in the game.

Chiptune started to earn recognition from the 1990s, particularly with the rise of the Nintendo Gameboy (if you are familiar with this console then the *Super Mario Brothers'* theme might spring to mind). Music creators have become more advanced in digital composition, by experimenting with step sequencers and tracker interfaces.[19] However, when VST started to loom (see Chapter 1), creators experimented with chiptune, such as blending the sounds with other styles. Not only did this result in more polyphonic and textural sounds, but chiptune also became recognized as its own style and (sub)culture (as well as having its own fan base and club nights such as the UK's "Gamerdisco"). Artists of this style include Anamanaguchi, Crystal Castles, and Chipzel, all of whom created full-length tunes (sometimes with featured vocals too) based on chiptune.

Chipzel and Super Hexagon

Northern Irish chiptune creator Niamh Houston, better known as Chipzel, has been a lifelong devotee of the video game and its music. Even though she comes from a musical family, Houston was always drawn to electronic music and production, in particular, chiptune. She excitedly says that her passion for this style sounds "really futuristic and weird and nerdy. I just loved everything about that aesthetic."[20] After creating chiptunes using

LSDJ (Little Sound DJ) software,[21] she became recognized for her music. Her big break came when her music was used in the computer game *Hexagon*, designed by Terry Cavanagh who hired her to create the soundtrack for the game's sequel *Super Hexagon* in 2012.

Super Hexagon is a frantic minimal twitch[22] app game designed for devices, such as smartphones. The gamers have to imagine (or virtually place) themselves as the tiny triangle (which is actually the users' pointer/ guide), and escape a spinning maze of hexagons within a time limit.[23] When looking at the game, it seems there are, indeed, minimal visuals to look at (a maze of hexagons), but do not be tricked by that. As soon as the game proceeds (activated and controlled by either side of the screen),[24] it guarantees a dizzying and psychedelic journey, as the tiny triangle quickly rotates through a whirlpool of shapes situated within the hexagon while simultaneously changing colors. Depending on the difficulty level of the game, the shapes can spin extremely fast, creating a hypnotic experience for the gamer and a feeling of being lost. Houston created three tracks for the game, with each corresponding to three difficulty levels: "Hexagon" (hard), "Hexagoner" (harder), and "Hexagonest" (hardest). The added effect of the music intensifies the gamer's fixation and experience.

Houston's three levels eventually graduate to a faster speed and higher complexity: "Hyper Hexagon," "Hyper Hexagoner," and "Hyper Hexagonest."[25] The "Hexagonest" (the hardest and fastest level) is aptly called "Focus," and requires plenty of concentration for the gamer to stay in the game. Created entirely on the LSDJ software, the music syncs in nicely with the speeding and rotating maze as well as the robotic vocal prompts ("begin," "line," "triangle," "square," "pentagon," "hexagon," "excellent," and "game over."). An experienced gamer should successfully complete this level in over a minute. It begins with a repetitive, tiny but effective, strong synth hook (discreetly responded to by an internal hook), supported by a piercing electronic clap and faint kick. As the game changes slightly, prompted by the robotic voice which announces "triangle," the classic and flutter-coated "chip" sound (think of it as a chirpy sound) enters and is heard at a high pitch, and is accompanied by a four to the floor[26] kick. This repeats throughout the "square" level but transitions into a harder level ("Pentagon") where the high-pitched chip sound, along with bleeps, is diffusely altered and panned around creating a dizzying experience for the gamer, especially as this is synced with the graphics. The tension reduces slightly when the chip sound, kick, and tempo are vacuumed by the saturated bleeps, informally hinting a sense of conclusion ("Hexagon" level). As the game ends (prompted by "excellent" and "game over") the music slows down, and the hooks melodically descend with each note accentuated by the sounds of the exhausted snare.

Overall, every musical layer/sound collage is memorable, ranging from the snare to the high-pitched hooks, and as the shape changes throughout the game, so does the music. These visual and audio qualities prevent the gamers from digressing, keeping them focused on the game. If the audio version of "Focus" was played without the video game, the non-gamer would hear it as a dance track—and this music is compatible for playing in clubs. Chiptune music in general brings a sense of retro-ness to the creator, gamer, and fan. It brings on that childlike or youthful innocence that erases panic and brings a sense of hope, in addition to celebrating their playful past.[27]

Jazz: *Cuphead*

A successful and nostalgic video game is *Cuphead*, released for Xbox One and PC in 2017. Both musically and visually, instead of bringing the past into the present, the past appears to stay in the past. Not to be considered

FIGURE 5.1 Cuphead *(artwork for the soundtrack album)*. © 2021 StudioMDHR *Entertainment Inc. All Rights Reserved. Cuphead™ and StudioMDHR™ are trademarks and/or registered trademarks of StudioMDHR Entertainment Inc. throughout the world.*

as 3D, CGI, or high-quality digital created games, where game designers create an immersive hyperreal experience for the gamer, *Cuphead*, instead, uses nostalgic animation, and a jazz soundtrack (Figure 5.1). Categorized as an "indie" game, where creators have more freedom to design the game and its music in any way they like, *Cuphead* was devised by Canadian brothers Chad and Jared Moldenhauer, and was created in StudioMDHR.

The main attraction of *Cuphead* is that it references 1930s animation, an era the brothers were inspired by when watching old videotapes of vintage cartoons. The game references "rubber hose" style, an early characteristic of twentieth-century animation, where the character's limbs are drawn in a way that does not resemble humans, but, instead, they are in the shape of rubber hoses (it can look very bendy and curvy). The creators were also inspired by early animators such as the Fleischer brothers (of Fleischer Studios), who created famous animation such as *Betty Boop*, and *Popeye the Sailor*. A distinctive feature of the Fleischer brothers' works was the use of dysmorphic characters (where the head may appear larger than the rest of the body), and this is featured in *Cuphead*. To give the impression that the video game was somehow created in the 1930s, every frame of the video game was hand-drawn rather than digitally designed, thereby maintaining past practices of animation. Furthermore, the visuals were embellished with scratches, color bleeds, pigment fades, and marks to simulate the worn-out look, resulting in "visual damage."[28] The combination of the 1930s animated style and the way the characters are graphically presented in *Cuphead* offers what David McGowan calls a "modern retro"[29] experience for the gamers, where they can gain a sense of past animation life, and relive their childhood memories by watching cartoons. As most familiar viewers/gamers would not have been alive during the 1930s to witness this particular style of animation, these cartoon characters have always been apparent in popular culture, including television and online video platforms such as YouTube.

While it is considered a "modern retro" or, more fittingly, a modern nostalgic, experience for the gamer/viewer, there are actually nostalgic signifiers to other animated characters from different decades that the familiar viewer will recognize, such as "Tom and Jerry" (1940) and "The Iron Giant" (1999).[30] These references to popular culture based on a visual medley of other cartoons enhance the nostalgic postmodern and fantastical adventure for the gamer.

Cuphead is categorized as a "run and gun" game, where a lone character carries a weapon of some sort and travels by foot to defeat enemies, or in this case, a string of bosses (known as boss fights).[31] The synopsis of *Cuphead* is clear at the beginning of the game: it is based on two brothers, Cuphead and Mugman, who are looked after by their guardian, Elder Kettle. Cuphead and Mugman are playing at the Devil's Casino where they are challenged to a game by the Devil. The prize is either the brothers will gain ownership of the casino, or the Devil will own their souls. When the brothers lose and plead for their lives, the Devil gives them the chance to save their souls by ordering them to collect his debtors' souls. The dippy turned hitmen brothers (mainly Cuphead) are advised by their guardian (Elder Kettle) to carry out the contracts, and they are given a magic potion that releases special powers. A game tutorial follows, detailing which buttons/keys to press to activate moves and gunshots. Each short level could represent an episode (almost like a traditional length of a cartoon) where Cuphead (i.e., the gamer) has to navigate from start to finish, and win boss fights to make it to the next level. Despite its very attractive animated and fairytale setting, together with magical and surreal characters, the theme of the game is dark, haunting, and scary, and it can be frustratingly difficult to play.[32] The non-gamer, that is, the gazer, can simply enjoy watching the game as a merry cartoon—or by dancing to the music. Both the gamer and gazer will be attracted to the music accompanying Cuphead, which is based on early jazz.[33] Brilliantly, the jazz music matches the theme and style of the video game.

Kristofer Maddigan—Composer for Cuphead

The music was composed by BAFTA-winning composer, Kristofer Maddigan,[34] with whom I spoke about the creative and thinking processes behind the soundtrack. Maddigan, an orchestral percussionist for the National Ballet of Canada, was approached by his childhood friend, Chad Moldenhauer (one of the game's developers) to compose the soundtrack. He warmly recalls, "when they started the game it was a lot smaller than it became as it was a very indie project with the two of them, a programmer, and an animator, and I was basically the only musician that they knew, so they asked me if I wanted to do the music for it."[35] Maddigan always wanted to compose music, but as a professional musician specializing in performance rather than composition, he had never had the opportunity until then. This was a four-year project that started in 2013, and as the game's concept developed and evolved, so did the music. The Moldenhauer brothers and Maddigan did not expect the game to do so well until a *Cuphead* trailer was previewed at the E3 conference in 2015 (also known as the Electronic Entertainment Expo), receiving attention from the indie game community and Microsoft.

Composing in the style of jazz was interesting for Maddison, as his musical background is more orchestral based. He was given sketches of *Cuphead* to work with and had to aim for a big band sound. This was interesting because 1930s animation was mainly supported by lively orchestral music, rather than jazz. However, the Moldenhauer brothers wanted a "vibe sound" and excitement in the music and, to achieve this, they wanted to inspire Maddigan by sending him their favorite big band tracks such as Benny Goodman's "Sing Sing Sing," (1936) and Cab Calloway's "Minnie Moocher" (1931). Maddigan did not need to create music for every scene/level/boss fight. Instead, he created over fifty-six linear music tracks that were later assigned to the scenes/levels/boss fights. As the soundtrack developed, the musical compositions stretched further than the big band sound, by including earlier jazz styles such as ragtime. Personally, when I hear the tracks, I am virtually journeying through the early history of jazz.

Interestingly, Maddigan does not extend musically beyond the year 1940 (the game is set in the mid-1930s). Additionally, as part of the four-year creative process, he conducted vast research on jazz music rather than the actual animation style. He recalls, "I didn't watch many cartoons but I spent a long time listening to big band, I was familiar with the music but never thought about it from a compositional standpoint."[36] He contemplates the time he studied ragtime conventions:

> how do you take those things and do something interesting with them . . . it's not like how can you take something that already exists and create something else that sounds like your own thing but it still sounds stylistically correct and that was a challenge. It wasn't four years of writing, it was four years of research alongside of that listening and reading about those [jazz] artists and that era.[37]

As part of his research, Maddigan studied old jazz scores, jazz theory, and the creative process of composers. To make sure he was on the right path with his jazz compositions, he hired a teacher, jazz specialist and film composer John Herberman to oversee his works, and serve as the conductor and arranger in the actual recording sessions. While Maddigan wanted the music to sound like the 1930s, he did not want it to be a direct simulation of it. However, he admits that the references to his favorite jazz musicians in the music really capture the 1930s jazz vibe, for example, Gene Krupa, drummer (known for playing weighty and catchy tom toms), Cab Calloway, Benny Goodman (clarinet), and Larry Hampton (vibraphone). Maddigan was also influenced by the music that accompanied the following dancers of that era: The Nicholas Brothers and Whitey's Lindy Hoppers. Additionally, certain innovative instruments at the time are heard in the soundtrack such as the American Fotoplayer[38] and Theremin.[39] Maddigan gracefully adds that he was very much inspired by the works of Duke Ellington and Scott Joplin (pioneer of ragtime), and he wanted to pay tribute to their works. For example, he was really inspired by how Duke Ellington successfully and daringly applied dissonance in his music, a musical feature that Maddigan used in "Pyramid Peril." He also wanted to pay respect to Scott Joplin's ragtime (in particular, "Maple Leaf Rag," 1916), by not directly imitating it, but by fostering a particular focus on thematic construction and variation. This is evident throughout the game as Maddigan turns the main feature of the music, "Inkwell Theme," into a leitmotif.[40] There are many variations of this theme played by various soloists throughout the game. At the same time, Maddigan also wanted to tease the listener/gamer to remind them that they are playing *Cuphead* in the twenty-first century by discreetly adding indirect references to other video games:

> There's definitely video quotes in there [such as *Final Fantasy* and *Ride of the Valkyies*] . . . I wanted to be authentic across the board essentially, I was more approaching it as not 2000s' composer writing 1930s music for an 1980s style video game, I wanted it to sound like "what if" the golden age of jazz and golden age of video games could co-exist at the same time. What would those composers in the 1930s be writing for video games? So that was kinda my mindset for a lot of the process.[41]

Overall, the music carries an erratic tempo (it is very fast) that matches the intensity of the game, making the gamer either more determined or, most likely, pressured to complete each level. To bring the music alive, Maddison carefully selected musicians to interpret his musical vision into reality but within a strict timeframe. He hired musicians from the renowned The Boss Brass as well as established session musicians. He explains his reason, "I wanted to get a group of musicians who knew each other and can play together, that was really important to the *sound* of the game."[42] After the musicians studied their individual musical parts, they had little time to rehearse together. The recording sessions took place in Canterbury Music Studios in Toronto, owned by well-known engineer and producer Jeremy Darby.[43] Maddigan took a breather from the performing process and sat in the recording booth to witness his musical creations come alive. The sessions took no longer than two and a half weeks in total (all recorded in various slots with minimal takes). It was the mixing of the recorded music, however, that took months to complete, including Maddigan playing additional musical parts where needed. Maddigan worked closely with Jeremy Darby in creating the vintage sound, so the music would sound like it originated in the 1930s, minus the inaudibility and unwanted sounds. Here, vintage microphones and vintage techniques were applied during recording sessions to maintain the video game and music's concept, and recorded sounds were digitally edited in the mixing process. Maddigan explains that this was very time consuming because, "on the soundtrack there are 56 tracks but because there are so many different versions within the game, there are different solos in the tracks—there are over 200 different tunes on the soundtrack itself and Jeremy had to mix the solos—he wasn't only mixing 56 tracks, but over 200 different tunes."[44]

After the mixing was complete, the music was transferred to the game developers and they assigned the music to the appropriate scenes/levels/boss fights. When the game was released in 2017, the music received positive responses:

> I was very glad it got a lot of strong reviews across the board, and people liked the game and music—there was a point around 2015 at the E3 when

the game got the buzz around the world and that's when we realized that we had a certain responsibility to do this as good as possible. I originally wanted to do a good job because my friend asked me to do a good job, and I wanted to do a good job because I respect the art form, but then there was a point where we needed to *nail* this because there's going to be a whole new demographic of people who may be listening to jazz for the first time, and we want them to check out the original artists from that era.[45]

Maddigan also loved that, on an educational level, the music inspired students to learn to play *Cuphead* music. He has rearranged scores for high school level after receiving requests from students and teachers. While the whole soundtrack took four years to create, the hard work has certainly paid off: not only has *Cuphead* received great responses for both the game and the music, it has also introduced a new jazz audience in the twenty-first century. Maddigan considers it an accomplishment that the music has attracted new jazz lovers: "the biggest reward is that not just people like it, people are looking into something otherwise not thought about checking out."[46] Personally, if I was not aware that the music was created for the game, I would have believed that actual old jazz vinyl records had been used—the vintage sounds presented in the music are very convincing. The dedication Maddigan applied to this lengthy project, including the exploration in jazz music, and his mission to pay "tribute to great artists that we love from the past,"[47] is revolutionary in video game music, as evidenced by his BAFTA, Audio Network Guild, SXSW Gaming, and The Game Awards.

Paul Novotny—Musician on Cuphead

In our interview, double bass player Paul Novotny (musician, educator, TV composer, and audio producer) fondly recounted the process of rehearsing and recording the music. He was hired to perform the music for the game, even though he was not aware of the visuals, only the game's concept. The musicians only had one rehearsal that lasted for three hours. While the idea of a one-off three-hour rehearsal for a jazz project sounds incredible, Novotny explains that session musicians with a high profile were hired only for a set time. While this may sound unusual to some, if you have heard the music, you can tell it is a very complex piece to listen to—after all, "it's Jazz"! While it was an ordinary job allocated for the double bassist, this session really stood out for Novotny, because it was a totally different experience from his other projects. Novotny passionately shares that the most striking and remarkable moment in playing the music was the tempo:

The first thing we did we undertook a rehearsal and everybody [the saxophone players, brass, and rhythm section] were all in disbelief at the tempos we were being asked to play at. It was the equivalent of "Mickey

Mouse" music that would have been sped up by tape but we were *playing* at that tempo. These were tempos at 300 bpm . . . and at that point none of us really understood the context of the game, only that there were going to be hand-drawn images that go back to the 1930s . . . it was only when we got to the recording session that the game developers were there, and we saw some of the developments visually, we could see where the whole thing was going to go.[48]

Novotny realized that this game was going to be a bestseller in the industry, and a game changer in the way video game music is consumed. It was the first video game to achieve the number one position in the Billboard charts (jazz category). While it could be considered as unusual for jazz to musically support a video game, the music is very fitting for the nostalgic 1930s animated style of *Cuphead*. The fast-paced music keeps the gamer engaged, but at the same time educates the unfamiliar listener and encourages him/her to find out more about jazz. Novotny describes the positive impact of the soundtrack because it "introduces the younger generation to another era of music."[49] As the soundtrack is so popular, the session musicians and Maddigan were invited to play the music live at the Kensington Market Jazz Festival in Toronto, Canada (2018). The Moldenhauer family also attended this event. Novotny fondly recalls that this live performance was special as it marked a momentous celebration for the game, design team, musicians, collaborators, and audience:

It's exhilarating because of the tempo of the music, but it astounded me to see the reception of the audience. I mean these people were just over the moon . . . it was really a celebration of the game and it was one of those moments where the fans and the music came together, and it was pretty amazing to be part of that.[50]

Novotny is so impressed by the soundtrack that he could not choose a favorite track or cue. He does, however, champion the song "Die House" (sung by Alana Bridgewater), which I will now discuss.[51]

Cuphead—*"Die House"*

In the video game, the character "King Dice" (the Devil's right-hand man) sings the outstanding song "Die House." Interestingly, King Dice's appearance bears a resemblance to the jazz musician Cab Calloway—in terms of dress code, the mustache, and facial expressions, but not his head, as this one is shaped like a dice.[52] In this section, the gamer directs Cuphead to a dice-shaped house. Inside the dice-shaped house, Mr. King Dice is having a dialogue with Cuphead, permitting him to enter the next isle. However, the musical accompaniment and lyrics then suggest otherwise with lines such as "I never play nice. . . . I cannot let you pass . . . bring me those contracts pronto, don't mess with me." The lyrics nudge Cuphead to realize he still has a challenging road ahead in collecting the soul contracts, but now he has encountered a major drawback, in Mr. King Dice. The song carries a nostalgic resemblance to Cab Calloway's "Minnie the Moocher" based on the vocal melodic shape, and the instrumental that is mostly directed by the swinging drums, piano, and steady bass line. Alana Bridgewater flawlessly portrays the character of Mr. King Dice by singing in a powerful deep tone that asserts his authority. The chorus is intended to sound terrifying as she sings in a threatening manner (e.g., "don't *mess* with me") and the lively male backing vocals forcefully echo her threats. This creates a worrying situation for Cuphead, and the gamer, who will feel under pressure to complete his/her mission. As with any video game music, this song is very memorable, and, in this case, it is a modern nostalgic and musical experience. Overall, while the music and game are powerful to hear and play, *Cuphead* enables the gamer to virtually experience a past era through gameplay based on the exciting vintage animation and jazz music.[53]

Popular Music: "Three Dreams of Black"

This chapter returns to Danger Mouse (Burton), who expanded his projects to include the first interactive music video game (and mini film) designed for Google in 2011.[54] The song used in the game, "Black" (sung by Norah Jones), is very fitting, so it is important that we gain an insight into the music first. The track is from Burton's collaboration with Italian film composer, Daniele Luppi, and their imaginary film soundtrack, *Rome* (2011).[55] As one would expect with the works of Burton, there is no set musical style pinned to "Black"; there is retro 1970s soft rock, soft pop, and 1960s spaghetti western—meaning the music is coated with both retro and nostalgic musical signifiers. The introduction has an oblique reference to the Eagles' famous guitar part in "Hotel California" (1977). The song's theme is traveling through a person's emotions, toward either loneliness, an exit of some sort, or possibly the end of life. The musical signs of 1960s spaghetti western are supported by a dynamic bass, in which its melody serves as a countermelody to the keyboard and vocals. The chorus is quietly supported by melodramatic strings, and a soft funk rhythmic pattern played by the drums with light sticks.[56] Here, the haunting backing vocals are sung by *I Cantori Moderni*, the same choir who sang for Morricone's soundtracks, demonstrating Burton's obsession with spaghetti western films.[57]

The visual accompaniment is a blend of a music video and game, where the gazers transition into gamers and have limited control over certain visual parts of the song. Nevertheless, they can get lost in the music and explore the virtual environment at the same time. Directed by leading digital artist,

Chris Milk, he and his collaborators, including fellow digital artist Aaron Koblin, created the visual, titled "Three Dreams of Black," into three interweaving sections. The Google Creative Lab, Mirada (design studio), and Radical Media designed the visuals for WebGL (Webs Graphics Library), which is a form of HTML (Hyper Text Markup Language) that allows 3D imagery on the web browser. This means the gamer can use the computer to control the game (by using mainly the mouse). Each of the three sections is presented differently, consisting of real-life imagery that occasionally blends with 2D and 3D graphics.

The gazer/gamer mostly views this footage in first person, making this an estranged experience as he/she is practically on his/her own and searching for survival (as opposed to *Cuphead* where the main character is always fighting for survival when confronted with villains). This concept is musically supported by the introduction, in which the indirect reference to the Eagles' "Hotel California" guitar melody nicely sets the haunting theme of the video game. Here, the viewer (who is also the girl in the video) is driving a car into what looks like a dystopian world. The girl is struggling for survival and ends up living on scraps in a neglected building.[58] The only way for her to escape from "reality" is through dreaming. In dream sequence/verse one (presented in 2D), the girl is driving, accompanied by random colorful birds signifying a sense of hope and freedom—if only she could find her way out of the dystopian world. As the chorus enters, the visuals transform into 3D where the gamer has the chance to participate in the video game through navigation only. This section deftly suits the chorus, as the character (i.e., the gamer) is trying to escape from her situation, but every time she attempts to drive out of the area (as guided by the gamer), she is faced with the same potential "exit," which consists of a gigantic morphed head with its mouth resembling a black tunnel. These images coincide with the somber lyrics "Until you travel to that place you can't come back . . . all that's left is black," and a chilling keyboard melody, until the second verse arrives. At this point, the video inactivates the user's function to control the game and the girl driving through the tunnel. This image transforms into dream sequence number two, where the girl is back in 2D graphics and is on a train to an unknown destination. When the second chorus enters, she finds herself in a beautiful 3D landscape, where the gamer can navigate the virtual environment again until another black tunnel appears. The third dream sequence sees the girl getting out of her bed in 2D and opening the door to a 3D utopian world. This concluding scene consists of a desert with floating random objects, sky structures, and colorful birds, suggesting the girl has managed to escape and the gamer has won. This scene is musically and blissfully supported by the Morricone-style choir, and evocative high-pitched strings suggesting a sense of relief and victory, but is it? This final sequence is significant as the gamer has slightly more control in navigation and speed, meaning that he/she can really explore the surroundings by "flying" at his/her own pace (fast or slow), as well as leaving a black and smoky trace of his/her direction. Just like the desert, the navigation of the area is infinite, suggesting there is no destination or way out. The gamer can try to fly through a random floating object, but nothing will happen, alluding to the feeling that he/she is immortal, and, indeed, in the "black."

Despite the limited interaction between the gamer and video (mainly in the 3D scenes/chorus sections), the gamer has the opportunity to create objects. On the website, there is a creator section with virtual tools where users can create animals and other items and, if lucky, it will be included in the final part of the chorus (hence the random floating objects). The computer becomes another type of disruptive technology where the gamer uses it as a game console, to play/control the game, and to create characters. Another incentive on the website is that there is an option to explore the desert in more detail. Here the gamer can navigate the desert and view more of the floating objects without a time limit, just like visiting a virtual museum. While the music and lyrical themes are dark, which ties in neatly with spaghetti western films, the music and surreal visuals are represented as a mystical dream, making it a restless but a retro-nostalgic audiovisual experience in the twenty-first century.[59]

Overall, this chapter focused on specific video game music to demonstrate the way the attentive creator brings past music into the present. The rebirth of these sounds expands in further ways for all to appreciate the music and visuals. The next chapter continues these themes by examining how artists shape their audiovisual performances and identities in the digital virtual era.

6

"Living in a Fantasy"

Performers and Identity

We may think that in the current digital era, creators in the music industry—in particular performers—are gaining greater control over their artistry. In most cases, though, "recruited" artists manufactured into disposable musical products are still the norm in the industry; after all, it is full of commercial businesses.[1] Thanks to technology, creators—regardless of musical expertise and experience—can similarly gain recognition and success without being tied to the major music industry; this is mostly due to distribution and consumption of music on the internet. However, there have been a few creators who are rightfully classed as multitalented—for example, in songwriting, playing, producing, and performing—and who have been fortunate enough to gain artistic control of their music, and identity. Some creators, such as Grace Jones and The Weeknd (in this chapter), have successfully taken control of their musical identities—I mean creators who have experimented with their visual identities and musically turned these into art forms. These creators can successfully manipulate their identities by revealing their virtual fantasies in real life, which, of course, may raise questions concerning authenticity and their "real" identities. Let's take a closer look on the concept of identity.

Understanding Identity . . .

The term "identity" may colloquially associate with one's character or personality. However, for the sake of this chapter we can briefly locate postmodern elements to help us understand the fascination behind the creators' thinking of and flirting with multiple identities. For those who wish to flirt with their persona in their creativities, their true identity is hidden from their façade. Sometimes, the individual (such as the creator, that is, the artist/performer) may wish to adopt or simulate another identity mainly through image, lifestyle, and personality.[2]

Mike Featherstone (1991) argues that individuals can apply postmodern identity in three different ways: by consuming images and signs; through recommendation or inspiration; or, by simulating an artistic and "original"/"authentic" identity founded in art, history, and bohemian lifestyle.[3] An example of the first mode of identity application is Madonna, who plays out her fantasies of different identities through audiovisual play. Perfectly labeled as the "queen" and "icon" of postmodernism,[4] Madonna reinvents herself continuously by simulating multiple identities successfully (e.g., being Marilyn Monroe one minute or a mysterious secret agent the next), leaving consumers to speculate as to who the "real" Madonna is, and to decide which virtual Madonna they prefer.[5] An example of this in the visual art world is the photographer Cindy Sherman, whom I consider the original "selfie" influencer (although I am aware that dubious honor is debatable!), since she experimented with different images of herself. Her most famous photo collection titled *Untitled Film Stills* (1977–80) is based on various images of her disguises in different acting roles, mainly female stereotypical types, such as the femme fatale and the innocent girl. Through the use of film stills, where Sherman is virtually acting out different roles, we are teased by the concealment of her "real" identity. As with Madonna, before the digital virtual era we were unsure of Sherman's authentic self, because every time there was a hint of exposure or reveal, she instantly switched her identity.

David Bowie (David Jones) is a great example of experimentation with high and popular cultures, musical genres/styles, and art forms, as well as a creator who was constantly self-reinventing. He has been celebrated as postmodern[6] and a chameleon[7] creator because, as Stan Hawkins says, "his music, his image was always undergoing changes."[8] Perhaps his finest moment was when he portrayed himself as "Ziggy Stardust" (1972), an alien-turned-rock star, in the glam rock era. He dabbled with various genres and styles, including disco, hip-hop, electronic, and drum 'n' bass, and as he progressed, "one mask fell off [and] others would appear from underneath,"[9] meaning that he created and wore a new identity for each project.

Featherstone's second type of identity is based on being influenced by other people in terms of attraction, which usually includes images, particular connotations, and lifestyles. This typically applies to gazing at people in the (social) media such as Instagram. Media influencers (who are also singers such as Gwen Stefani) usually recommend the latest trends of lifestyle and leisure, including fashion and music, enticing fans and consumers to believe they can transform their persona and lives.

Featherstone's third type of identity consists in bridging everyday life and art.[10] This type of identity exudes with creators, where their "life imitates art"[11] by carrying their look from bohemian lifestyles, and artistic scenes such as Dadaism in the 1920s.[12] This type of aesthetic lifestyle is otherwise called the "artist of life"[13] where image is not only a priority (e.g., Bruce Springsteen, Kanye West) but also the actual creators' way of living, and how they perform in their creations. Bowie also serves as a good representation of this concept. Despite experimenting with multiple identities that also matched his various lifestyles, music, and performances, he successfully stands out from other similar creators. Thanks to his performance art background, Bowie convincingly performed his different fantasies that complemented his image, fashion, music, and theatricality.

With all these in mind, what are the signs of authenticity, if the music is no longer considered unique or "one-off," and if people choose to play or switch roles by reconstructing their identities?[14]

. . . and Authenticity

The authenticity of popular music is well documented in terms of songwriting, music, and performances, and, of course, creators in other genres and styles freely and emotionally express themselves, and are labeled as authentic.[15] Nowadays, because of the ways in which music is produced (refer to the previous chapters), a sense of authenticity could be identified in *how* the music was created, including *how* the vocals were delivered—for example, do we perceive expression, emotion, and intonation in the song? Authenticity in music can open various debates concerning production, songwriting, performing, and maintaining self-identity.[16] Some critics may be puzzled to consider this music as "authentic" due to genre/style blending and recycling of past eras, and we often hear that nagging expression "there's nothing new about it if it has been done before." I maintain, however, that the music mentioned in this book deserves a sense of authenticity, and my claim is echoed by Andrew Herman and John Sloop, both of whom argue that authenticity is "far from being an act of piracy or plagiarism, appropriation is a gesture of respect and inspiration, where one uses an original source as a springboard for one's own creativity."[17] It is also echoed in Allan Moore's concept of the authenticity triad in music: first person (authenticity of expression), second person (authenticity of experience), and third person (authenticity of execution).[18]

While critics have argued that creators such as Madonna and Bowie, who play with multiple visual identities, may not be considered as authentic, I propose that the use of simulated images and imitation, with the addition of the creator's music, can result in an individual identity (or, indeed, multiple identities). This could be considered as "authentic inauthenticity,"[19] a notion examined by Lawrence Grossberg. He argues that creators who appear to be authentic can admit at the same time that they are inauthentic;[20] e.g., Bowie and Madonna acknowledge and affirm that they want to pass their influences via their art to their audiences.[21] Interestingly, Grossberg detects that authentic inauthenticity in popular music evolved in the 1970s where visuals and performance appeared to be more prominent than the music.[22] Glam rock, for instance, was perceived to be inauthentic in various ways, such as musically attacking experimental psychedelic and progressive rock, and resurrecting 1950s rock and roll in the 1970s. Glam rock was fluid in terms of visual presentation, and Philip Auslander highlights that theatricality in performance is a major factor to consider when questioning authenticity in glam rock because, in rock culture, a musician's "real" identity is important.[23] In glam rock, it was usual to observe performers displaying inauthentic identities through disguise, cosmetics, glamorous outfits, wild hairstyles, gender-play, and attitude. Glam rockers would also mask their identities by performing under different pseudonyms,[24] allowing them the liberation to self-invent and play out their fantasies.

A good illustration of this point is to return to Bowie. Auslander argues that Bowie's glam rock performances presented "challenges to rock's ideology of authenticity, [and] his desire to theatricalize rock performance."[25] As Ziggy Stardust, Bowie would wear heavy makeup, colorful body suits and sport bright-colored hair. Ziggy's identity would at first be viewed as inauthentic because of his play with images, yet at the same time, Bowie's character is authentic, due to the way he blended originality, art, his gender, and sexuality with playful images and characters. The birth of Ziggy Stardust was a groundbreaking moment in modern popular culture, and has inspired future creators to explore their fantasies visually and virtually, such as Lady Gaga, St Vincent, Janelle Monáe, and, more significantly for this chapter, Grace Jones and The Weeknd.

Grace Jones

Grace Jones is the missing creator in the trilogy of the postmodern greats alongside David Bowie and Madonna. Daring to step into biblical analogies, I would propose Madonna as Mother Mary (naturally), David Bowie as Jesus, and Grace as God. Moreover, I would not be surprised to hear Jones claiming to have given birth to Bowie and Madonna (the pop star)!

Immediate impressions of Jones can be described as fierce, fearless, and flamboyant, and she is widely admired for her eccentricity, art creations, gender-play, personality, philosophy, and beauty. Born as Grace Mendoza possibly around 1948,[26] in Jamaica, she moved to New York City in 1964 and became a successful model for designers Issey Miyake and Thierry Mugler, and appeared on the magazine covers of *Vogue* and *Elle*. She made her musical debut in the New York "Studio 54" disco scene from the late 1970s and has since experimented with her identities, music, and other forms of art, including acting and fashion. Her well-known songs include "Pull Up to the Bumper" (1982) and "Slave to the Rhythm" (1985). Jones's musical trademarks include her domineering vocals presented as *Sprechstimme* (half spoken and half sung) that have limited character, described by Timothy Warner as her distinctive way of "evoking a sense of presence to the listener."[27] However, do not be fooled by a seemingly limited style and range of vocals—she is very capable of producing various tones and timbres, such as the high, piercing vocals in the dub track, "She's Lost Control" (1980), and the hypnotic, authoritative vocals in the industrial track, "Corporate Cannibal" (2008).[28]

Her identity is striking and she is known to be "performatively hypermasculine."[29] Never afraid to play with her gender and tease the audience with various sensational and theatrical looks, her most memorable profiling image is circled around her perfectly toned body, chiseled cheekbones, and flattop haircut, and she is often spectacularly enveloped in power suits. Sheila Whiteley stresses that a female wearing a male suit is significant, as the suit masks her femininity "but, rather than constituting a denial of her identity, it was assertion of autonomy,"[30] and this is clear in Jones's performances.

Jones's gender fluidity is witnessed more in her performances where she constantly switches genders while singing from a male's perspective. However, she does not care for how the media labels her gender, as she asserts, "The future is no sex. You can be a boy or girl, whatever you want."[31] While critics may label her as compellingly androgynous or overly camp, Jones was simply "being me, not thinking about the color of my skin, or my sex—I was outside race and gender: I considered myself an energy that has not been classified."[32] Jones captivates the media and the audience's attention extremely well with her domineering looks (regardless of style). Interestingly, she appears solo in most of her videos, performing different identities including exploring her feminine masculinity.

Due to Jones's multi-identities, Francesca T. Royster persuasively asks, "[I]s Grace Jones a hologram?"[33] because she performs her fantasies through experimenting with her music and image. With her stage performances as with her videos, Jones mostly lives out her fantasies in solo, and almost in nonhuman/post-human/part-machine form. Part of her vision in playing out her fantasy while honing her gender fluid/less body and championing her blackness was brought to reality with her artistic collaborator (and former lover), Jean-Paul Goude, who helped in styling her, as well as creating and contributing to the artwork on album covers and music videos. The following comment by Jones refers mainly to her performance art event *One Man Show*, but could equally apply to her videos, performances, and herself:

There was also a robotic quality to my performance. A mix of the human, the android, and the humanoid. . . . Theatrically, I was not thinking. This is a way of finding a different way to be black, lesbian, female, animal. I didn't want my body language to betray my origins, I wanted to use my body to express how I had liberated myself from my background, ignored obstacles, and created something original, based on my own desires, fears and appetites. I was using my body as a language. A language that comes from a dark continent. And dark is dangerous.[34]

Her comment is reflected in videos such as "La Vie En Rose" (from *One Man Show* in 1982), where she plays the accordion on the stairs, with her body silhouetted behind her. The use of mundane stage props and block lighting supports her performance, but she captures the viewer with her vocal range style (and seductive French accent), her perfectly semi-motionless shaped body, and the way she displays her facial expressions with her supermodel looks and a contoured face that would make Instagram influencers envy her. Another example is "Corporate Cannibal" (directed by Nick Hooker in 2008), a digitally enhanced black-and-white video, where Jones is a distorted object with her body mutated into various shapes and sizes. You cannot help but gaze at her mouth and eyes throughout the video, and witness how they contort and sync with the music. At the end of the video the screen turns to black, as Steven Shaviro notes, "as if it had been entirely consumed by her body."[35] Although Jones does not appear in all of her music videos,[36] when she does, the viewer's focus is on *her*. Typical visual characteristics of Jones are not entirely focused on her dress sense but, rather, on how she uses her body, catwalk-ready makeup, and sinister stares. She maintains these visual gestures to coincide with her songs, regardless of genre/style, and timeframe.

"Love You to Life"

The 2010 music video "Love You to Life" (from the 2008 album *Hurricane*) showcases different identities of Grace Jones while maintaining her visual trademarks (body, makeup, and stares).[37] The song was written by Grace Jones, Bruce Woolley, and Mark Van Eyck, and produced by Ivor Guest. A dark song aching for everlasting life that is supported by the wordplay of the main hook ("love you to life" instead of "love you to death"), the music is demurely drenched in reggae and dub, and Jones's experimental vocals: she talks in the verses and sings in the choruses.[38] A major highlight of this music video is the lighting, which comes across as haunting and futuristic—a perfect alliance for Jones. It was created by photographer and light artist, Chris Levine (Figure 6.1), who was introduced to Jones by haute couture milliner, and creative director of Jones's *Hurricane* tour, Philip Treacy. Levine was hired to do the laser lights installation for Jones's concert at the Royal Festival Hall in London. Throughout the *Hurricane* tour, Jones wore a signature crystal-encrusted bowler hat designed by Philip Treacy.

FIGURE 6.1 *Chris Levine and Grace Jones at the* Stillness at the Speed of Light *Exhibition, 2010 (the portrait in the image is based on the "Love You to Life" music video). Credit: Dave M. Benett/Getty Images.*

Levine recalls he was nervous about meeting Jones, but knew he had to captivate her: "I met Grace standing on stage at the Royal Festival Hall and told her that if she stood on this cross on the floor all light would break loose from her head. Luckily my theory worked and it looked awesome."[39] Jones then hired him to direct the video and experiment with light in the visuals. Levine's specialism is light design, an art form he has always been fixated on. He passionately reflects, "Light is intrinsic to the way we perceive reality and by working with it, particularly with laser as a very pure form of light, I do get the sense of tuning into a deeper realm of awareness. It is innate within us but somehow the circuits need firing up and it's to do with energy and flow."[40]

Levine was determined to reflect his devotion to light in "Love You to Life," but was apprehensive as it was his first time creating a music video, along with the added pressure (and pleasure) of working with Jones. He recollects, "It could all go very wrong and Grace would exterminate me. So I got a really good team [The Why Not Associates] around me and it came together nicely . . . though using high technology I like to keep it raw."[41] Being well aware of the visual trademarks of Jones in her videos—and to make sure her fashion did not clash with the lights—he filmed her naked.

While light is a major part of Levine's vision, he does a fantastic job of making sure that both light and Jones work equally well together, with Jones triumphing over the visuals—or does she? This is not a bright and colorful light show, but a subdued texture of illuminating lights channeling aura in a dark space. To begin, a luminous pink light semi-vanishes in the black space that is quickly seized with black-and-white blinkering signs showing the words "love" and "life," and an opaque image of Jones's mouth—the only noncolorful images featured in the video. After these quick, passing black-and-white shots, the music begins and is visually supported by a cloud of aurora-specter lighting and a laser beam with a star-shaped focal spot. The viewer is drawn to the star, and, like an optical illusion, a shimmery, covered but under-exposed, Jones hazily appears and is dancing, embodying a *danse macabre* (dance of death). As the first verse begins, we are mesmerized by an infinite wave of colors, gradually joined by breaking lights of rainbow and evaporating streaks of aurora. While we are so engaged with the gradual speed of colors and lighting effects, as well as hearing the frantic walking bass line, wandering drums, and faint sounds of strings and rhythmic wah-wah guitar, an apparition of Jones dancing hazily appears, leaving us to wonder when we will see her properly. She keeps us guessing, by leaving us to gaze on the close-up shot of her eye represented as her iconic stare (as she contemplates the word "question"). The visuals in the chorus section are saturated with 3D-stereoscopic lighting that changes shape with each repetition of the line, "I love you to life," and is musically supported by a deep rolling bass line, an organ playing detached chords, and march-style drums. We see a semi-silhouetted Jones transforming into an orb of light that gently ruptures to colored circular waves of pink, white, and green. When the final line of the chorus is heard, the circular waves of the light turn into stripes that mutate into Jones's face and then it evaporates like a ghost—you have to watch very closely at this point as the ghost of Jones's face is delicately displayed.

Before the second verse, we get a full glimpse of Jones in her signature crystal-encrusted bowler hat, alerting us that we may get to see her "in real life" after all. That thought is temporarily dashed when we are treated to a psychedelic experience to match the sound effects of the dub music. Here, Jones is dancing, with different colored light flares reflecting off her naked body. We are then enticed by close-up shots of her moist skin, delicately wearing a beam of green laser light. In the bridge section ("dark heart"), the stereoscopic circular wave of lights returns, but this time with a piercing laser beam focal spot alternating with close-up shots of Jones's iconic velvety-textured lips. As the bridge intensifies with strong militant beats and the rising dynamic female backing vocals (that are singing against her descending speech on the line "Falling like a star"), we are finally exposed to zooming shots of Jones, staring at us. Her face displays her classic makeup, and she is visually overlaid with random stripes of stereoscopic lighting. To ensure your attention is not distracted from Jones to the colors, Levine places a bright piercing laser beam focal spot on her face. We witness Jones singing the second chorus and, from the audience's perspective, we are indulging in a light show thanks to the lasers beaming off her crystal-encrusted bowler hat. Here, Jones appears to be robotic, with her expressionless face, non-body movement (except for moving her hands in strict time), and iconic stare (enhanced by her colored lenses).

In the final verse and chorus, a now non-robotic Jones still holds her motionless body, but her eyes are closed. She is gently reinforced with a jittering bass and staggering whispering strings, hinting that Jones's desire for eternal life has not succeeded. Jones's fears are confirmed when all the lighting effects mentioned so far—aurora, stereoscopic and laser beams—including a spectrum of focal spots, evaporate from her body. With the thought that she may have lost her mission for eternal life, Jones is captured in dark exposure, with her body coated in a blue metallic sheen, and her face and body contours highlighted by dark lighting and a single pink laser beam. The color blue brings out a melancholic Jones as she expresses the final chorus with her body, and more significantly, her eyes that emotionally display defeat and torment especially on the lyrics: "Don't you die for me." These words vocally clash with dub music (especially the drum and bass), the haunting sounds of the organ, and the canon and polyphonic voices that dramatically respond to Jones with the word "life." As the ending of the chorus peaks, Jones's struggle for control of her feelings is suddenly halted on the words "I won't die for you." At this unmerciful ending, the music stops, the imagery turns darker, and the glowing focal spots return to dazzle around Jones and then vaporize her, turning the screen black.

Unlike in her other videos, where we see Jones successfully controlling her identities and dominance in her performances, in "Love You to Life," we revisit the iconic looks of Jones in a different light (pun intended!). While we witness Jones performing her fantasies as a dancer, controller (through her piercing stare), robot, and ghost, we also view her emotional side. Jones's different identities all come from her and her naked body, and she is accentuated by lighting effects, and not fashion or fancy props (with the exception of the bowler hat). Chris Levine flawlessly captures Jones's inner spirit and energy with the use of textural lights. While she is always in control of her performances, she appears to have reversed that role for this video, by allowing the lights to digitally and virtually control her actions but at the same time, giving her the liberation to explore her emotions, and for us the gazers, to luxuriate in a forever hyperreal and gracious Grace Jones.

The Weeknd

Abel Makkonen Tesfaye, better known as The Weeknd, is a Canadian singer, songwriter, and producer. He was born in 1990 of Ethiopian heritage, and I would describe him as a modern musical chameleon who is not tied to any one particular genre or style, and is constantly reinventing his musical creativity and artistry. In 2011, The Weeknd anonymously released three mixtapes that did exceptionally well, and since then, he has been marketed as a pop/R 'n' B/hip-hop/experimental artist, and rightfully so, as he is influenced by the likes of Michael Jackson, Prince, Aaliyah, and David Bowie. Tesfaye is praised for his creativity, collaborations (including with Rihanna, Daft Punk, and Drake), hyped promotional campaigns (such as having a pop up store in Selfridges in London or posting cryptic Instagram posts), and vocal talent. However, he has had a turbulent life, as observed in his works, and is mostly known for his dark-themed songs and visuals, based mainly around sexual encounters, voyeurism, bitter failed relationships, drugs, and violence.

While these dark themes are present in his music, perhaps as a form of catharsis and virtually placing his obsessions and imaginations in his songs, he has been described as exhibiting signs of "hegemonic masculinity,"[42] by exerting his male power in visual performances and songwriting through violence, driving expensive cars, and sex. With his songwriting, he asserts, "I'm not walking around like I'm macho man or anything, [writing lyrics] is like an escape sometimes. You see what's going on in the real world. And sometimes, you go into your own world, where you create what's going on."[43] While the average Weeknd fan may momentarily forget these thematic elements and prefer to get lost in the sound of his voice and identity play, Tesfaye's fantasies in his visual performances have attracted attention. He has a creator's vision that is slowly and painfully stretched out throughout his musical projects.

Take, for example, "Wicked Games" (2012) from his mixtape, *House of Balloons*, which is a minimal black-and-white video. Visually, Tesfaye's role of being a hegemonic masculine is reversed (in juxtaposition to the lyrics), as he appears as the traditional creator we became fixated on, that is, the vulnerable, mysterious, and stoned singer, along with his iconic hairstyle inspired by artist Jean-Michel Basquait. In the video he is oblivious to an attractive model trying to seduce him with her dance moves and silhouette. The visual narrative is easily misleading through the play of binaries, thanks to Tesfaye's play with identity and angelic vocals. While the visuals display the woman as the dominator and seducer of the fragile "Weeknd," in the audio version Tesfaye clearly displays signs of the hegemonic masculine in his lyrics (in particular, in the line, "bring your body baby . . . just let me motherfuckin' love you"), where he dominates and controls the relationship.

Fast forwarding to 2016, we witness Tesfaye as a superstar and visual artist. His critically acclaimed album *Starboy* and the single (bearing the same title) is a collaboration with French electronica duo Daft Punk, and carries a musical display of pop and electronic music. Visually, in this slick video[44] we witness Tesfaye killing his former self (including his once iconic haircut) and reinventing himself as "Starboy." That could be a reference to Bowie's 1972 glam rock song, "Starman," (or to Ziggy Stardust) which is about a character coming down to earth to save the world. In the case of "Starboy," Tesfaye resurrects himself as a mega superstar who has a luxurious lifestyle, only to destroy it. He is torn between his fragile past and accepting his fame, causing egotistical friction, and driving him to chillingly sing to himself, "look what you've done, I'm a motherfuckin' Starboy"; and this is intensely and musically acknowledged by the thick combined snare and clap beats and the vocoder "ha ha" countermelody—reminiscent of Laurie Anderson's "O' Superman" (1982), but also a common musical trait in Daft Punk's music.

The "Starboy" video is shot in dark exposure, with Tesfaye appearing almost in silhouette form. However, he is more confident and alert (and is not stoned). He is wearing designer gear and a noticeable cross pendant (as opposed to his former life where he would wear casual gear). To completely annihilate the old Weeknd, the only vivid prop in the video, a massive glowing red neon cross, catches his attention. The sign of the crosses (his necklace and the neon cross) signifies that Tesfaye has accepted his rebirth of becoming an icon, and his newfound power. He illustrates this concept by using the neon cross, whose red color suitably represents chaos and determination, to violently trash his pad including his music awards and gold record discs. The hegemonic masculine Tesfaye is in full form and to complete his transformation to Starboy and remove himself from his past, he sets his home on fire and drives away in his McLaren P1 with his domestic cat, which later magically transforms into a panther. The car and panther signify masculinity and power, confirming Tesfaye's resurrection and authorship of his actions.

Regardless of time frame, the visuals in Tesfaye's videos have fairly been described in what Kai Arne Hansen calls a "spectacularization of violence"[45] where the visuals (and music) could almost be considered as psychotic. The violence is not glamorized, as such, but presented in a sense where we can understand Tesfaye's intentions and emotions, which can be viewed as disturbing, delusional, and surreal, as already demonstrated in "Starboy."

"The Hills"—VR Video

Returning to video game music, Tesfaye allows us to participate in his videos, such as the game version of "The Hills" (2015).[46] To set the concept of the song, Tesfaye frustratingly and obsessively reveals he is involved in a destructive and secretive relationship. This song is supported with remixes and two videos. At the time of writing this chapter, the main video for "The Hills" has over 1.4 billion views on YouTube and is one of the platform's most watched videos.[47] The dark setting of this particular visual shows the typical traits of a "Weeknd" video: scenes of disturbing material (e.g., an injured Tesfaye, in addition to "random" female acquaintances, car wreckage, car explosions, a deserted place/location), minimal color setting (with a hint of an aurora background also noticeable in "Starboy"), and Tesfaye presented as a semi-silhouetted figure.[48] With these observations in mind, it is actually the second promo video that is more intriguing for the viewer. This promo, which is based on a remix featuring rap artist, Eminem, is a GoPro Spherical 360-degree virtual reality video directed by Nabil Elderkin (on behalf of GoPro Productions).[49] This allows the viewer to have an immersive experience of the video, provided they have access to Google Chrome or the YouTube app.[50] Upon immediate viewing, the video appears to be disorientated (including Tesfaye) as well as static, until the viewers realize they can control the navigation of the video. The navigator on the screen allows the viewer to experience the video in two ways: (a) as the inquisitive spectator examining the surroundings and not so much The Weeknd and, (b) as being The Weeknd virtually, and experiencing his dark and seedy world. The latter allows the viewer the opportunity to see what Tesfaye sees in the video. The setting of the video is a combination of the original music video and a promo advertisement for Apple Music. When the viewers choose the role of the spectator (and, indeed, the navigator), they will see that it is a dark and deserted virtual location. There are buildings on fire, and scantily clad women dancing by their apartment windows. Furthermore, the whole area carries a dystopian theme due to the smoke from random explosions, fire, and firing of rockets. The only appealing view to gaze at against this bleak setting is a sky blanketed with aurora lights.

Back on the ground, the viewer sees Tesfaye, who appears to be in a drug/alcohol-induced state, and not fully absorbing what is happening around him. He is the only human outside and on the ground, and appears unaware (or maybe he is?) that he is about to be killed by a rocket. This feature almost serves as a video game where the "controller" (that is, the spectator and navigator) can *explore* the situation. The main difference is that he/she cannot *control* the situation and save Tesfaye from his demise. As the viewers are now familiar with the format of the video, this should encourage them to watch it again, but this time, to position themselves as The Weeknd. This results in a different sensation for the viewers, as they are about to have an immersive experience of the surroundings and music, and more importantly, to be The Weeknd virtually. In this situation, Tesfaye appears to be leaving a gig, oblivious that he is walking into dystopia. The disorientated artist is walking through smoke and being exposed to fire sparks, yet does not seem fazed by the explosions (including the burning cars) around him. As he turns around and walks toward the empty limousine, the music stops, and he is hit by an explosion. While Tesfaye does not panic in this situation, the viewers who are virtually experiencing themselves as The Weeknd may stimulate (or even simulate) feelings depending on how involved or sensitive they are to this immersive experience. For example, the experience may evoke bodily senses by gaining a virtual sense of the smell of smoke and burning cars, including the feeling of being hit by sparks and, eventually, the explosion. Music-wise, the viewer hears high-pitched and distorted screams, Eminem's agitated rap, and Tesfaye's distorted singing that all sounds distressing, and is supported by a pounding sub bass and kick to extra-intensify the dark timbre of the song.

While this visual serves as a promotional video for GoPro, Apple, and the music collaboration with Eminem, this exciting (yet extremely dark) immersive experience invites the viewer to participate in The Weeknd's world, or to be the artist virtually (for one minute and thirty-seven seconds). This draws the viewer/listener to engage and fully experience the audiovisual.

"Blinding Lights"—The Late Show with Stephen Colbert

Tesfaye continually invites his audience to participate in his music, as demonstrated in December 2019 on *The Late Show with Stephen Colbert*.[51] Here, as a live performer, the once disorientated/impassive, now over-confident superstar seemed to be going through a 1980s phase, living his fantasy as an out-of-control, injured, gambling, and car-speeding daredevil in a yuppie/*Miami Vice* suit.[52] On the show, he performed his 1980s retro/synthwave[53] and synth-pop song, "Blinding Lights" (from the album *After Hours*) to a seated audience (and television/streaming viewers).[54] His live vocal performance is remarkable as he sounds flawlessly like the audio recording (with the added ad-lib). What is alluring about this visual performance is that the staging is simple, and the lighting is somewhat controlled by the seated audience, which creates a different kind of immersive experience for the singer, audience, and viewers. The visuals on the screen are in black and white, but the artist is displayed in dual screen where the TV/stream viewer can observe the front and back of Tesfaye. Here, he is caged inside a neon-lit cube (Figure 6.2), which has mirrored walls (note that the live audience can only see the cube and not the dual screen). At this moment, Tesfaye cannot see the audience, but, instead, sees infinite reflections of himself because of the mirrored walls. He does, however, refrain from looking at himself in the mirrors by disguising his shyness with dancing.

In addition to this engaging spectacle, the neon lights change correspondingly to the beat of the music, while the simple stage lights bounce to the ceiling, caught by an audience holding mirror-reflecting cards. As the audience hold the cards toward a dancing Tesfaye, the light from the cards reflects to the mirrors in the cube, which creates both strobe and camera flash effects. The light effects match the song title "Blinding Lights" and it certainly gives the impression that Tesfaye is "blinded by the light." The black-and-white visuals and the pulsating light transmitted from the audience create a hazy and trippy experience for the viewer at home (they may feel that they are also "blinded by the lights"). This changes, however, when Tesfaye focuses his attention on the seated audience. He steps out of

FIGURE 6.2 *The Weeknd on* The Late Show with Stephen Colbert. *Credit: Scott Kowalchyk/CBS via Getty Images.*

the cube and directly sings to the audience, who are still flashing the mirror cards at him. He then encourages the audience to sing with him, which further enhances their involvement with his performance.

For the viewer, the visuals remain confusing because Tesfaye is still displayed in dual effect, surrounded by strobe/flashing lights controlled by the audience. The viewer can only see the back of Tesfaye and full frontal of the audience. While it may look as if the "staged" performance has now transformed into a mini concert for the seated audience (who are all singing along with Tesfaye), the viewer at home may feel left out. Yet, I would propose that Tesfaye invites the viewers to join him virtually on stage, allowing them another opportunity to experience being The Weeknd again—just like in "The Hills" VR video. While the video of "The Hills" is digitally made, the live performance of "Blinding Lights" is more simplified in terms of visuals only. The main difference is that the viewer cannot control the performance, yet is offered the opportunity to have a VIP experience of viewing the performance with a "backstage" view. This lets the viewer have a closer gaze at the performance from virtual and intimate levels, just as close friends would have in a live concert, and witness the effort and emotions that Tesfaye is putting into his performance.

Just as in "The Hills," but this time with a seated audience, the participants can experience being "The Weeknd." Tesfaye is a gifted and musically informed creator in his music, performances, and his identity, and when the opportunity arises, he invites the audience to join him on his virtual musical journey in the digital era. The Weeknd declares, "People tell me I'm changing the culture,"[55] and therefore, he is certainly a contender to be placed along the postmodern greats of David Bowie, Madonna, and Grace Jones.

7

"Showroom Dummies"

Live and Simulated Performers, Performances, and Audiences

How do we consume the use of space, place, and liveness in the digital virtual era? Is the audience's role in performances more significant than ever due to the rapid evolution of technology? Virtual reality is experienced and observed in various types of performers and performances, whether it is in the form of a simulated or live performance. The various types of VR in visual performances are infinite and are rapidly evolving thanks to digital technology, allowing creators to be experimental and imaginative with their visions. While this is an exciting development in the digital virtual era, I will question how virtual performers and their performances impact and communicate with real-life audiences. For instance, familiar observers of this development will have noticed its rapid progress in this century, led by the likes of digital virtual performers such as Gorillaz and Hatsune Miku. This in turn may offer an opportunity for the viewers to interact with the creation (with some form of digital media) and, if relevant, allow them to "virtually" participate in the musical experience. The viewer is more likely to be engaged in viewing the whole performance—perhaps repeatedly—and, if relevant, interacting with the performance.

Situating Liveness in Space and Place

One major aspect to consider when exploring performance in the digital virtual era is the importance of space and place. Traditionally, creators and consumers were confined to spaces and places, both to create and to consume music. Today, we can choose how we use our space to create and consume music, and the same applies to participating in or watching a performance. Sheila Whiteley emphasizes the importance of music and space by indicating that they both play "a significant part in the way that individuals author space, musical texts being creativity combined with local knowledge and . . . impose collectively defined meanings and significance on space."[1] We have been witnessing this in the previous chapters involving video games, Grace Jones, and The Weeknd, where manipulation of their space generates fixed codings within that particular performance. Furthermore, space is becoming more infinite now, when technology is involved, and, as a result, produces further meanings and intentions. This concept correlates with Jem Kelly's thoughts that technology today is enabling windows of opportunities for further expression as "[t]he incursion of audiovisual technologies has produced mixed effects that either amplify and extend or attenuate notions of presence, representation and self-expression in pop performance."[2] Just as we observe genre/style blending with music, we witness the blending of media and art forms, and we cannot detect (or choose to deny) if the performance is, indeed, implemented as a music concert, theater, film, music video, or animation. With this notion in mind, for the consumer, the meaning of place can sometimes be irrelevant in this era, because if we have access to suitable technology we can experience performances in our own personal and preferable space without needing to physically strategize or conform to how and where we partake in such events.

When we think of the digital virtual performance today, there can be opportunities for interaction with the audience, where they (the audience) can simply join in or control the performance in real time, or asynchronously. Furthermore, digital virtual performances encourage collaboration with other creators (such as musicians and performers) with online virtual jams/recording sessions, or by performing live with holograms. When we perceive the virtual performer or performance, this spectacle is the result of what Thomas Conner calls "a burgeoning commercial content-generating machine." In what is otherwise known as virtual labor,[3] many creators in the creative industries are involved in making the spectacular a reality, and in making the viewer believe that the virtual performer is in control of his/her performance, just like a standardized manufactured pop artist is made up of agency belonging to the music industry and beyond, but even more so in this setting, regardless of how the virtual medium is presented.

The term "performance" may bring infinite definitions and responses, especially in the digital virtual era. When we think of the term "performer" or "performance," we immediately associate it with liveness, or more appropriately in this century, a concept of liveness,[4] or what I would describe as *some kind* of liveness. Theoretically, this notion has been raised by Philip Auslander, who claims that how we traditionally perceive "liveness"— that is performed and watched in real time, for example, in the theater—is nonexistent.[5] Therefore we can consider that "liveness," and the mediatized (i.e., some kind of presentation of recorded material such as music, film, or television) are blurred together and not separated.

"I Was There . . .": Audiences in the Digital Virtual Era

It goes without saying that audiences have a vital role in music. As Lucy Bennett argues, "music audiences are currently situating themselves, and the processes that are impacting upon musical experience, meaning making and value judgments."[6] The virtual audience can offer great value in music in various forms. While the traditional mass audiences serve as fans,[7] spectators,[8] or consumers,[9] more opportunities are accessible on the internet where audiences can participate through other means in celebrating music, and this supports Richard Peterson and Andy Bennett's observation that "participants in virtual scenes are widely separated geographically . . . virtual scene participants around the world come together in a single scene-making conversation via the Internet."[10] While the opportunity to physically socialize may be obliterated, audiences can find other means of interacting on the internet in online (fan) communities, chat rooms or social media groups (including live chat at an online event),[11] virtual visuals such as concerts or games (especially where audiences can virtually attend events as avatars or participate through other means such as wearing virtual goggles/headsets or navigating/controlling spherical videos), and online creative collaboration. While the immersive experience of music is evolving and contributing to the current shaping of society and cultures (depending on the accessibility and availability of technologies), this creates other opportunities in consuming music, either as an individual or as part of a virtual community. For example, music promotion is more accessible now with the aid of the audience (through mailing lists, viral videos, adverts, social media, personal blogs/vlogs, and websites). The barrier, then, between the audience and the industry becomes blurred, and with the help of online engagement and communication, the audience builds awareness of the music.

Virtual audiences are becoming more implemented into live and simulated performances. Say for example, when we attend a live concert, we can instantly share our experiences with acquaintances who are not in attendance, but are likely to be on social media in real time. While paying attention to the performers and their performance, fans may film footage or take photos and immediately share them online. As Rebecca Bennett states, the recipient of messages or followers of the concert attendee "deepens offline audiences' authenticity and downgrades online-only participation to a secondary not 'quite as real' version,"[12] but still giving them a light hint of illusion that they are at the concert. With livestreamed concerts, the virtual audience is witnessing both the performers and the live audience simultaneously. If it is a direct livestream affair between the performer and virtual audience only (i.e., the concert is not at a venue and not open to public), issues that could arise are the awkward interaction between the performers and audience, especially on platforms such as YouTube, Twitch, and Zoom. The performers will have to stage their interaction without receiving any verbal responses from the audience apart from the reaction presented as emojis or text via live chat. Whether a virtual audience is observing a real-life audience or not, it is questionable if the virtual audience *is* really the audience although experiencing the emotions and intimacy at a concert is debatable, and will, of course, depend on the individual. However we may view it (especially now as I edit this section in early 2020, when most of the world has been forced to move to online platforms during the pandemic), we are moving to another whole new level of music consumption in the digital virtual era, where virtual live performances and virtual audiences are becoming immensely and logically pragmatic for health, safety, and sustainability reasons.

In addition to the examples already mentioned, there are performances aided by immersive technologies to consider, in video games and concerts. With video games, for example, gamers and spectators can participate by controlling sounds or navigation, and experience being the subject. There are opportunities for audiences to place themselves virtually in a concert, usually aided by headsets, and they can navigate the venue, seating, and back or front stage—such as the following concerts by Paul McCartney (created by Jaunt, 2014), Imogen Heap (created by WaveVR, 2018), and Post Malone (created by Melody VR, 2018). The participation of the virtual audience in performances is an ongoing evolvement, and breaks boundaries between the performer and the spectator—this also applies to live concerts presented only in audio. While some may oppose these exciting changes in virtual performances, arguing that these type of concerts lack social and emotional engagement and that the liveness of the event is imperiled, and may prefer to keep it traditional by physically attending a live concert, virtual concerts, in particular in VR, open up amazing and considerable opportunities for those who cannot attend in real life (for whatever reason, be it health, life-conditions, geography, affordability), where they too can experience the live performance and get to say those immortal words, "I was there. . . ."

Variations of Virtual Performers and Performances

There are different variations of liveness and simulation in the digital virtual performance, and with the virtual in particular, this has been evident in popular culture for over two centuries in various mediums such as animation, theater, musical, and film, where we observe characters and momentarily forget that they are either technologically controlled (and created by agency) or actually "performed" by a human (or, indeed, by celebrities portraying specific roles). Our position as the audience, then, is simply to be entertained and immersed in the feature by engaging *in* (and not *with*) the performance, even though in reality these characters are not real, and we may be aware that there is a controller involved. This corresponds with Louise Jackson and Mike Dines's approach when discussing early Japanese Banraku puppetry. Here, they note that, while three puppeteers control the puppet, the audience can see only the lead puppeteer controlling the puppet, meaning that the so-called virtual performance is both illusionary and real.[13] The audience are not dissuaded by this, however, and become more fascinated with how the lead puppeteer makes the puppet more "alive," and welcome him/her as part of the performance (perhaps unaware that there are actually two other puppeteers who are hidden and covered in black clothes).

Animation, Film, and Music Video

As might be expected, many virtual performers (including established human performers presented in virtual form) do not offer any indication that they are operated by controllers (unless something harsh happens with technology, in a real-time performance, for example). For instance, let us revisit 1930s animation and the Fleischer brothers, and turn to their popular animated character, *Betty Boop*, an endearing jazz flapper who is always being scolded by her parents for being mischievous. One of the cartoons featured a special guest, jazz musician Cab Calloway in 1932.[14] The episode, fittingly titled "Minnie the Moocher" (the title of Calloway's most famous song), features Calloway and his band introducing the animation by playing a steady instrumental version of "Minnie the Moocher." After the cameo of Calloway and his band, Betty Boop is again being scolded by her parents and decides to run away with her anthropomorphic cat-boyfriend, Bimbo (who is part-human/cat). While the concept of watching an innocent cartoon with fun characters, let alone featuring a well-known jazz star, sounds very appealing and exciting, this is actually a surreal (and for some, scary) animation for viewers—very suitable for Halloween. As Betty Boop and Bimbo run away, they are confronted by Calloway disguised as a singing walrus. He sings a revamped rendition of "Minnie the Moocher," but as the song develops, so does he, as he magically morphs into different characters. We do not see the extravagant friendly singer we are familiar with but, instead, a plump tired-looking walrus (who tries to maintain Calloway's signature dance moves), who transforms into a ghost, a prison guard, a witch, and a haggard cat, all presented with grim scenarios. Betty Boop realizes that running away is not for her, so she and Bimbo return home. While this feature was a great promotional tactic bringing animation and jazz together, as well as an example of an early music video, we witness Calloway performing as different characters, virtually. Viewers will be more fascinated with the fact that it is Calloway performing in their favorite cartoon than with the technicalities and the creators who made this feature possible.

Another example is the jazz musician Louis Armstrong who appeared in the film, *High Society* (1956).[15] Presented as a self-reflexive character, not only does he appear as himself, but also as a character and the narrator of the film. While the film included a respectable cast, the starring of a high-profile musician was not only a crossover between mediums but also a form of a mixed reality where we witness Armstrong not only performing as an actor in the film who is instructed by the film director on how to perform, but at the same time, also playing a "live" musical performance (with his band) as one would expect from this incredible musician.

From the late 1950s onward, there was a gradual surge of virtual performers in television, film, and animation, with *Alvin and the Chipmunks* and *The Archies* as leading examples. The music was a significant part of the animation and the characters served as a neat simulation of a real-life band (in human form). Popular music dominated popular culture during the 1960s, with certain genres and styles, such as rock, soul, and pop, and certain bands/artists—The Beatles, The Rolling Stones, Dusty Springfield, Jackson 5, Jimi Hendrix—defining the sounds of the decade. While commercial popular music was predominately aimed at the youth, it made sense that these animated features with virtual bands that included cute characters and novelty pop songs (e.g., *Alvin and the Chipmunks*) were targeted on children. As the popularity of cartoons grew along with popular music, it came as no surprise that creators began to imitate animated characters based on actual real-life bands.[16] Other famous features followed, such as The Monkees (a comedy show based on a fictional boy band) and the Muppets (a puppet television music show).[17]

Music videos became more recognized and visually conceptualized from the mid-1970s onward.[18] Previously known as a promo, where artists/bands would mime/simulate a live performance of their single for a television show, the music video started to be more creative in terms of narrative and performance. The music video was a game changer in the music industry where the creator could be innovative with the visual representation of the music. Like a mini movie, "live" performance, surreal creation, imitation of a video game, or "visual" album, the music video is appealing to the spectator as they can engage with the visuals, and have the choice to decode any intentions presented by the creator, performer, and music. Virtually, this enables the artist/band to conduct their ideal representation of their music regardless of visual style.

In terms of early consumption of the early music video, if the consumer had access to a VHS/Betamax home video recorder, they could record their favorite videos and rewatch them at their own leisure. The music video also acquired its own television programs with MTV in the United States and *The Chart Show* in the United Kingdom.[19] Sunil Manghani asserts that, in this century, the "traditional music video" is now an "empty visual product"[20] due to the evolution of digital technology including the internet. With this debatable statement, it is arguable that there is *still* a demand for music videos, as premieres of highly established artists on YouTube have proved; however, it does depend on budget and access to resources. Manghani noted that a "new video" is in place where both music and internet videos merge together as a result of the rise of amateurs/new performers on vlogs, YouTube, and similar platforms. It is safe to say, then, that the music video has successfully flourished and continues to be innovative thanks to digital technology. While emerging artists may not be able to access the traditional music video route, they can virtually and visually present their performances, live or simulated, on digital platforms such as YouTube, Facebook, TikTok, and Instagram.

The Rise of Digital Virtual Performers

The rise of digital virtual performers certainly becomes interesting in the current century and more prominent in music videos, video games, music (audio and creation), and live performances. How performers are presented in digital virtual form is quite intriguing to explore. The impression of how we could imagine performers of the future presented in digital form has actually arrived. Take, for example, the female cyborgs in digital form[21] confusing our perceptions of what is real, unreal, past, or present, as they all appear as one, thereby confirming Donna Haraway's argument that the "boundary between science fiction and social reality is an optical illusion."[22] Female cyborgs including Noodle (Gorillaz), Hatsune Miku, and Miquela have their own unique qualities, strengths,[23] and unknown origins as they are perfectly presented as hyperreal. Arguably, these virtual figures carry a sense of independence (in terms of performance only) and mission in the way, Haraway argues, "They are wary of holism, but needy for connection— they seem to have a natural feel for the united-front politics, but without the vanguard party."[24] This can be observed with Noodle of Gorillaz. While their music is socially motivated anyway, she advocates her beliefs through connotations of symbols and logos presented on her attire, surroundings, and identity. While she appears to be an independent woman, she feels safe with Gorillaz, with whom she can freely be herself and be guarded by her group when needed. Miquela, on the other hand, is opinionated and an advocate for many causes, as demonstrated on her social media accounts and vlogs. She also carries the impression of independency as demonstrated in her short-lived romantic relationships, monologue vlogs, and her music videos.

In terms of virtual space, its relevance and usage are also equally symbolic, for both the performer and viewer/consumer, allowing the opportunity for interaction without being physically face to face or confined in a particular space, a trend started by Second Life. As John Richardson and Claudia Gorbman highlight, "Much of our experience of so-called virtual reality involves a kind of cinematic immersion, just as this sensibility is finding its way into installation art, multimedia theater, live action role-playing games (LARP) and environmental sound art. We are increasingly made to feel as though we are part of the work or performance."[25] Methods of digital virtual interaction are ongoing and can involve collaboration, control, and immersion, therefore inviting participants to intensify their musical experience. Furthermore, with the use of digital technology, wannabe performers, amateurs, and rising creators have the opportunity to share their ambitions on digital platforms and apps such as YouTube, SoundCloud, Instagram, and TikTok, resulting in alternative and independent ways of finding musical success (some will be eventually snapped up by a known major or indie label, while others will remain independent).[26]

Virtual Performers

Gorillaz

Gorillaz (Figure 7.1) are an interesting, and a fun band to explore, not only for journalists and scholars but for students and fans, too. Damon Albarn and Jamie Hewlett have successfully managed to keep the band together for virtually twenty years, fulfilling their agenda of creating the "ultimate" manufactured band, bypassing other disposable manufactured bands that would normally last for five years—if lucky. Do you remember when you discovered Gorillaz? If, during the first decade of this century, you were a toddler, child, or teenager, you would be more familiar with the animated music videos, and the incompatible characters, that just somehow work and look so good together. If you had just graduated from university or were a hard-core music fan recovering from the 1990s "daze," then you would know that it was really Damon Albarn (and his crew) behind this intriguing and fascinating group.

My personal experience of learning about the group was when I graduated from university and worked at a music venue. It was Gorillaz's live performance at the BRIT awards that got me and my colleagues (as well as the nation) talking. While we were amazed that the virtual

FIGURE 7.1 *Gorillaz, Damon Albarn, and live band. Credit: Suzi Pratt/WireImage.*

project was led by co-founder Albarn, we were more excited that he was experimenting with hip-hop and dub. Fast forward a few years, when I was researching for my PhD, and Gorillaz were in Phase 2 (second album) of their story; I decided to investigate further, mainly because Danger Mouse (Burton) was the producer for the *Demon Days* album. As Gorillaz's admirers would be aware, the group are a gateway to many topics of discussion including virtuality, digital technology, identity, authenticity, gender, sexuality, racial awareness, postmodernism, cultural memory, popular culture, creative industries, and, clearly, experimental music. I was particularly drawn to the construction of the virtual group and their music production, in addition to questioning Albarn's identity. While I wrongly presumed that Phase 3 (*Plastic Beach*) would be the last installment of the project, due to Albarn comfortably "representing" or collaborating (delete as you decide is appropriate!) with Gorillaz, he has successfully continued the project to Phase 6 (at the time of writing), and yet, despite knowing that Albarn is one of the main brains behind the virtual group, the audience are still fascinated by how the group is evolving—that is, the virtual group, including the real-life group that consists of Albarn and his friends.[27]

The musical project created by Albarn and Hewlett[28] was a response to the surge of manufactured groups and celebrity culture at the turn of the twenty-first century. While Gorillaz was also a perfect opportunity for Albarn to experiment freely with music (and a successful attempt in temporarily shrugging off his "Blur" musical brand and Britpop reputation),[29] it was also a good time for Hewlett and his team to develop the virtual characters of Gorillaz due to the quick progression of digital technology. The characters are not a typically standard manufactured group, but the way they are (de) constructed is very appealing as demonstrated in their visual stories, music videos, and "live" performances.[30] To elaborate, the virtual group are not uniform in age or identity; instead, their "looks are unconventional, and it is the peculiar animated modification of their bodies along with their distinctive personalities that makes the band appealing to the audience,"[31]—thus classifying them as a hyperreal group. In reality, if Gorillaz was in human form, the members would probably be considered incompatible with each other, because of their lifestyles, attitude, and age-range.

Characters

For those unfamiliar with the virtual lineup of Gorillaz, it is Murdoc Niccals (bassist), 2D (lead singer, multi-instrumentalist), Russel Hobbs (drummer), and Noodle (guitarist). Murdoc is the "founder" and oldest member of the group. Murdoc is from the West Midlands in the UK, which is a metal music hotspot, and he portrays the image of a metal and rock star with his black clothing, by wearing religious crosses, and displaying his obsession with Satanism. He also comes across as alien and devil-like due to his green skin and multicolored eyes, as well as carrying the attitude of a debauchee rock star. 2D is the visually impaired laidback/zombie-like/attractive singer (he has nice face contours) with bright blue hair, from South of England. He is obsessed with electronic, punk, and reggae music (and his vocals are represented by Albarn). The drummer, Russel Hobbs, is from New York. Influenced by hip-hop music, Russel is an interesting character due to his size and his fatigued/laidback/zombie state (after all he was possessed by the ghosts of his friends). Then there is Noodle, a Japanese guitarist who joined the group at the age of ten. She carries multiple identities at once, including an anime superhero, fembot, soldier, tomboy, and ninja. Her background story (along with those of the other members) is gradually described through the phases (each album) and there are clear references to Japanese popular culture as well as her heritage.[32]

The staging of Gorillaz's "live" performances has varied, always attempting to keep in line with the developments of digital technology. Ranging from their acclaimed 2001 BRIT Awards performance (with the characters projected on screens), to their 3D collaboration with Madonna and De La Soul at the 2007 Grammys, the use of digital technology to showcase the group has always been uncertain. Ideally, Albarn and Hewlett would love to consistently present the group in virtual form, but are aware of the technical hiccups of the visuals and sounds that could occur in a live situation thereby giving away the illusion (as they discovered while rehearsing for the *Demon Days* tour). Instead, they resort to showing projected interactive visuals of the band with live musicians representing them on stage. Over time, the setup has changed, ranging from Albarn silhouetting himself at the back of the stage to owning the performance with his band in front of the stage. This gradual reveal of Albarn over the phases shows he is comfortable that, despite his "Blur" branding, he can freely experiment with music and collaborators, and that he revels in being the "ambassador" for Gorillaz.

Exploring the Virtual Worlds of Gorillaz

As digital technology progressed over this century, so did the homes of Gorillaz. Their changing virtual worlds demonstrate that they are in line with the fashionable changes of technology and allow them to change how they virtually interact with their fans through CMC (Computer Mediated Communication). In Phase 1, their debut self-titled album (2001) included a CD ROM that invited their fans to explore their first home, Kong Studios. This setup extended to their website Gorillaz.com, which was originally used not only as a PR base (to announce concert dates or news) but also as MUVE (Multi-User Virtual Environment), where fans could enter their favorite members' bedrooms and explore their property; go to the recording studio; watch videos; and, virtually chat with other fans. While Phase 2 (*Demon Days* album)[33] was in development, their "home" was renovated, with more added perks for the fans (such as exclusive demos), as well as launching a competition called "Search for a Star" for their fans to showcase their talents. They also unleashed their "Reject False Icons" campaign (a protest rejecting celebrity idols) where they encourage their fans to graffiti the slogan in public and post pictures on the internet (it was also a clever but discreet marketing tactic to promote their second album).

In Phase 3 (*Plastic Beach*), Gorillaz's Kong Studios was transformed into an island.[34] Along with its usual perks, the website was in AR form and the island served as a video game, where the fans could navigate and search for objects, such as sea treasure. In Phase 4 (*Humanz*, 2016), their world became more mobile as the fans were treated to two smartphone apps.[35] The Gorillaz app was a mobile version of their new and haunted home called "The Spirit House," where fans could still continue to explore their home, or watch music videos and content. This phase was emphasized by the 3D music video of their single, "Saturnz Barz (Spirit House)" where the viewer could navigate their house and their virtual outdoor surroundings. The second app, "The Lenz," in collaboration with Telekom Electronic Beats, enhanced ways for fans to interact with the group in AR not only in their personal space but also in public space. When the app is active, the user can point his/her camera phone to any magenta-colored surface (such as a wall or a moving bus), and the surface will display videos, live performances, and filtered images of Gorillaz. Fans can also immediately share their experiences as images or stories on social media such as Instagram.

The Gorillaz app, along with the website, was still active for Phase 5 (which coincided with *The Now Now* album in 2018) but with no novelty perks this time, due to the quick turnaround of the album.[36] In 2020, Gorillaz took another approach in releasing music as a series of EPs, which will eventually be compiled as an album called *Song Machine*. Moving away from interacting with fans on their website and apps, Gorillaz took advantage of promoting their music on social media platforms, including TikTok, Twitter, Snapchat, and Instagram. As part of the interaction, fans are invited to participate in question and answer sessions, download filters that they can experiment with (e.g., where they can virtually morph themselves as their favorite member of Gorillaz and post and share it with virtual friends), and view visual telegrams (in the form of vlogs).

Music Video—"Tranz"

The music of Gorillaz is not tied to one genre or style, but to a plethora of genres/styles. This was Albarn's opportunity to experiment with music in disguise. While exploring the music catalog of Gorillaz, expect to hear elements of hip-hop, rock, reggae, dub, punk, electronica, and dance. The lyrical content usually includes critical social and climate awareness and nondirect political issues. The music videos are experimental, ranging from narrative to a nonlinear collage of visuals, but seldom a full-length simulation of a live band performance, until now as demonstrated in the synth-pop-rock-trance song, "Tranz."[37] This track is from the album, *The Now Now* (2018). Murdoc the bassist is not included in the video, because he is in prison, so he has been temporarily replaced by *The Powder Puffs'* villain, Ace (who carries similar body features to Murdoc). The absence of Murdoc is significant because it gives 2D the chance to take control of the group and own the visual performance.[38] The video itself is psychedelic, with interchanging colored lighting and kaleidoscope effects swirling in the background.[39] The main focus throughout the video is on 2D, as he is the lead singer. This differs from the other videos in which the other characters are usually shown equally, so the audience can engage with them fully, but remember, 2D is taking advantage of Murdoc's absence. As this is a "live" performance, the rest of the characters are simply "acting" their performance. Russel is well alert and happily playing the drums (as opposed to his usual sleepy trance and lethargic character), and Noodle is, surprisingly, mostly shoegazing while playing the guitar (as opposed to the fun and cheerful girl we used to know).[40] The stand-in for Murdoch, Ace, is enjoying his moment by excitingly being involved in the music as if to suggest that all his birthdays have arrived at once.

The music is steady and dominated by the throbbing bass, beats, and agile sonics, while 2D's singing is doubled by an octave. The dominance of 2D is highlighted in the chorus that can only be described as what Timothy Warner would call "a textural complexity that is musically impressive, while still retaining a strong and direct sense of character . . . and a determined, almost relentless, momentum."[41] As demonstrated in the line "do you dance like this for-ever," the compressed vocals are multitracked with a range of 2D/Albarn's voices that almost depict an unusual exalted (Albarn-esque) choir. Here, each vocal layer, including timbre, is exploited with sonics of muffling and loudspeaker effects pushing against 2D/Albarn's mainly woolly and angelic alto voice that lingers, into a stuttering tinny sound. The chorus blends with the glowing light rupturing from 2D's eyes as he stands like a transcendent and iconic figure with his arms wide open, followed by footage of him playing the keyboard, and ending with close-up shots of his face in anaglyph 3D. Later, the performance becomes surreal in the bridge section ("do you look/feel like me") where the audio space is swallowed by the cascading voices, intensified by the piercing and pulsating electronic sounds, creating a psychedelic reminiscent of Krautrock and Pierre Henry's "Psyché Rock." These psychedelic sonics visually match the characters, whose bodies are distorting to the bright trippy-effect background, which creates a surreal experience for viewer. As the final section of the music progresses, so does the chorus—it becomes more of a dreamy or hallucinogenic state, fused with speeding random mixed reality aesthetics being thrown into the visuals: claymation of 2D; scenes from black and white horror movies; hand animation; sprouting magic mushrooms; 2D's rotting tongue (yes); and, anthropomorphic creatures. As the music stops, 2D drops to the ground like a puppet only to reveal a green screen in the background,[42] bringing a devious reminder to the viewer that Gorillaz are a virtual (fictional) band, and are controlled by real-life "puppeteers" (Albarn, Hewlett, and their crew). This video enables us to witness the spectacular first "live" performance of the Gorillaz in its entirety—and in this particular situation, the audience are simply the spectators.

Now Albarn has a strong presence in the group, he is comfortable performing live and is no longer concealing his identity, and this does not bother the fans. As the albums and phases of Gorillaz develop, they gain new fans. While it is shamelessly obvious that there are connections between Albarn and 2D (with his distinctive singing voice aside), he insists he is not the lead singer of Gorillaz. He is, however, dedicated to seeing how much more he can push his experimental ideas in this project, by collaborating with musicians he admires—yet he still insists he is not 2D. When approached by a journalist who said *The Now Now* album should be retitled *The Damon Albarn Album* as it is all about 2D, Albarn dismissed this suggestion: "It's 2D singing, and 2D has a slightly different voice from Damon Albarn. I refuse to refer to myself as the third person."[43] Besides, he adds more confusion by teasingly declaring, "I feel quite strongly that Gorillaz is an American band. The band I'm in is American"[44]—this statement could be credible as the guest collaborators are mostly American; however, his alter ego 2D may not entirely agree, especially with his strong British accent, which is supposedly from the South of England. . .

With the long-standing success of Gorillaz, questions may arise as to why and how they have sustained their longevity in the digital virtual era. Other virtual groups exist but they are not as widely celebrated as the Gorillaz. Is it due to the unpresentable and incompatible characters that grasp our attention? Or the experimental music that can appeal to anyone at any one time? Or is it because of Gorillaz's association with Albarn? While other virtual performers exist, they have received a mixed reaction as well as a diverse audience. Without doubt, a positive point when observing virtual performers, as demonstrated with Gorillaz, is the interaction with the audience and therefore the breaking of barriers between them. Another example is Japanese virtual idol, Hatsune Miku, whose controllers encourage her fans to create, modify, and alter her music and image.

Hatsune Miku

Hatsune Miku was originally branded for Yamaha's Vocaloid software (a voice synthesizer) but has since become a global singer. The software allowed the operator-turned-creator (i.e., user) to compose vocal melodies and lyrics on the software that would be sung by preinstalled vocals (the Vocaloid).[45] The preinstalled vocals were recorded as samples of syllables and words, offering an illusion that it is Hatsune Miku's voice when, in fact, it belongs to the actor Saki Fajita. Moreover, the vocals have been digitally generated and modified to add a sense of an identity for Hatsune Miku, by making her vocals sound part-human and part-cyborg, presenting further assimilation between the real (human) and synthetic (cyborg/machine) vocals in the digital virtual era.[46] Furthermore, the user is not restricted to genre/style; therefore, he/she can create any type of music to accompany the vocals (ranging from J-pop to metal) and, from there, create visuals based on Hatsune Miku, then upload and share them on the internet.[47] This makes her an open-source singer—literally anyone can have a go in constructing her music, identity, and performance.[48] The fascination clearly lies within the character's identity. Hatsune Miku is a sixteen-year-old high school girl, who is a dancer, 158 centimeters in height, with noticeable neon blue hair— and it is at this moment that the presentation of her character may divide opinions. I have found that, while the concept of the Vocaloid software is so appealing, the visual characteristic features of the virtual idol do not impress my students. They are irritated by their observations of a young cutsimo[49] wearing revealing outfits while dancing provocatively—they blame the creators (Crypton Future Media) for creating what they consider a perverse concept. My students often complain that her presentation is overtly sexualized, which is why they prefer to watch the Gorillaz. I have to explain here that I have discussed Hatsune Miku in lectures for quite a while now, and it is not a question of cultural clash that my students are experiencing; they consider that the visual presentation of the concept is peculiar and a form of an uncanny valley[50]—yet at the same time, they are intrigued by the "live" performances.

The situation is different in Japan where, as Suzanne Livingston explains, people are more receptive to ever-changing technology as it is "much more interconnected and there is much more acceptance of the human's place within that wider world."[51] Fans who do take Hatsune Miku seriously include the male *otaku*,[52] who include her in their lives, and schools in Japan where Vocaloid is taught in the curriculum[53] and practiced as an open-source creative tool. The fans like to believe that Hatsune Miku is a "real" person, even though she is controlled by technology and by her fans,[54] confirming that, in Japanese culture, people take technology extremely seriously—not only using technology for everyday life, they are living for technology to confirm their existence—as recently demonstrated by Akihiko Kondo, a thirty-five-year-old male who paid around two million yen to "marry" the hologram of Hatsune Miku in 2018.[55]

While the concept of Hatsune Miku's character will divide opinions, she does have an international fan base (over 2.5 million fans) consisting mainly of children, youth, and hard-core J-pop culture fans. This has sparked opportunities within the music industry as she has performed live on stage with Lady Gaga as well as at the Coachella Festival, and collaborated with Pharrell Williams. Hatsune Miku performs as a hologram and is supported by four real-life musicians on stage. Her performances are interactive and musically polished for her fans, hence the profiling of her concert series as "Expo," a convention where fans can celebrate their dedication to the virtual idol by dressing up as cosplay,[56] buying souvenirs, celebrating the music they may have created, and meeting up with other fans they have met online. While the average concert attendees (i.e., non-Miku fans) may feel left out of the Hatsune Miku party atmosphere, they may find themselves gazing at the devoted audience (including the interactive light show and the real-life musicians if they are lucky to spot them), rather than an appealing hologram being projected on stage, as was demonstrated at the Expo concert in London in 2020.[57] Here, Hatsune Miku's concert involved a nonstop two-hour set with performances broken up into segments that consisted of other VR idol performances[58] while Hatsune Miku was taking digital "breaks." The human band (drummer, bassist, guitarist, and keyboardist) were situated on the sides of the stage, gently blending in the background but still visible to the audience, to give the feeling that it was a live concert (and they were actually playing live). Hatsune Miku was projected on a mirror screen, and mimed to the already recorded vocals accompanied by the live band. She was at the same time, however, collaborating with the devoted audience who were corresponding to the beat of the music with their glow sticks, and had their appearance and actions reflected on the mirror screen on stage. Their reflection on the mirror is intriguing because it creates an illusion that Hatsune Miku is surrounded and worshipped by her fans, when, in fact, her fans have stepped into her virtual world. Thinking from a Baudrillardian position, the reflection of the audience on the mirror "cannot imagine the real any longer, because it has become the real. It can no longer transcend reality, transfigure it, nor dream it, because it has become its own virtual reality,"[59] confirming that the fans are also virtual, making the whole experience a hyperreal performance. The nonvirtual audience—the regular but curious concert attendees and parents accompanying their children— may be skeptical about this connection, but this particular performance was about experiencing a virtual community that originated online (whether as fans and/or collaborators), and was finally celebrated together by congregating in the actual same space, in real time. While the concept of Hatsune Miku was unleashed by Yamaha and Crypton Future Media (the Vocaloid and brand), it opened new ways in bringing the performer and fans together, through a creation on which they create and "control" the musical vision.

Miquela

Nineteen-year-old Brazilian-American Miquela, aka Lil Miquela (digital birth name Miquela Sousa), is a multi-hyphenate, consisting of a supermodel, social media influencer, trend setter, social activist, music journalist, and singer. Unlike Hatsune Miku, she is not animated but presented as CGI, which makes her realistically and alarmingly hyperreal. By this, I mean, if the viewer is unaware she is not real, they would be convinced she is human. She was created by Trevor McFedries (better known by his musical alias Yung Skeeter) and Sara DeCou, the co-owners of creative agency Brud. They are thus responsible for creating the first CGI social media influencer.[60] The imagery of Miquela is that of a stereotypical Instagram social influencer, displaying the perfect model and flawless looks (big brown eyes, full lips, distinctive hair style) enveloped in designer clothes (by names such as Chanel, Burberry, and Moncler). The appealing aspect of this avatar is that she has a very ambiguous ethnic background, something that is more of a publicity stunt than an attempt at raising critical racial awareness by her creators. Miquela is also a social activist, campaigning on behalf of women, for racial equality (although she and her controllers do not address her own race—as yet), for LGBTQI+ people, and for displaced youth; she is also an advocate for Black Lives Matter. All this has made her one of the "25 most influential people on the Internet."[61]

While her 2.2 million followers and fans (known as Miquelites) on various social media platforms see her as a role model, they are also in awe of her Instagram posts, where they can witness her selfies, videos, and self-motivated caption messages. While her targeted audience are teenagers and young adults, Minna Fingerhood claims that they do not seem to be disturbed by the fact that Miquela is not real. They are "enthralled by her existence because she represents a departure from the norm and a challenge to established ideas . . . her appeal is all the more magnified by her artificiality."[62] What is fascinating about her fembot/cyborg virtual presence is that while she convincingly appears more human than human (the hyperreal) and is perfectly saturated in designer wear, she comes across as no different from the average Instagram user, with regard to utilizing the virtual social space to construct a perfect identity. Many social Instagram influencers, as well as the average user, will manipulate their image with the app's filters and effects to virtually beautify themselves and conceal any unwanted features. So are the users any different from Miquela? In which case, are they hyperreal too?

What distinguishes Miquela from humans is that they often claim to be posting a "realistic" and idealistic image of themselves, when in reality, they may be concealing another image and story. In a theoretical sense, for Miquela, there is no concrete image for her to originate from: the more she is enhanced, the more she is mirroring the ideal representation, and the immaculate image and lifestyle of Instagram's average user. Unlike Gorillaz and Hatsune Miku,[63] the intentions of Miquela's existence are not entirely clear. Her Instagram account took effect in April 2016 and instantly gained followers. As her popularity grew, the media became suspicious of her existence as being simply an advertising ploy. She is always branded with designer gear and has appeared in marketing campaigns for the likes of Calvin Klein and Samsung. She is also associated with "logomania"[64] where the display logo of the designer brand becomes more important than the actual design of the clothes—and therefore she translates to a status symbol—a likely promotional tactic as well as a signifier for capitalism; after all, the maintenance of her popularity is funded by sponsorships.

To follow the thought on the concealment of her robotic presence is to turn to Miquela's voice. It is obvious there is a voice-over for her spoken and singing vocals. The singing vocals in particular, as one would expect, are laced with autotune and effects to match her persona. However, the real identities of the voices are undisclosed (unlike with Gorillaz and Hatsune Miku), making the concealment and the mystery of her robotic persona stronger. This is reflected in the 2019 music video, "Money," where "her" vocals feature more than her presence.[65] Whether this is to do with budget, creativity control, or technology is unclear but the director Charlotte Rutherford and creative team do a convincing job of maintaining the spectator's attention on the video. The colorful video is set in a house party in Los Angeles, and every character has a unique and very appealing identity. While Miquela appears only in certain scenes (and for a short time only), it is the characters (including the celebrities featured, such as Zuri Marley, Josephine Lee, Alanna Pearl, and Sophie Meiers), colors, and song that keep the spectators engaged. They can momentarily forget and forgive the lack of Miquela's presence, and, instead, indulge in the eye-catching clothes, artifacts, and attractive characters that appear in the video. Miquela performs as a cute and shy girl in this bubblegum pop song. Her face and upper body do most of the moving, and she perfectly resembles a human (and not a robot), and blends in well with her friends. Her facial expression, however, is more evident in her eyes that hauntingly reveal that her mouth is not brilliantly syncing with the lyrics at all, briefly reminding the spectators that she is not real. She does, however, remind the spectator of her status by posing for her friend's smartphone for an Instagram post, and through the long close-up shot of her in the pool where she just gazes into the camera. "Money" is a novelty video for her fans—and for the curious with limited interaction with the CGI star. Even though her huge and acceptable fan base confirms Miquela's success and status as a virtual celebrity, she has yet to perform "live."

Marshmello and Fortnite

At the time of writing, Marshmello's live appearance in the video game Fortnite, in 2019, is another development in bringing various digital cultural mediums together. While this is not the first time a "live concert" has been presented in a video game (for example, one may be reminded of Minecraft's take on the Coachella, known as the Coalchella Festival, in 2018,[66] and of various music performances on Second Life), Marshmello attracted over ten million virtual players at the concert. Arguably, an intriguing feature of this performance is the relevance of the American EDM DJ, Marshmello (real name Chris Comstock). He is known to conceal his identity in live performances, by wearing a marshmallow mask that covers his head and face.[67] Marshmello as the playful music character (and much in demand DJ) performing in Fortnite, serves as a perfect combination of bringing music and video gamers (users) together.[68]

To participate, gamers had access to only one mode, called "Showtime," where they could not challenge their rival avatars (e.g., fight or shoot each other), but, instead, navigate the location, Pleasant Park (situated in an area of Fortnite island), and dance to the music. While this broke tradition in attending a concert, the event still evoked emotions for the "performer" and participants. As Katherine Isbister comments, "Game designers combine avatars and actions to generate rich possibility spaces for emotionally meaningful social interaction. The game worlds they create may be imaginary, but the social dynamics are not."[69] In this context then, this concert serves as an opportunity for all users to be part of the performance. While watching the playback,[70] participants (avatars) are jumping in the air as well dancing. You can also hear Marshmello encouraging the audience to dance by signaling music cues or shouting, "who is ready to fly with me . . . let's go!" and everyone starts to fly. The social interaction is also heightened through chatting on the voice chat feature.

This platform enabled users to "hang out" and interact with each other (for about ten minutes—the length of the performance). Furthermore, this event was an opportunity for the young audience to attend a concert in real time, bearing in mind that there could be barriers if this was IRL (in real life), such as age restrictions or location. More significantly, this concert reached out globally. Digital consultant, Sammy Andrews, reflected on the positive outcome of the event by suggesting that

> what's new here is the sheer level of integration, and the scale of exposure and engagement to a far larger and more receptive audience . . . [t]his was a seriously deep integration which undoubtedly had mass impact . . . the scale of Fortnite can't be estimated, it's a near global platform—though yet to launch in a few countries.[71]

With this in mind, I would proclaim that this exciting development of (virtual) social interaction and integration invites further ways for users in attending and/or participating in a concert. For example, users who may be unable to attend a concert in real life for whatever reason (be it location, economic situation, health, or lack of access) could participate and experience an immersive musical event.

The Fortnite event was shared by users posting videos of themselves having a great time at the concert while interacting on their devices. This was championed by Marshmello who tweeted on February 3, 2019, "What makes me happiest about today is that so many people got to experience their first concert ever. All the videos I keep seeing of people laughing and smiling throughout the set are amazing." The crossover of music performances and video games brings in exciting opportunities for all involved. While it is obviously great marketing for the main players involved (including Marshmello and his label), this demonstrates how the development of technology continues to be innovative for the creative industries, and yet at the same time, allows the consumers the sensational chance to experience a music concert in a video game setting, and from their personal space.[72]

Immersive Virtual Concerts

Virtual performances can be attended by anyone with access to technology, making the fan or participant more connected with the atmosphere of a performance. While climate awareness and maintaining a healthy revenue for the music businesses is important, the music industry is warming speedily to profiting from fresher musical content by recognizing the significance of virtual as well as traditional live performances. Obviously, the emotional and social engagement is debatable, but this is all down to personal choices, tastes, and situations. Those who have been fortunate enough to attend concerts and have had unforgettable experiences can forever document those memories through conversations with friends, images, souvenirs or merchandise, recordings, tickets, or wrist bands. For those who have not had the experience, or want an alternative way of participating in a concert, immersive virtual concerts are the solution. Various tech companies have been developing various ways of making this possible, such as MelodyVR (see below), Jaunt, NextVR (in collaboration with Live Nation), WaveXR (in partnership with Roc Nation), and Sansar. Examples of consumption and participation in virtual concerts of this kind may involve wearing a headset (e.g., Samsung Gear VR) or viewing on a smartphone via an app.

MelodyVR

The UK-based company, MelodyVR, offers pay-per-view live concerts filmed in VR/360° that can be viewed live or asynchronously. Co-founded by Anthony Matchett and Steven Hancock, MelodyVR was launched in 2018, and includes a huge roster of artists and music events, such as Wiz Khalifa, Imagine Dragons, Lewis Calpaldi, and Mabel, including festivals and clubs.[73] Their model resolves the following factors that may prevent people from attending a live concert such as age and geographical restrictions, personal circumstances, affordability, and ticket availability. The last two factors are especially relevant as the demand for live performances of established artists is costly and tickets tend to sell out quickly. With these factors in mind, Steven Hancock promises that attending a virtual concert on MelodyVR "allows the fan and artist to get a level of engagement that's just never been available before [such as] putting you on stage, in the dressing room, in a recording studio, or in a jet plane with your favorite artist in full VR."[74] This offers the fans various experiences of enhancing their participation in the concert, which would not happen in real life, bearing in mind also that they would not actually "interact" with them (i.e., speak or sing with them), but only share their space. Currently, there are two ways of gaining the immersive experience: by investing in an Oculus Go Headset or Samsung Gear VR, or downloading the app on the smartphone. While both choices offer the same concerts and options, for the deep immersive virtual interaction—such as jumping on stage—fans prefer to invest in the headset. The more affordable option is the app, and while the users can still explore and enjoy a concert, they will be simply watching and navigating the visuals (just like The Weeknd's "The Hills" in Chapter 6). The cost of performances varies, for example, there are options to purchase the concert in full, or per song, and additional content.[75] Furthermore, concerts are stored on the app, meaning the participants can relive their experience again and again. Each event is accompanied by "jump spots" where the users can virtually transport themselves to their ideal position (such as standing with the crowd, dancing on stage, walking backstage, or standing next to the drums), all from the comfort of their personal and physical space.[76] For example, when experiencing Jamiroquai's 2018 concert at the 02 Arena, London, on MelodyVR, I can choose where I want to position myself. I can try to have a dance-off with Jay Kay, the lead singer of Jamiroquai, when in reality I am dancing by myself in the kitchen wearing a headset.

As music concerts are still very much in demand, it is likely that live performances are rapidly moving toward a digital virtual setting via various platforms. In these, the audience have a choice on how to participate, which, of course, may be based on their musical tastes and access to certain technology. Expenses also need to be taken into consideration. While investing in a headset, smartphone, or other equipment will work out to be cost effective in the long term, pending virtual admission to concerts and data usage charges, it will be interesting to observe if it is cost effective for the service provider, music industry, or artist. Creators will need to maintain the use of technology and create quality content, while the industry will see this as a profitable investment opportunity in which their artists/musicians/ publishers may not reap fair financial gain (unless they are independent). For the consumers, however, whatever their choices or needs are, they have some kind of access to live music that can be stored and relived repeatedly. Whether it is livestreaming, audio, synchronous collaboration, simulcast, recorded performance, or the various forms of the virtual concert, we are continuously being furnished on how to consume, experience, and appreciate music, while the performers—whether they are constructed and controlled or not—can eliminate the boundary between themselves and the audience in the performance.

8

"Take Control"

Creators, Fans, and the Internet

What the Internet is going to do to society is unimaginable . . .
—DAVID BOWIE[1]

In the twenty-first century, it is no surprise that established and upcoming creators want to maintain a sense of control over their music. Many creators (musicians, composers, producers) have little control of their artistry in the music industry, yet, we are now witnessing a remarkable digital DIY culture where creators have the freedom to share their music online, and gain success at their own merit thanks to their dedicated and interconnected fan base.[2] What we mainly observe in the twenty-first century is that there is a sense, if not a lot, of musical independency among creators, but why? Although the major music industry is continuously monitoring copyright/intellectual property issues, and is still in a powerful position in seeking other ways of building revenue (e.g., streaming), it does not appear to be overly threatened by the multitude of successful online independent music creators. The music industry steps in by opening up opportunities for one-off collaborations with other creators in music and creative industries (fashion, film, video games, or sport), and/or try and sign them to their label. There are even occasions when the music industry supports its major artists in exploitable ways by interacting with their fan base through music and technology.[3] We will look at how creators and innovators are now encouraging fans and audiences to interact with them and their music online.

Creator + Fan = The Ultimate Collaborators?

Eventful occasions when established creators, fortunate enough to have creative control of their artistry, have used the internet and associated technologies to produce innovative projects and directly share them with their fans, such as Björk's *Biophilia* (2010) interactive album app (consisting of music creation tools, interactive visuals, and games)[4] and "Björk Digital" (2017), a VR exhibition (where the visitor can interact with Björk through installations, audiovisuals, film footage, and performance, and virtually play with her tonsils like I did). Other examples are Nine Inch Nails, who offered multitracks of their records for their fans to remix and gain an intimate experience of their music;[5] Kanye West who released albums on selected streaming platforms (e.g., *Life of Pablo* on Tidal in 2016) and did live album launches on streaming apps (such as the WAV app for the *Ye* album in 2018); Massive Attack who celebrated the twentieth anniversary of their *Mezzanine* album by channeling its recorded stems through a neural network installation in which its sounds were controlled by people's body movements to remix the music;[6] and, Amanda Palmer, who ran a successful crowdfunding campaign where her fans donated over $1,000,000 for her *Theatre is Evil* album (2012) and art book project (incentives for the fans included albums, art books, VIP party invitations, gig tickets, and dinner with Amanda Palmer).[7] This demonstrates that established creators appear to be in control of their music online and have introduced innovative ways of releasing music to their fans.

With creators taking control of their music, the internet is a convenient way of building interaction between the creator and the fan, "shifting the balance from a passive audience to an active user of the [digital] media,"[8] making the role (or, indeed, dedication) of the fans more valuable as they can be relied on to distribute information of the music online. This direct way of sharing music with the fans through various digital means encourages more of an intimate way of virtual interaction and promotion. As Nancy K. Baym observes, fans use their favorite music to create "remixes, stories, covers, art, videos, designs . . . archives of musical information on websites [and] blogs. . . . They are the ones who spread the word [and] . . . They are the ones who 'make things happen.'"[9] While the fans are spreading the word at their own expense, either individually or collectively, their loyalties to the creator result in more musical incentives for them. While it is obvious that creators are in favor of gaining a sense of control of their music, it is also important that they want some form of direct interaction with their audience, but why? Some creators such as David Byrne and Metallica observe the internet as a threat (mainly to do with piracy and lack of streaming royalties), while others view it as an opportunity to directly engage with fans, yet at the same time amplifying ways in promoting music (that is, conveniently digitally and virtually distributed by the fans).

Taking these points into consideration, we will look at how Bowie predicted that the internet would revolutionize musical creativity and interactivity with fans. We will also look at Radiohead's approach in using the internet to distribute their music as now independent creators. Finally, let's look closely at music apps[10] where fans can gain an audiovisual experience of music including remixing, where the users can explore and manipulate recorded music of their favorite artists.

The Internet According to David Bowie

Bowie was considered not only as the King of Postmodernism, but he should also be considered the King of online music. While we were getting to grips with the internet from the late 1990s onward, Bowie correctly predicted that innovative virtual methods in musical communication between creators and fans would be majorly successful in the twenty-first century. During the 1990s, he was already experimenting with ICTs, and in 1999, he said, "I appreciate that there's a new demystification process going on between the artist and audience . . . we're at the cusp of something exhilarating and terrifying . . . [and] the interplay between the user and the provider will be inseparable."[11] This quote was received with skepticism from the media at first, but later proved to be true. To put this concept into practice, he introduced the following ways in bringing the fan and the creator closer with digital technology.

In 1994, his CD album release, *Jump,* included a CD ROM[12] that the fans would insert into the personal computer, and once it was loaded they would be presented with a 3-D virtual skyscraper, and an interactive music video of "Jump, they say" where the user could remix the audiovisuals. The CD ROM also featured other music videos and an interviews section. This was a unique way of fans virtually interacting with Bowie through musical creativity (remix), intimacy (exclusive interview content), and gazing (music video). Bowie then released his digital single, "Telling Lies" (1996) on his website, which resulted in over 300,000 downloads. In 1997 he held a cybercast concert, the 1990s equivalent of a virtual concert, shown live from Boston, but with its setbacks. Due to internet capacity at the time (exhibiting a lack of data and speed), virtual fans were regularly cut off on the internet. The following year Bowie collaborated with tech developers Robert Goodale and Ron Roy and launched his own internet service provider, "BowieNet," to make it easier to distribute music and novelty content directly to fans. "BowieNet" included Bowie's website, where fans could navigate through images, music videos, interviews, blog, and news. Those who had internet access and subscribed to "BowieNet" (mainly in North America at the time) at $19.95 per month were allocated 5 mb of web space to create their own sites, obtained their own personal "@davidbowie.com" email address, and became social media users where they could chat with fans including Bowie (under his pseudonym "Sailor").

As the website and "BowieNet" developed, fans were treated to Bowie's music tracks, concert footages, and even his own short-lived bank (called BowieBanc). As well as having "Bowie internet,"[13] fans were invited to mash up his album *Reality* (2003), with the winner's track supposedly featuring on an Audi car commercial as well as winning an Audi TT.[14] The website offered stems[15]/samples of Bowie's music and a demo version of software Acid Pro that fans could work with. Christopher Moore notes that this event was not all cracked up to be as the available stems/samples included only specific sounds for the fans to work with (which were actually quite limited), and that the winning song did not feature in the advert after all, but, instead, included the high-profile mash-up DJ Mark Vidler's remix, "Rebel Never Gets Old."[16] The winner received $30,000 instead of an Audi TT and built his own recording studio. Whether the reason for not including the winning track was a marketing ploy, intellectual property issue, or an industry decision, it was perhaps a relief for DJs who did not prefer the mash-up to be viewed as a novelty factor as this defeats the concept of recognizing unknown talents and amateurs gaining recognition for their creativities, especially when remixing their favorite music. A positive side to the story is that the competition winner, David Choi, had a head start in the music industry.

Bowie's adventures with digital technology demonstrated his high status as a creator: by showing appreciation for his fans by inviting them to partake in his "world"—including communication with other fans virtually. Bowie was experimental not only with his identity, art, and music, but with technology too, in particular the internet.

Radiohead's Okaying the Computer

When British experimental-rock group Radiohead (formed in the mid-1980s in Oxford), known for the albums *The Bends* (1995), *OK Computer* (1997), and *Kid A* (2000), fulfilled their music contract, they decided not to extend their relationship with EMI in 2006. With advice from their managers, Chris Hufford and Bryce Edge, they decided to maintain independence with regard to their music, including its distribution. Unreleased tracks contributed to the 2007 album, *In Rainbows,* and were released to their fans in an unconventional way. Bearing in mind that they had the funds to distribute the album on the internet (such as providing the platform), the band insisted it was not an attempt to profit from it but to share their unreleased music with their fans before it was officially released to the public. Colin Greenwood (bassist) remarks, "If we set out to do this to make lots of money, we'd have signed to Universal Records. . . . No sane person would have released a record like this for financial gain."[17] Radiohead honored their statement by releasing *In Rainbows* as an honesty box method where fans could choose how much they wanted to pay to download the album (between £/$0 and £/$99). The promotion was led by Radiohead's guitarist Jonny Greenwood who posted the following message on their website "Hello everyone. Well, the new album is finished, and it's coming out in 10 days. We've called it In Rainbows. Love from us all. Jonny."[18] That message alone—and minus a PR team—was enough to motivate their fans into buying the album. Various media reactions have stated that this venture was a flop, in that Radiohead did not make much money[19] and that the sound quality of the MP3s was inadequate. While Radiohead hesitantly acknowledge that there was always going to be a risk of loss of profit, they claim that as they had cut out the middleman, the profits reflected money they would have lost if the album had been released by a major record label. Regarding the sound quality, Radiohead continue to assert that they wanted to reach out to their fans with the music first before releasing the album officially, regardless of audio attributes. Therefore, this was not a case of "try before you buy" but more of a gift (in exchange for money) for fans. The project did not flop after all when the CD format was released and distributed via independent label XL and returned a healthy profit. Thom Yorke argues: "We have a moral justification in what we did in the sense that the majors and the big infrastructure of the music business has not addressed the way artists communicate directly with their fans,"[20] suggesting that this method of releasing music was a better way of communicating directly with the fans and that there were no gatekeepers or parties involved—the whole process of the digital release of *In Rainbows* was controlled by Radiohead (and their managers), proving that like Bowie, they too could find and offer a direct way of interacting with their fans on the internet.

In 2014, Radiohead found another opportunity for their fans to interact with their music. Collaborating with their music producer Nigel Godrich, graphic artist Stanley Donwood, and digital arts team Universal Everything, Radiohead released an app, *Polyfauna,* for Android and iOS. This is an AR video game set to the music of Radiohead's album *The King of Limbs*. *Polyfauna* is easy to play as the instructions are stated on the app and website, "Your screen is the window into an evolving world. Move around to look around. You can follow the red dot. You can wear headphones."[21] By following the red dot on the screen, the users will journey through different virtual dark landscapes of forests, mountains, sunsets, moonlight, weather, and animals. As they tilt the screen the image also tilts; as they turn, the image also turns. However, for the game to be effective and for the red dot to move, the users have to move around and explore the virtual landscape, in addition to being exposed to surprising images that may flash to them. It is so easy to get pulled into the virtual space, and this is dangerous (as I have found out myself), as this game should not be played in a public space—

therefore, the users must be aware of their physical surroundings for safety. Another interesting feature is that the users can draw on the screen—their finger swiping across the screen will generate images that correspond to the scenic virtual environment (the mimic sketches could translate into birds, bats, thunderstorms, and illuminating colors). These images blend nicely with the atmospheric music. While this app is promoted as a video game, it does not involve any challenging levels or competitions as such. Instead, it may come across as a novelty game for the fans and curious users where they can explore the virtual world and hear Radiohead's virtual album. There are no technical restrictions, such as installing complicated software or plug-ins; all the users need is a compatible device and they are set up—it should be noted, however, that the app only includes the game and that there are no features such as the MP3 files of the album tracks (the fans would have to purchase the album separately). Despite the simple interface, this is actually a nice convenience for the fans, especially if they are technophobes, as they will find this a user-friendly app.

As well as using the app as a game and enhancing their multisensory experience of the virtual album, fans can also treat *Polyfauna* as an extended music video or film, where the users have control of changing virtual landscapes, surreal images, and colors that sync with the music, thereby creating their own virtual version of the audiovisual soundtrack. While the users cannot capture their experience or share with others, Radiohead invite their audience to take control and experience the audiovisual in their own space, and ensure that they have a brand new adventure every time they play *Polyfauna*, as well as enjoying the virtual album *The King of Limbs*.

Return of the App?

Compared to the success of nonmusical apps,[22] the album app has yet to be recognized as a companion to existing music formats as well as a stand-alone format, despite its existence since 2008 (starting with Brian Eno's *Bloom* and, more significantly, with Björk's *Biophilia* spearheading this trend in music). Georgiana Bogdan observes apps as "companions of the album, primarily intended for marketing,"[23] that tend to be more effective with established creators such as Radiohead and Björk.

Album apps are a way for the user to interact with the music and have a unique audiovisual experience. For the album app to be effective, attractive visuals and musical activities need to be implemented—and that is likely to be costly—hence the reason why such established creators as Björk and Radiohead have found this platform successful. There is an appealing feature of the format that is perhaps more in favor with the music industry than the average consumer, as Jonathan Shakhovsky and Rob Toulson note, stating that the album app is an "attractive method for musical delivery because it is relatively secure, i.e. once the app is created it cannot be tampered with. . . . It is also much more difficult to pirate and distribute unauthorized copies of album apps."[24] While this app could have been the answer to reducing piracy issues in the industry, and was originally considered to replace digital formats such as the MP3, those ideas were prematurely dashed when streaming became massively popular. However, there is still a demand for music apps that cater for fans and audiences who have a general interest in this music format. The following two examples, variPlay and Massive Attack's *Fantom Mezzanine*, demonstrate various ways in which the user can interact with the music through apps.

variPlay App—Rob Toulson

variPlay was a five-year music app project with Warner Music Group that focused on enhancing the audio experience for the users by allowing them to interact with the digital format on an iOS device. The app contained specific features that enabled the users to manipulate the music and change the style to suit their mood, yet at the same time, maintain the general shape of the song without drastically altering it into a transformative work. variPlay was created by Rob Toulson (app developer and music producer).[25]

Toulson explains that the concept of the app was not only to interact with but also to explore sound in a song, and how it could enhance the listener's experience in a virtual and nonvirtual setting:

> The concept was that nowadays a song is never a "thing," one song have 10 or 100 different embodiments, such as classical music where different orchestras would perform a score and it would sound different everytime, so there would always be interpretations . . . and with artists doing cover versions of their own songs [here he refers to Radio 1's *Live Lounge* and MTV's *Unplugged* where musicians would play different versions of their own songs such as Nirvana and Oasis]—where you take the song and it doesn't matter if you play it on a guitar in a rock band or in *a cappella*, or with a electronic background. It demonstrates that lots of artists have more than one [musical] personality or taste.[26]

Therefore, not only he had the user in mind, but also the artists. While commercial artists, in particular, are known for creating music in a specific genre or style, they may want to experiment with other music while maintaining their fan base, yet may feel restricted in doing so. However, there are artists that are fortunate enough to be able to experiment with their music, such as when artists create different versions of the same song. While the user could previously access such mixes on the single format (or, indeed, downloads or streams), Toulson wanted to develop a similar feature for the app, meaning that the different styles of music would be instantly accessible to the user. He elaborates:

> Take for example a song that you hear on the radio, it actually has 3 versions (including a dance version), which demonstrates the artists' openness to a variety of genres and styles, and so the app was the version for that—we wanted to build an app allowing the user to *explore* the song and the artist's creativity.[27]

With this in mind, variPlay consisted of Interactive Recorded Music (IRM) that included "a number of playback strategies where the listener maintains a level of active control of prerecorded content within a single song."[28] To execute this, the technology had to be simple to keep it user friendly and in addition, to simply provide a platform for playing music. The app allows the user to change the style of the song by playing with the available stems permitted by the original creator (e.g., artist), and this may consist of the drums, guitar, bass, strings, keyboards, and vocals. The users select the style they want (e.g., rock, electronic, or dance), and change the volume of the individual stems, including selecting the ones they want to hear the most (or less of), therefore effectively "putting the mix in the hands of the listener—they can't mess it up."[29] As such, the music in the app was specifically created for the mix or remix to not sound atonal, displaced, or out of time—it was important for the creator and app developer that the music maintained the shape of its song. Therefore Toulson explains that collaborating with the artist and producer was important, offering them the opportunity to select the parts of the song the user could modify in addition to creating additional styles. The artists in question welcome this idea as the user experience benefits them (as well as the listeners), and their experience and exploration of the music is also enhanced. Toulson elaborates on this notion that the technology (app) for the artist "enables a new way of thinking" with music.[30]

Toulson also insists that the design of the app's interface should be visually appealing (like an album) but its use should be kept simple: "the fewer buttons the better—users don't want to play a game while listening to music."[31] Take one app developed by variPlay, for example: Daisy and the Dark's *Red Planet* (2015), an independent musical project fronted by singer-songwriter Sarah Foster, with the music produced by Toulson. This app is an EP (extended play—a mini album) and when loading the app, I am presented with the app's attractive cover of the music (equivalent to a single or album cover—Figure 8.1). On the virtual EP cover, there are four virtual buttons: "Extra" (includes links to the band's website, social media, videos, contact details, and instructions on how to use the app), "Gallery" (images of the band), "Band" (biography section and EP's credits), and "Music" (music player and songs).

FIGURE 8.1 *Daisy and the Dark App. Credit: variPlay.*

To activate a button is to drag it toward the center of the virtual EP cover. After selecting and dragging the "Music" button, I have four songs to choose from. On selecting its main track, "Red Planet," I am presented with a graduated colored red and purple circle/planet (i.e., the mixer—Figure 8.2) with a white dot in the middle. When the music starts, I keep dragging the white dot across the circle (mixer), and explore the various sounds of the

FIGURE 8.2 *Circle mixer. Credit: variPlay.*

song, and detect various styles such as acoustic, pop, different variations of electronic, and a capella.

If I swipe left on the screen, I am presented with instrument stem faders (Figure 8.3) where I can adjust the sounds by reducing the volume of the guitar, muting the drums, or increasing the dynamics of the synthesizer. With practice, I become more familiar with the different sounds and I have the choice of how I explore and adjust the sounds to my liking. For example, if

FIGURE 8.3 *Instrument stem faders. Credit: variPlay.*

I want to listen to the electronic style but with more focus on the drums, I can set it up, and likewise for acoustic, or whatever effect I want. I can still follow the song as it has maintained its melodic shape including form and structure—it is only the texture and timbre that has changed.

Personally, I would have benefited from an app such as this in the late 1980s, when I became obsessed with hearing remixes of my favorite songs and wanted to create my own versions—I had to make do with very limited resources, instead. This app offers the listeners the opportunity to enhance their enjoyment of the music, and, more importantly, to explore and detect the different sounds presented in the music.

Other variPlay releases followed, such as Ximena Sariñana (Warner Music Mexico, 2018), Defab1 (Regent St Records, 2018), Ofenbach (Elekta France, 2019), and Jack Harlow (Atlantic Records, 2018). While these apps received great attention from consumers, Warner Music Group were not committed enough to market the app (as streaming had become so popular). This style of app is still popular, however, and has stretched to other uses such as providing the accompaniment to a performer—which is great for performers, who do not need to rely on average-quality backing tracks—they can sing or play with the original music, and modify it to their taste, and, more importantly, perform with the original version. While the app may not suit the major music industry's best interests (yet, this same thought was also applied to streaming), other artists are offering similar apps to their fans (see next section). Not only does it provoke them to create and experiment with a piece of music that their fans can mix, but they are also virtually connecting with their followers through their music—further confirming the blurred distinction between the creators and fans. As Toulson says, variPlay "justifies a new type of artistry—it allows the artist to be greater"[32] in the digital virtual era.

Massive "App" Attack

As we are aware, the music app serves as an "add-on" feature of the album, focusing on the interaction where the user can directly experience and, if available, alter the audiovisuals. The app can also momentarily build an emotional attachment between the product and the consumer. Whereas earlier, a consumer would explore and admire the images, album cover, lyrics, and credits while listening to the music, that multi-engagement was briefly lost when the MP3 and early streaming arrived (but this has since changed—see the following endnote)[33]—the album app, however, changes that by bringing back the novelty and nostalgia, by including revamped features of the album along with the visuals, with Massive Attack's *Fantom Mezzanine* app serving as an example.

Massive Attack is an electronica group (notably known for trip-hop) from Bristol. Their *Fantom Mezzanine* app was released in 2018 to celebrate the twentieth anniversary of the *Mezzanine* album, and the concept was co-created by group member Robert Del Naja.[34] The app is a "sensory music experience"[35] where the fan can visually remix the album's stems by using the iOS device's "sensor functions such as camera, acceleration and location for sampling, recording and unique playback."[36] When opening the app, you are presented with the album's track list with a black and white background including x-ray images of animals. A link to iTunes is also provided (should you wish to purchase the album), along with instructions.[37] With the imagery and style of font (all presented in capital letters and embellished with symbols), it does leave a haunting impression for the fan, hence the title of the app "Fantom" (realizing the play of words here from "phantom" to "*fan*tom," but this could also be an innocent way of dedicating the app to the "fan").

Using the app's interface is straightforward, for example, the camera image is automatically set to "selfie" or normal mode (depending on the track) and it controls the music, so when I move (the image of myself, that is), the music

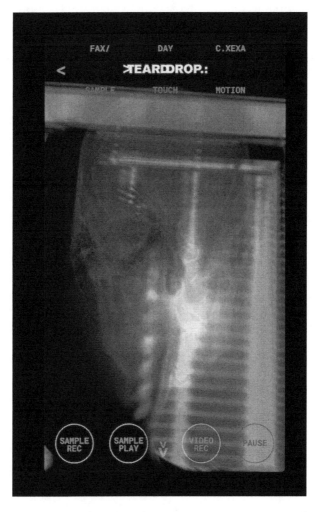

FIGURE 8.4 *Image of author using the* Fantom Mezzanine *app. Credit: Author.*

alters. Smiling into the camera activates the vocals and closing the eyes will make the vocals stop. The finger controls the tempo as I slide it on the screen in fast or slow motion. If the device is moved around, it has an effect on the chords: the more force it receives, the thicker the texture of the sounds becomes. Also, the sensor can detect whether it is day or night, resulting in different music timbre each time—therefore headphones should be worn to experience the full effects of the music. If I go deeper into the experience based on the track "Teardrops," the sensory part is that I am manipulating the music through my facial expressions, body movement, and personal recorded samples. The faster I move and tilt the device with force (while trying not to drop it at the same time), the music distorts. If I gently smile and randomly close my eyes, the music goes softer and more ambient-like. It is so easy to co-coordinate with the music in a trance state and control the audiovisuals with my body and leave my scattered fingerprints transferred onto the app. The light behind me (Figure 8.4) also plays a part in the experience by adding extra sonics to the music, confirming that the app responds not only to the sensory movements of the human body but to the environment, too. When I get lost in the music, a skeleton appears that prompts me to carry on controlling the music. Overall, the app enables fans to get closer to the music in their own space, and they can record their experience and remix, and share, online.

While the app may be observed as a novelty add-on to the album (and memorabilia) and is designed for only one user to manipulate, it will be interesting to see whether the album app will eventually take over streaming. One drawback will be that the user's device will need large amounts of storage space for apps, and a very high battery life. In the meantime, this is another exciting example of the ongoing developments in the way the creator can digitally interact with the fan, and vice versa, via music and visuals. Overall, as demonstrated in this chapter, the creators explore their opportunities in building interaction with their fans by creating an experimental, experiential, and exclusive digital platform for fans to remix, enhance, and virtually engage with the audiovisuals and, where possible, share content instantly online.[38]

9

"Digital Witness"

Online Communities, Networking, and Virality

If you see something going around the Internet, people want to join in.

—LIL NAS X[1]

It is arguable that the barriers between the creator/artist, industry, and consumer/fan are now erased in the digital virtual era, which this final chapter will continue to explore. While the music industry depends on the masses to maintain its successful global business, consumers are more relevant now and, arguably, have an unofficial role in the music industry. A practice in which they can really engage with the creators' works is online networking. Previously, consumers and fans were assets in promoting music either individually or collectively. The importance of the consumers/fans/online users in the digital virtual era is that they are the "media" as they assist in their favorite creators gaining exposure immediately by sharing music online, and they digitally witness the outcome of the success by networking with virtual friends, and by sharing their feelings, opinions, gossip, news, blogs/vlogs on the internet.

Online Communities and Music

Before the wave of online communities, it was pretty challenging to celebrate music as a collective unless you "belonged" to a group of people who shared similar interests, such as a scene or subculture, or socialized at a concert, event, or club. For the creators, valuing their fans and offering a sense of connection was via fan clubs, meet-ups, secret events, and conventions—and even then, the fans seldom got to talk to the creator/artist. To gain information on new music, gigs, or gossip, the fan would rely on the music/local/national press, record shops, posters, radio, television, and word of mouth. The barrier between the fans and creators started to ease around the 2000s when "street teams" became popular where the music industry, especially low-key record labels, would "recruit" fans to help promote music by distributing fliers, stickers, bringing friends to shows, and collecting contact details of concert goers for a mailing list. This tactic almost gave a sense but false illusion that the fans were working for the industry when in reality they were working for free (with the exception of receiving perks such as free access to gigs).[2] However, this was a step further in bridging a closer connection to their icon, yet often not for the creators as they were not always aware of the promotional work carried out by their fans. Despite this, the street team member meets other people who share similar musical tastes.

Moving forward, digital technology provides the space for "online communities who can participate, interact, and influence music in the virtual world of the Internet [that] has often led to an all-encompassing interpretation of social equality."[3] This concept can be approached in various ways that perhaps lead to delusions of equality on the internet, particularly in music; however, the virtual world provides the means to give users the opportunity to freely participate in online activities. At first, online forums and message boards arrived where fans could virtually connect and chat about their favorite artist. While fans could not physically see each other, the digital space allowed people to congregate together globally from their own safe space. This development in online communication is significant because participants were not pressured to physically meet people. They also had a digital space to virtually socialize regardless of their background or personal situation that might prevent them from experiencing networking in the "real world" (e.g., disability, health, geographic location, or financial position). As Baym notes, it took a while for the creator and the industry to realize that they could use music to directly communicate with fans online,[4] making distribution quicker and easier to spread awareness of the music and its content on the internet. This concept aligns with Leah Lievrouw, who argues that the internet has "created unprecedented opportunities for expression and interaction, especially amongst activists, artists . . . and cultural groups around the world who have found new media to be inexpensive, powerful tools for challenging the givens of mainstream or popular cultures,"[5] making this a remarkable way of interacting with other fans and creators, bringing in exclusive ways to share and discuss music online.

Social Media

While the music industry was dealing with online piracy in the early twenty-first century, it was missing out on investing in new musical talent when social media platforms started to become popular (with the likes of MySpace, YouTube, SoundCloud, and Twitter). Social media is an ideal platform for independent creators to instantly share music and interact with fans online. Another advantage is that creators could receive musical recognition without belonging to a record label, while at the same time, the record labels could scout for talent on social media and monitor the reception of the fans for free before investing. A networking site that initiated this trend of sharing music as well as discovering new talent was MySpace. Launched in 2003, this was the precursor to Facebook where any user can sign up and follow/communicate with followers and celebrities as well as uploading images, music, and videos. Creators could upload their music and build a fan base in which in return the fans could also post links or comments on their page. Famous musicians who took this route included The Arctic Monkeys, Lily Allen, and Sean Kingston.

YouTube gradually became the main platform for streaming music videos once the music industry eventually saw this as a business opportunity to make profits. While the user does not pay to watch the video,[6] the clicks, and adverts generate revenues for the industry. The users can comment and share the video link on social media, emails and other mediums, resulting in more attention for the artist. This is also a preferred platform for premiering exclusive music videos (e.g., The Weeknd) rather than a website, as the site and its search functions are easy to find and navigate. Besides, YouTube would recommend other videos to view, which increases the user's time spent on the site as well as increasing engagement for the artist.

SoundCloud[7] is a music-sharing platform where unsigned creators can upload their music in the hope of receiving attention from fans and maybe a record deal, as well as networking with other creators. The fans can comment on the creators' profile and distribute the music by posting a link on their social media page or blog, thereby increasing and promoting the music. This once "average" site surged with unknown American rappers who used this platform to promote their mixtapes, and its success resulted in the "SoundCloud Rap" genre. This genre received attention from the hip-hop magazine *XXL*, boosting the popularity of SoundCloud Rappers such as Lil Uzi and Juice WRLD.

Twitter[8] is also a popular platform for music. Although it is not primarily used to post music, creators/artists can tweet their activities, opinions, and promote music, with a link. Their social position on Twitter is regulated by the number of "followers" (e.g., fans) they have—the higher the number of followers, the more likely their posts will be shared, thereby increasing engagement on the social media platform. The platform enables the users (fans) to communicate with their artist, by mentioning them in their post (using @ and their user name to grab their attention) and share tweets. Furthermore, creators, labels, and fans create hashtags (#), making it a promotional tool (and tactic) to generate interest in a specific song or album. An example would be the controversial Robin Thicke, T.I, and Pharrell Williams's 2013 track "Blurred Lines" in which the video is plastered with the overly sized "#Thicke" hashtag in red font, not only making it a direct and clever marketing tool for the artist's brand (that is Robin Thicke) but also encouraging the viewers to type it on Twitter and stalk and reply to the tweets posted by tweeters—this increases engagement and impressions (i.e., appearing in timelines) for the artist.

Other social media platforms include Facebook[9] where fans can join and "like" their favorite artist's page and get information, videos, and performances, and chat with other fans; and, Instagram,[10] which has a visual appeal as artists post images, snippets of videos/stories, and integrate with their fans—but with the disadvantage of not allowing clickable links.[11] Social media is a great promotional tool if executed well and if fans engage with and share the content. Other than "spreading the word," there is one particular trend in online social networking where sudden spectacular moments are divulged by the artist (or media) such as a single release, music video drop, gossip, or experiencing an embarrassing/scandalous or celebratory moment, that instantly sparks a reaction from the public prompting them to share across the social infrastructure, and is exposed to other users immediately, resulting in virality.

Virality

Virality is best defined as a "social information flow process where many people simultaneously forward a specific information item over a short period of time within their social networks, and where the message spreads . . . [to] distant networks resulting in a sharp acceleration."[12] "Virality" is not a new term to be used in the media; in fact, it has been present in culture for many decades, but implemented in various ways, mainly for marketing purposes, displaying awareness of current affairs (politics), or a random incident that just happened to be documented and received attention from the public. Karine Nahon and Jeff Hemsley argue that the usage of this term can be traced back to the 1950s, when people would record extraordinary events by using the "telephone, hand-bills and word of mouth."[13] The difference between how the term was observed in the past and the way it is in the present is in the use of technology and the duration it takes for the event to spread globally. In the past, it could range from a few days to a couple of hours for a mediatized segment to go viral—but today, it is much quicker as online reactions to the first posting can become viral thanks to digital technology.[14]

It is worth noting that the concept of virality is not solely about spreading news around for a limited time, but also about *why* it grabbed our attention in the first place. Is it for pleasure (music), humor (satirical content), shock/anger (violence, social matters), or to eliminate boredom (cute cat videos)? Whatever the reason, it may catch our attention regardless of whether we are concerned about the topic or not. Obviously, we cannot deny that we may come across messages where the censored is uncensored, and the unknown becomes known, regardless of subject or situation or whether it is presented in a good or bad context—just because a story/visual has gone viral, it does not always carry good intentions yet creates a sense of engagement. Some factors contribute to making material go viral regardless of the subject, and typical examples include social currency (crafted intentions that leave lasting impressions), emotion (that generate feelings), and stories (that get people talking and embellishing the narrative)[15]—these particular factors can be applied in music.

Contagious music and its random events online can grab anyone's attention whether they like the artist or not. It gets people talking and results in checking out the viral information for curiosity's sake, especially on social media sharing platforms such as YouTube, Facebook, and Twitter. With music in particular, the following signs of virality will involve a famous artist and creative content that engages with users/fans inspiring them to share online. There are various types of music virality to consider: the music video that hugely permeates online and receives appraised attention (due to gimmicky content, a catchy song, or the known artist);[16] a viral campaign that is carefully planned (for promotional purposes) that is sometimes accessible for the user to remix and share online; and a viral source that is unplanned (i.e., accidental and unintentional with no direct input from the creator/artist and industry). We can associate these types of music virality with the following: Drake, Baauer, David Bowie, Kendrick Lamar, and Lil Nas X.

Drake—"Hotline Bling"

If we look briefly at a planned music viral campaign, it would involve an anticipated music video release or hashtags (as mentioned earlier), or anything related to Canadian singer Drake (Aubrey Graham), as demonstrated in his 2015 "Hotline Bling" video.[17] The video was Apple Music's first content visual to mark their debut in the streaming market and culture. This memorable video is actually visually minimal, in terms of narrative and use of props, but there are elements to consider about why this video has become successful. First, it was a feature of two super brands:

Drake and Apple, which guaranteed success in their own right, and second, the video (and music) displayed unique audiovisual content that the fans could remix, create memes with (to be discussed shortly), and get people talking. The song title is catchy although the simplified lyrics may suggest otherwise (the topic points toward a bitterly failed romantic relationship). Drake shamelessly asks his fans on Instagram to help his track get to the Billboard Hot chart's number one position.

Although he ended up only at number two,[18] his video was certainly a talking point in popular culture, as the minimally designed visual was totally owned by Drake. The set is made up of a confined space in a cube with its walls illuminated with block pastel colors and passing shots of silhouette dancers. The video is obviously dominated by Drake, who displays the ultimate bad dance routine by himself, and with himself only—it is the equivalent of going clubbing and finding a bloke dancing by himself regardless of what other people think. Drake is trapped in the cube and offers some interesting moves as if with the confidence that no one is watching (but we are!), with no dancers or props to enhance his performance—he does not need any. In fact, the gaze is set on Drake and his body movements and gestures, therefore a visual background is irrelevant—he might as well have been dancing in front of a green screen.

The simple, attractive setting serves as an accessible source for the audience to manipulate, resulting in mostly parody and hilarious memes. Examples of remixing include syncing Drakes' dance moves to any song and style; replacing the visual background with a virtual set (of literally anything); and enhancing his motions with activities such as playing tennis or holding lightsabers. There have also been parody versions of the song where fans (including celebrities) change the lyrics and feature themselves in the video. Drake's video serves as an extension to connect with the audience by making his song shareable, as well as a smart promotional tactic that may not have worked with an unknown artist. As the video is both comical and genius to watch, the viral reaction it received brought Drake's brand even more (virtual) global recognition.

Baauer—"Harlem Shake"

An example of an unplanned viral music video is Baauer's "Harlem Shake" (2012). The dance track was originally an underground hit and had no accompanying video, until a comedian, "Filthy Frank," used the music for a thirty-second video (it included characters in fancy dress doing a novelty dance). Without the knowledge of Baauer[19] or his label, this turned out to be a happy moment for them because the video instantly garnered views on YouTube and the dance moves were imitated and uploaded by users and shared on social media. The original viral video, along with its user-generated videos, boosted the music sales of Baauer's "Harlem Shake" without his or his team's involvement, and naturally did not legally challenge the creator of the video.[20] Like Drake, this video went viral because the content was accessible to manipulate and share online, and in this case it imitated the dance moves of the "Harlem Shake" and not the actual music or original video.

David Bowie

Music virality does not always need to involve visuals or be implemented as a marketing tool. Social media has enabled a space where users can unite and share stories, and mourn the loss of their favorite artists. In this space, otherwise known as "iMourning,"[21] users (e.g., fans and nonfans) can use the world of social media to "grieve" for the artist, whereas before they would have dealt with "loss" personally, or with friends, without having the opportunity to express their feelings publicly. The deaths of high-profile artists including Prince, George Michael, and Michael Jackson prompted users to express their thoughts directly to strangers instead of calling their friends, and by making their posts personal as if they really knew the deceased artist—momentarily neglecting their parasocial (one-sided) relationship[22] with the artist in question. As Hilde Van den Bulck and Anders Larsson suggest, "an interest in and a feeling of closeness to a celebrity are no longer restricted to the—once believed 'special'—category of fans but has become part of everybody's lives."[23] Therefore, fans and the nonfans can congregate on social media where they can network with others online and share their emotions together, instantly.

Bowie's untimely demise shocked his fans and (social) media, especially as it happened right after he released what became his final album, *Blackstar* (2016). With his death announced on social media, users (fans, celebrity friends, industry colleagues) immediately flocked online to express their loss. Twitter, in particular, became the main platform, where users were enabled to find posts under the hashtag "#bowie." Users were not only expressing their virtual mourning online, but some curious users were also using the hashtag to curate information and narratives surrounding Bowie's death,[24] suggesting that people were also glued to seeing how the event unfolded online (rather than referring to the usual media outlets). Additionally, users, whether Bowie fans or not, would post tributes such as images and videos. The multitude of shared emotions and information that are rapidly shared on social media platforms encourages inquisitive users to understand, appreciate, and provoke conversations on why Bowie was a respected music creator and performer.

Meme: Kendrick Lamar and *Damn*

An offshoot of virality is a meme (based on the term mimema)[25] which has developed into its own culture. A meme is based on cultural information such as an image, text, music, and video, where its content is imitated and

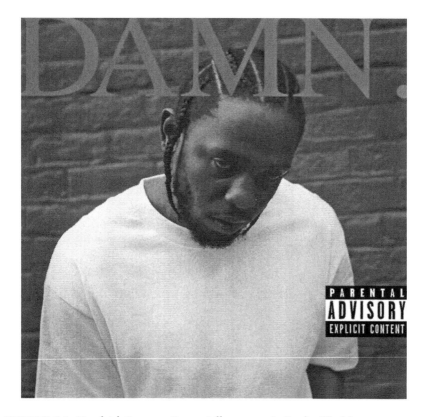

FIGURE 9.1 *Kendrick Lamar—Damn (album cover). Credit: Vlad Sepetov.*

modified, then passed around through some form of communication such as social media to gain attention. A meme is not always socially friendly as it can be seen as an insult, parody, bad humor, and disrespect for the original creator or subject of the source. However, it has been widely used in music (e.g., Drake) mostly in a positive manner and has served as another worthy and guerilla marketing tool, because like a viral video, a meme that permeates online guarantees success.[26] An example would be Kendrick Lamar's 2017 conscious hip-hop album, that is simply titled *DAMN* (Figure 9.1). While the title alone is specific and snappy, the album cover is unusually mundane to look at. While a typical hip-hop album cover is usually visually appealing and dynamic, Lamar has done the opposite: he is looking at the camera, wearing a plain T-shirt, and looks fed-up/emotionless/lost/miserable. This image is fostered by the title of the album, *DAMN*, which is presented in big and bold red lettering.

The combination of Lamar's image and the massive title erases the visual dullness of the artwork and immediately brings a relatable and lasting impression for the viewer. Furthermore, the image was exposed on social media before the release of the album, making it a clever promotional tactic, as it became a meme. Users were quick to imitate or make jokes about the artwork and attempted to apply it to everyday scenarios. While this meme quickly spread on the internet, many realized that this was clever marketing—accusing Lamar and his label of creating the meme as a deliberate tactic. It certainly got people discussing and sharing, or to be precise, promoting his album, for free.

Social Media + Virality + Meme = Lil Nas X

A perfect example of a viral audiovisual is American rapper and singer Lil Nas X and his 2018 song "Old Town Road." Lil Nas X (born Montero Hill) was a meme creator on social media, therefore he knew how relevant virality is in popular culture. Always aspiring to be a musician, he created a buzz in presenting the unpresentable by making the country and trap song "Old Town Road."[27] The timing of Lil Nas X promoting the song on social media was perfect as the meme culture was recognizing the "Yeehaw Agenda."[28] This is a movement reflecting "a moment of transition in which the very idea of American identity is being contested"[29] and challenged by African American fans of country music. It was also an attempt to make the genre more accessible to nonwhite Americans, no longer aimed only at white American cowboy stereotypes—as the genre sadly appears to be cemented in its white American musical origins. The historic elements of African American music that inspired so much about country music appear to be forgotten. While the meme helped to make the movement popular but with humor and parody, Lil Nas X cemented its relevance in culture with his song by creating memes himself and distributing it on social media. As he explains, "I saw the power to make something bigger from social media because it's done so often nowadays, I didn't want to miss my chance, I went for it."[30]

Lil Nas X teased his followers by posting various meme videos on Twitter (and later on Instagram), and what helped it to be so attractive was the soundtrack's catchy musical excerpt of "Old Town Road." One meme example is a Twitter post on December 3, 2018 consisting of a short clip of a cowboy dancing by himself and being ridiculed by the audience at a public event. What makes this meme funny and smart is that the clip is dubbed with the "Old Town Road" audio excerpt, and Lil Nas X cleverly uses the caption "country music is evolving" on his Twitter post—a hint that the music has tapped into trap music territory, but it is also a sassy ploy to trigger a response from the country music community.

This meme (along with 100 others all carrying the exact same music) caught on with his followers who retweeted the tweets. The followers would then promote the song by creating and sharing videos of themselves based on the song-inspired game, the "Yeehaw Challenge," by imitating cowboys in comical ways and dancing to "Old Town Road" on the app TikTok—an amateur video making/sharing platform app and social network targeted on teenagers and young adults.[31] The success of the TikTok videos exposed Lil Nas X's music on social media and radio, and to keep the momentum moving, he remixed the song by featuring the famous country singer, Billy Ray Cyrus. Lil Nas X also marketed the song on SoundCloud and iTunes as country music, making it easier to promote as he may have dealt with fierce competition if he had labeled it under another genre/style (e.g., hip-hop and rap).

Within four months of the memes going viral, the remixed version of the song made the number one position in the Billboard Hot charts for nineteen weeks.[32] As well as the song officially overtaking Mariah Carey's longest chart reign of the 1995 hit "One Sweet Day" (a duet with Boyz to Men), Lil Nas X scored a record deal with Columbia/RCA Records and a fashion deal with Wrangler clothes.

Lil Nas X uniquely combines the distinctive ingredients in making the song viral by using memes and social media. Not only did he know that visual content had to be made appealing by using various memes as mini music videos, but he also had an agenda to make sure his plan worked. Originally an online DIY creator, he used his existing experience in creating memes that proved to be valuable and a great promotional tactic, as these visual contents accompanying the catchy "Old Town Road" illustrated. To execute his plan, he had to create shareable content that could be manipulated by users to guarantee its virality—which worked with the added bonus of users making amateur videos on TikTok that secured the success of the song, only to be further enhanced by Lil Nas X's collaboration with Billy Ray Cyrus.

If playing with musical genres or styles was not enough for it to go viral, it was certainly the memes, and social media users, that helped the song to be a success and create a buzz, without the aid of the major music industry. The barrier between the creator and fans continues to blur in the digital virtual era through user-generated and shareable content including virtual conversation, pushing the music to be a success and appraised, as well as building connections with each other through a particular event like "Old Town Road."

The division between the creator and fan/audience/consumer rarely exists in the virtual world, thanks to technology, because interacting with performance, music, and social media, makes their relationship with music stronger in the digital virtual era—as neatly summarized by Lil Nas X, "It paints a picture and allows people from any place to just join in and feel a sense of togetherness."[33]

Conclusion

Rewind or after the Future?

The future has arrived. The unimaginable, unthinkable, unexpected, that is, the virtual, has been made possible in music, thanks to digital technology. While the discussions presented in this book focused mostly on highlighting exciting developments in creativity and consumption of music, including interactivity, we can also debate the challenges brought on by the developments of technology. These have affected the relationship between the music industry and creator, but at the same time have strengthened the virtual connection between the creator and the listener/gazer/consumer.

Having just lived through the turbulence of the first half of 2020, I realized I needed to reexamine and revise this conclusion, because suddenly the world was witnessing and experiencing a global pandemic. This has affected everybody in some way—or, perhaps, in many ways—and this turbulent time of living through history will be discussed for years to come. Needless to say, the pandemic and its consequences have brought yet more new challenges for the music industry and music businesses, but even more so for the creators. Music-streaming culture has become embedded in the digital virtual era, and it is unlikely it will disappear any time soon, due to the easy access it provides to music and other related content. However, the debate about creators receiving fair royalties still continues, particularly now when real-life performances, festivals, and even much-loved music venues are in jeopardy, because of the pandemic. This crisis has resulted in the suspension of real-life music entertainment all over the globe, meaning that artists are needing to seek alternative ways of making an income.[1] While, at the time of editing, some resolutions in alternative live performances are in place, for example, via Zoom, Skype, or Twitch—where live performances can be presented from a musician's bedroom, backyard, or an empty music venue— it looks more likely that virtual performances will begin to compete with real-life performances, and will be presented in innovative and conventional ways. These changes will increase possibilities for everyone to deliver and have access to music.

As already mentioned in the Introduction, there are also other means by which creators can sell music and perform directly to their fans, for example, via blockchain or online music services such as Bandcamp. It will be interesting to observe if, in the "future," music-streaming services (including performing platforms that labels may invest in), or perhaps an as-yet-unknown new format that will replace streams, will offer a financial resolution in which the "real" creators will receive their fair share of royalties. If this debate about royalties is not resolved soon, then the fans/audiences/consumers will need, now more than ever, to support their favorite creators and artists directly, via channels such as social media and crowdfunding.

Returning to the scope of the book, I have endeavored to identify and explore how music has been shaped by virtuality and digital technology, and the impact that this has had on culture, including for all those involved, through both creation and consumption. I have offered an insight into how virtual music and digital technology build relationships with sound, music, and image, in addition to monitoring how the digital virtual era is constantly evolving and pulsating with exciting musical ideas. One theme I kept returning to is the presentation of unimaginable, unthinkable, and unexpected ideas in virtual music. This has been achieved through experimental music, remixing, identity play, interactive music, and virtual performances. The combination of mixing incompatible sounds, fusing genres and styles, teasing the audience with the creator's vision, engaging with the music (rather than just listening to it), and experiencing virtual performances (in real life and simulation) has enabled opportunities for all to explore and appreciate music in various ways.

A sense of dystopia made possible by digital technology has been evident mainly in sound and video games where the consumer can "experience" the unpleasant without actually having to undergo the situation. This particular theme can actually be portrayed with virtual performers (such as Gorillaz, Hatsune Miku, and Miquela), where it appears that they are becoming more prominent than humans. In Chapter 7, I explored how fans or an audience can become too emotionally involved with the virtual performers (especially Hatsune Miku and Miquela), meaning that they might sideline their connection with everyday life, including with other humans. This dependence on technology might be seen as the need to fill a void of some kind, such as loneliness, and this is an aspect of virtuality that needs to be considered and explored.

There are also virtual performances by "resurrected" performers to consider—that is, by deceased performers brought back to life through holograms, such as 2Pac/Tupac Shakur, Whitney Houston, and Michael Jackson. As digital technology continues to develop, it is possible that viewing past performers could become a norm in the future, and it will also give rise to debates between fans, some of whom may cherish the notion of being able to experience their favorite (dead) artist once again, while others may feel unease or heartbreak—and, of course, there may be many legal issues raised by the family members of estates of the deceased, who may not welcome the idea.[2] Similar debates on posthumous albums can be examined, where previously unreleased material of a deceased artist is released for public consumption. While fans may never know if the artist's intentions had been to release the unreleased tracks, as with virtual performances, fans can gain an insight virtually into previously private music recordings.[3] Fans may either relish this new music from their idol, or they may find the experience unearthly, leading back to the concept of hauntology, where the past is inside the present. This concept could also be stretched to virtual collaborations with the dead.[4] Just like the "marmite" episode in experimental music where you might "love it or hate it," the same could be applied to any posthumous music presented as audiovisuals or stand-alone albums, where listeners and viewers could, conversely, see them as being in either good or bad taste. Whatever the fans' feelings about this issue, the stark reality is that the music industry sees this as a money-making opportunity—and this is increasingly true as digital technology exceeds in ever more ways in presenting the unimaginable. A fine example of this is the global launch of Avicii's posthumous album *Tim*, as a VR experience on Oculus.[5]

A less ghoulish way of reviving the past is to rewind music back to its future by embracing its retro and nostalgic signifiers in modern creations. Most of the music we hear today is made up of a plethora of genres and styles, reminding us of the past and evoking a fascination for the origins of the previous sounds (including compositional and sampling techniques). This gives the modern audience a virtual taste of "other" music and allows them to experience its transformative outcome. While the music as discussed in Chapters 4 (remixing) and 5 (video game music) were influenced by earlier genres and styles, it is crucial to remember that creators apply their own knowledge and research in creating this music. This accessing of previous music to inspire them to recreate works is not derivative but a homage to previous eras of music —with many of these modern compositions leading the new audience to interact with musical history.

Interactivity has broken the barriers between creators and their audiences, meaning that there are opportunities to virtually converse, explore, and mix existing recorded sound, allowing the audience to personify their audiovisual experience of the music (e.g., through apps or remixing). Furthermore, creators online (such as Lil Nas X), particularly DIY creators, use social media as direct marketing, to promote their music in the hope that their followers will take over in spreading the word. It is not always the creator/artist (or their label) that initiates promoting the music; it may also be the fans that help to generate interest through the use of social media, or their own platforms, such as blogs, websites, and vlogs. This confirms the importance of the fans and audiences in the music industry and the media, and the significance of their virtual relationship with their favorite artist.

Another development that contributes to the virtual relationship between the artist and fan, is that, where relevant, the fans can now glimpse at their artist's "true" identity, thanks to social media. While, in the past, we were left mystified by artists who successfully concealed their personal identities, many today—including Madonna—are comfortable in presenting their personal image to the public online through social media platforms. This "exposure" of an artist's identity, however, runs the risk of disappointing fans and followers as they can no longer play the guessing game as to what his or her future musical projects may reveal, yet it could delight them, leaving them to crave more insight from the artists, including about their personal lives. Some artists are able to balance their true identity while maintaining their creative vision, and welcome their fans to interact with them in their performances (e.g., The Weeknd), while some have yet to reveal their true identity (e.g., the singer providing the vocals for Miquela). There are, of course, artists who cannot help but continue in confusing the audience with their "real" and virtual identities as demonstrated in a virtual performance with Damon Albarn performing a duet with himself/alter ego/ Gorillaz's 2D over a Zoom conference call—leading fans and audience to continue speculating, conversing, and appraising Gorillaz online, as well as directly sharing their thoughts with the group on social media platforms such as Instagram and TikTok.[6]

As music changes, so does the language around music. While the relationship between the creator, audience, and music—as well as the constant shifts in creating and consumption practices in the digital virtual era—has expanded, there is increasing ambiguity in using the terms "digital" and "virtual." I offered examples on how we can apply these terms, including my own suggestion that in music, the virtual consists of creative thoughts and imagination that can either be transformed or *nearly* transformed into reality and actuality, through digital means. As I explained, in my view the term "creator" (which is arguably ambiguous too) was my preference when referring to the composer, musician, producer, and other creatives. It has become clear that the term "user" is also ambiguous and, perhaps, is a more suitable term to use in the digital virtual era. By this I mean, in true postmodern (or, insert your preferred term here, reader!) form, there is no distinction between the creator and audience/consumer anymore, due to the increasingly innovative ways of using digital technology. Therefore, the term "user" could now represent the creator, musician, producer, recording/ sound engineer, artist, performer, DJ, listener, consumer, audience, gazer, participant, or viewer. As Arjun Appadurai says, "we are all 'users' of tools, apps and devices that define much of our humanity and sociality."[7]

It is impossible to predict how virtual music and digital technology will evolve in the digital virtual era, but it should be exciting to think about what "after the future" music could bring to us in terms of creativity, performance, distribution, consumption, and interactivity. What might not work in our favor is the growing use of AI (artificial intelligence), where computers and machines simulate humans' ways of thinking, with an ability to control and create music (e.g., bots).[8] While this thought could be one (of many) concept(s) in the future, this obviously raises questions and concerns about the future of creators and the industry. I do not think human creators will be disappearing anytime soon, especially as we are obsessed with music's past and its history, and still wanting to embrace it in the present. As we are unintentionally experiencing the past in the present, it delights me when I hear that the younger generation are aware of the Sony Walkman, are collecting records, and can identify retro/nostalgic elements in current music. Other examples of experiencing the past in the present are the comments on YouTube with viewers typing, "[W]ho is still loving this timeless 2008 song in 2019?", not forgetting that even the videos we watch on YouTube (no matter how recent they are) are actually playback, and, therefore, from the past.

As digital technology evolves, music will certainly become more virtual than virtual, while maintaining its origins and the history that made it possible. However we perceive the digital and virtual, or the virtual and digital, in the digital virtual era, we cannot deny it has certainly strengthened our relationship with music. And, if I am finally lured into advocating an interpretation for "virtual" (let's face it, defining the "digital" is straightforward), then I am persuaded by Jaron Lanier's definition that the virtual is a "cross between music and perception."[9]

NOTES

Introduction

1 Finley Quaye, "Broadcast," recorded 2000, on EMI, song.

2 Gorillaz, "Tomorrow Comes Today," recorded 2001, on EMI, song.

3 Arjun Appadurai, *Modernity at Large: Cultural Dimensions of Globalization* (Minneapolis: University of Minnesota Press, 1996).

4 David Harvey, *The Condition of Postmodernity: An Enquiry into the Origins of Cultural Change* (Oxford: Blackwell, 1990).

5 Sheila Whiteley and Shara Rambarran, eds., *The Oxford Handbook of Music and Virtuality* (New York: Oxford University Press, 2016).

6 Jean Baudrillard, *Simulacra and Simulation*, trans. Sheila Glaser (Ann Arbor, MI: University of Michigan Press, 1994), 125.

7 Other P2P sites that encouraged file sharing of not only music but also films, video games, software, and books include KaZaa, Limewire, Gnutella, and Pirate Bay.

8 Record labels included Warner Bros. and Sony. Napster later resurrected itself as a legal streaming music platform.

9 Bill Thompson, "The Rootkit of All Evil?" *BBC News*, November 4, 2005, http://news.bbc.co.uk/go/pr/fr/-/1/hi/technology/4406178.stm.

10 XCP was developed by the UK software company "First 4 Internet."

11 See Chapter 4.

12 Also, the following Acts protect misuse of digital piracy: UK's Digital Economy Act 2017 (http://www.legislation.gov.uk/ukpga/2017/30/contents); EU's Copyright Directive, otherwise known as the Directive (EU) 2019/790 of the European Parliament and of the Council (https://eur-lex.europa.eu/eli/dir/2019/790/oj). Also see Siva Vaidhyanathan, *Copyrights and Copywrongs: The Rise of Intellectual Property and How It Threatens Creativity* (New York: New York University Press, 2003), and Joanna Demers, *Steal This Music: How Intellectual Property Law Affects Musical Creativity* (Athens and London: The University of Georgia Press, 2006).

13 Popular streaming platforms include Spotify, Apple Music, Deezer, and Tidal.

14 Sofia Johansson and Ann Werner, "Music, the Internet, Streaming: Ongoing Debates," in *Streaming Music: Practices, Media, Cultures*, ed. Sofia Johansson, Ann Werner, Patrik Åker, and Greg Goldenzwaig (New York: Routledge,

2018), 12–24; Lee Marshall, "Let's Keep Music Special. F__K Spotify: On-Demand Streaming and Controversy over Artist Royalties," *Creative Industries Journal*, 8 (2015): 177–89; Tim Anderson, *Popular Music in a Digital Music Economy: Problems and Practices for an Emerging Service Industry* (New York: Routledge, 2014); Patrik Wikstrom and Robert DeFilippi, eds., *Business Innovation and Disruption in the Music Industry* (Cheltenham: Elgar, 2016); David Arditi, *iTake-Over: The Recording Industry in the Digital Era* (London: Rowman and Littlefield, 2017).

15 Musicians such as David Byrne, Taylor Swift, and Thom Yorke of Radiohead. Musicians are finding alternative ways of making royalties with blockchain such as UJO and Mycelia. The aim with blockchain is for musicians to receive fair royalties for their services and music streams and to make sure that all creators involved in the music are paid. There is also Bandcamp to consider (founded by Ethan Diamond in 2008). Creators (artists/groups) can sell music and merchandise directly to fans and interact with them. The creators keep 80–85 percent of royalties and the remainder covers Bandcamp's processing fees and revenue share (https://bandcamp.com/about).

16 The major labels are Sony Music, Warner Music Group, and Universal Music Group.

17 Rowan Oliver, "Bring the Beat Back: Sampling as Virtual Collaboration," in *The Oxford Handbook of Music and Virtuality*, 65–80.

18 Paul Draper and Frank Millard, "Music in Perpetual Beta: Composition, Remediation, and 'Closure,'" in *The Oxford Handbook of Music and Virtuality*, 248–65; Paul Théberge, "The Network Studio: Historical and Technological Paths to a New Ideal in Music Making," *Social Studies of Science*, 34, no.5 (October 2004): 760.

19 Jason Stanyek and Benjamin Piekut, "'Deadness': Technologies of the Intermundane," *TDR: The Drama Review*, 54, no. 1 (Spring 2010): 35.

20 Ruth Finnegan, *The Hidden Musicians: Music-Making in an English Town* (Cambridge: Cambridge University Press, 1989); William Duckworth, *Virtual Music: How the Web Got Wired for Sound* (New York: Routledge, 2005).

21 Christopher Small, *Musicking: The Meanings of Performing and Listening* (Middletown, CT: Wesleyan University Press, 1998), 12.

22 Mihaly Csikszentmihalyi, *Flow: The Psychology of Optimal Experience* (New York: Harper-Perennial, 1990); Mihaly Csikszentmihalyi, *Finding Flow: The Psychology of Engagement with Everyday Life* (New York: Basic Books, 1997).

23 Derek B. Scott "(What's the Copy?): The Beatles and Oasis," Beatlestudies 3: Proceedings of the Beatles 2000 Conference (University of Jyväasklä, Finland), 201–11.

24 Mark Grimshaw, ed., *The Oxford Handbook of Virtuality* (New York: Oxford University Press, 2013), 2.

25 The combination of the two terms "digital virtual" is rare but it has been scholarly applied before, see Rob Shields, *The Virtual* (New York: Routledge,

2003); Mike Molesworth and Janice Denegri-Knott, eds., *Digital Virtual Consumption* (New York: Routledge, 2012).

26 Andrea Hunter and Vincent Mosco, "Virtual Dystopia," in *The Oxford Handbook of Virtuality*, ed. Mark Grimshaw (New York: Oxford University Press, 2013), 727.

27 The inspiration in presenting such themes in virtuality usually derives from dystopian fiction, such as the works of William Gibson's *Neuromancer* (1984). For further information, see Hunter and Vincent Mosco's "Virtual Dystopia."

28 Whiteley and Rambarran, *The Oxford Handbook of Music and Virtuality*.

29 An app (short for application) is a software mainly used in portable devices such as smartphones and tablets (e.g., iPhone and iPad).

30 Crowdfunding platforms include Kickstarter, Patreon, and Indiegogo.

Chapter 1

1 Paul Théberge, "'Plugged In': Technology and Popular Music," in *Cambridge Companion to Pop and Rock,* ed. Simon Frith, Will Straw and John Street (Cambridge: Cambridge University Press, 2001), 3.

2 Théberge, "'Plugged In': Technology and Popular Music," 3.

3 David Tough, "Virtual Bands: Recording Music Under the Big Top," in *The Oxford Handbook of Music and Virtuality*, 307.

4 Mark Katz, *Capturing Sound: How Technology Has Changed Music* (Berkeley, CA: University of California Press, 2004), 4.

5 Antoine Hennion, *The Passion for Music: A Sociology of Mediation*, trans. Margaret Rigaud and Peter Collier (Farnham: Ashgate, 2015), 284.

6 Simon Frith, "The Popular Music Industry," in *Cambridge Companion to Pop and Rock*; Paul Théberge, *Any Sound You Can Imagine: Making Music/ Consuming Technology* (Hanover: Wesleyan University Press, 1997); Katz, *Capturing Sound*, 26–52.

7 Richard James Burgess, *The History of Music Production* (New York: Oxford University Press, 2014), 3.

8 Ibid., 3–4. For a more detailed history, read the works of Richard James Burgess and Jonathan Sterne's *The Audible Past: Cultural Origins of Sound Production* (Durham, NC: Duke University, 2003).

9 Christopher Cox and Daniel Warner, eds., *Audio Culture: Readings in Modern Music* (London: Continuum, 2004).

10 "History of Recorded Music Timeline," EMI, accessed May 8, 2018, https://www.www.emiarchivetrust.org/about/history-of-recording/.

11 Kieran Downes, "'Perfect Sound Forever': Innovation, Aesthetics, and the Remaking of Compact Disc Playback,'" *Technology and Culture* 51, no. 2 (April 2010): 313.

12 Burgess, *The History of Music Production*, 10.

13 "Alan Blumlein and the Invention of Stereo," EMI, accessed May 8, 2018, https://www.www.emiarchivetrust.org//alan-blumlein-and-the-invention-o f-stereo/

14 Jonathan Schroeder and Janet Borgerson, "How Stereo Was First Sold to a Sceptical Public," *The Conversation*, December 12, 2018, http://theconversati on.com/how-stereo-was-first-sold-to-a-skeptical-public-103668.

15 Evan Eisenberg, *The Recording Angel* (New Haven and London: Yale University Press, 2005), 53.

16 The speed was achieved using a 3,600 rpm motor and 46 tooth gear, generating 78.26 rpm in the United States on a mains frequency of 60 HZ. The main frequency in Britain was lower at 50 HZ, therefore the speed was set at 77.92 rpm—however, it was still marketed as a 78 rpm disc. See Richard Osborne, *Vinyl: Analogue Record* (Ashgate: Farnham, 2012), 18; Gordon Mumma, Howard Rye, Bernard Kernfield, and Chris Sheridan, "Recording," *Grove Music Online*, 2003, https://doi.org/10.1093/gmo/97 81561592630.article.J371600.

17 Richard A. Peterson, "Why 1955? Explaining the Advent of Rock Music," *Popular Music 9*, no. 1 (January 1990): 100–1.

18 Sean Wilentz, "The Birth of 33 1/3: How Columbia Records Won the Battle of the Speeds," *Slate*, November 2, 2012, http://www.slate.com/articles/arts/ books/2012/11/birth_of_the_long_playing_record_plus_rare_photos_from_t he_heyday_of_columbia.html.

19 See Will Straw, "Dance Music," in *Cambridge Companion to Pop and Rock*, 158–75.

20 Examples of creators who experimented with *turntables* can actually be traced back to Sefan Wolfe, Darius Milhaud, John Cage, and Pierre Schaeffer (see Chapter 3).

21 Technics SL—1200 turntable was the desired and esteemed staple for DJs, see www.technics.com.

22 Thomas A. Edison, "The Phonograph and Its Future," *North American Review*, 126/262 (May–June, 1878): 530 cited in Osborne, *Vinyl: Analogue Record*, 32.

23 See Cox and Warner, *Audio Culture: Readings in Modern Music*, 400; Burgess, *The History of Music Production*, 45.

24 "Sound on Sound," Les Paul Foundation, accessed May 8, 2018, http://www .les-paul.com/timeline/sound-on-sound/.

25 Musicians who experimented with analogue sampling include the Beatles. Furthermore, analogue sampling can be traced to dub (reggae), in particular the "version." Also known as cover versions, instrumental reggae songs along with all their musical parts are modified and remixed while maintaining the feel of the original tracks.

26 David Traub, "Art and Telecommunications Glossary," *Leonardo*, 24, no. 2 (1991): 254.

It should be noted that Casio launched the first DAT recorder "DA-7" in 1992, see "Recording and Sound History: Playback and Recording Equipment," British Library, accessed May 10, 2018, https://sounds.bl.uk/Sound-recording-history/Equipment/029M-UNCAT01XXXXX-0002V0.

27 Bob MacNevin, "DAT as Storage Medium," *Computer Music Journal*, 20, no. 4 (Winter 1996): 5.

28 Elizabeth Corcoran, "Have You Heard DAT?" *Scientific American*, 258, no. 5 (May 1988): 30; Dave Laing, "Record Sales in the 1980s," *Popular Music*, 9, no. 2 (April 1990): 236; Jim Horner, "The Case of DAT Technology: Industrial Versus Pecuniary Function," *Journal of Economic Issues*, 25, no. 2 (June 1991): 450.

29 For further insight on the recording history, see Michael Chanan, *Repeated Takes: A Short History of Recording and Its Effects on Music* (London and New York: Verso, 1997); Greg Milner, *Perfecting Sound Forever: The Story of Recorded Music* (London: Granta, 2009); Albin J. Zak, *The Poetics of Rock: Cutting Tracks, Making Records* (Berkeley, CA: University of California Press, 2001).

30 Keith Negus, *Producing Pop: Culture and Conflict in the Popular Music Industry* (London: Edward Arnold 1992), 25.

31 Jude Rogers, "Total Rewind: 10 Key Moments in the Life of the Cassette," *The Guardian*, August 30, 2013, https://www.theguardian.com/music/2013/aug/30/cassette-store-day-music-tapes.

32 For digital back copies, visit http://doctechnical.com/sfx/.

33 Andrew Blake, *Popular Music: The Age of the Multimedia* (London: Middlesex University Press, 2007), 28.

34 Meaghan Haire, "A Brief History of The Walkman," *Time*, July 1, 2009, http://content.time.com/time/nation/article/0,8599,1907884,00.html.

35 Quoted in Haire, "A Brief History of the Walkman."

36 Robert Grayson, *Sony: The Company and Its Founders* (Minnesota: ABDO Publishing Company, 2013), 9.

37 Michael Bull, *Sound Moves: iPod Culture and Urban Experience* (London: Routledge, 2007); Jean-Paul Thibaud, "The Sound Composition of the City," in *The Auditory Culture Reader*, ed. Michael Bull and Les Back (New York: Berg, 2003), 329–42; Raphaël Nowak and Andrew Whelan, *Networked Music Cultures: Contemporary Approaches, Emerging Issues* (Palgrave Macmillan, Hampshire and New York, 2016).

38 Paul du Gay, Stuart Hall, Linda Jones, High Mackay, and Keith Negus, *Doing Cultural Studies: The Story of the Sony Walkman* (London: Sage, 1997), 10.

39 Paul Théberge, *Any Sound You Can Imagine*.

40 Thomas W. Patterson, "Player Piano," *Oxford Handbooks Online*, November 2014, https://doi.org/10.1093/oxfordhb/9780199935321.013.16.

41 Arthur W. J. G Ord-Hume, "Player Piano," *Grove Music Online*, November 2001, https://doi.org/10.1093/gmo/9781561592630.article.21928.

42 Mumma, Rye, Kernfield, and Sheridan, "Recording."

43 Stuart Jeffries, "Music on a Roll," *The Guardian*, March 28, 2003, https://ww
w.theguardian.com/music/2003/mar/28/classicalmusicandopera.artsfeatures.

44 Lisa Gitelman, "Media, Materiality, and the Measure of the Digital, Or,
the Case of Sheet Music and the Problem of Piano Rolls," in *Memory
Bytes: History, Technology, and Digital Culture*, ed. Lauren Rabinovitz and
Abraham Geil (Durham, NC: Duke University Press, 2004), 212.

45 The keyboard, as music technology, has a very interesting history of its own as it
has been transformed in various ways ranging from electric pianos to machines
(synthesizers), and from samplers to virtual instruments (e.g., apps). For a quick
guide, visit: https://sound-unsound.com/who-invented-the-keyboard-piano/.

46 Edmond T. Johnson, "Theremin," in *Grove Music Online*, January 2014,
Oxford University Press, http://www.oxfordmusiconline.com/subscriber/articl
e/grove/musi c/A2257364.

47 For more details, visit www.moogmusic.com.

48 Andrew Blake, *The Music Business* (London: B.T. Batsford, 1992), 54.

49 Downes, "'Perfect Sound Forever': Innovation, Aesthetics, and the Re-making
of Compact Disc Playback," 313.

50 Mark Katz, "The Amateur in the Age of Mechanical Music," in *The Oxford
Handbook of Sound Studies,* ed. Trevor Pinch and Karin Bijsterveld (New York:
Oxford University Press, 2014), 459–79; Shara Rambarran, "'DJ Hit That
Button': Amateur Laptop Musicians in Contemporary Music and Society," in
The Oxford Handbook of Music Making and Leisure, ed. Roger Mantie and
Gareth Dylan Smith (New York: Oxford University Press, 2017), 585–600.

51 The first nondigital drum machine was developed in the 1930s, for example,
Leon Theremin's Rhythmicon.

52 TB stands for Transistor Bass and it was used by musicians such as the
famous jazz pianist Oscar Peterson.

53 Phuture consisted of the late Earl "Spanky" Smith Jr., Nathaniel "DJ Pierre"
Jones, and Herbert "Herb J" Jackson. The group helped to develop acid
house music. The TB-303 was a major feature in acid house.

54 DJ Pierre in Idris Elba's *How Clubbing Changed the World*, produced by Sam
Bridger, aired August 24, 2012, on Channel 4.

55 Thérberge, "'Plugged In': Technology and Popular Music," 17.

56 VST (Cubase) created by Steinberg in 1996.

57 Paul White, *Basic Sampling* (London: Sanctuary Publishing, 2003), 36.

58 Mitch Gallagher, "Insider's View of the Modern SAW," *Sweetwater Music
Instruments and Pro Audio*, 2008, http://www.sweetwater.com/featyre/daw/
daw_defined.php.

59 Nelson George, "Sample This," in *That's the Joint! The Hip-Hop Studies
Reader*, ed. Murray Forman and Mark Anthony Neal (New York and
Oxford: Routledge, 2004), 437–41.

60 George, "Sample This," 439. Also, other types of digital samplers integrated
in synthesizers included the Synclavier.

61 Quoted in Kodwo Eshun, *More Brilliant Than the Sun: Adventures in Sonic Fiction* (London: Quartet Books, 1998), 20.

62 George, "Sample This," 439.

63 Andrew Hugill, *The Digital Musician* (New York: Routledge, 2012), 144.

64 Nick Prior, *Popular Music, Digital Technology and Society* (London: Sage, 2018), 80.

65 Benjamin O'Brien, "Sample Sharing: Virtual Laptop Ensemble Communities," in *The Oxford Handbook of Music and Virtuality*.

66 Paul Théberge, "The Network Studio: Historical and Technological Paths to a New Ideal in Music Making," 760.

67 Rambarran, "'DJ Hit That Button': Amateur Laptop Musicians in Contemporary Music and Society"; Adam Patrick Bell, "D.I.Y. Recreational Recording as Music Making," in *The Oxford Handbook of Music Making and Leisure*.

68 Berlin city, for example, is known for being a music technology city housing software and music companies such as Ableton, Beatport, Spotify, Native Instruments, FATdrop, and so forth. For more information see, Paul Hanford, "Berlin's Love for Techno Has Turned It into a Music Setup Powerhouse," *Wired*, December 12, 2019, https://www.wired.co.uk/article/berlin-music-tech.

69 Such as the Yamaha Tenori-On, which was released in 2007 and has since been discontinued. Who knows, it may become popular one day (it should be popular).

70 For more details, visit http://jonathansparks.com/nomis/.

71 For more information on the Optron, visit http://www.myoptron.com/.

72 The lights also help the user to locate the notes/sounds on the keyboard.

73 For more information on the Du-Touch, visit https://dualo.org/en/.

74 For more information, visit https://skoogmusic.com/.

75 For more information on MI.MU gloves, see https://mimugloves.com/.

76 Hugh G. J. Aitken, *The Origins of Radio* (Princeton: Princeton University Press, 1985), 209; Priya Satia, "War, Wireless, and Empire: Marconi and the British Warfare State, 1896-1903," *Technology and Culture*, 51, no. 4 (October 2010): 829.

77 "Radio," BBC, accessed May 12, 2018, https://www.bbc.co.uk/bitesize/guides/z2s97hv/revision/1.

78 Frith, "The Popular Music Industry," 40.

79 Ibid., 41.

80 Peter M. Thall, *What They'll Never Tell You About the Music Business: The Myths, the Secrets, the Lies (and a Few Truths)* (New York: Billboard Books, 2006), 229.

81 Paul Cesarini, "I Am a DJ, I Am What I Say: The Rise of Podcasting," in *Small Tech: The Culture of Digital Tools*, ed. Bryon Hawk, David M Rieder, and Ollie Oviedo (Minnesota: University of Minnesota Press, 2008), 9.

82 Ben Hammersley, "Audible Revolution," *The Guardian*, February 12, 2004, https://www.theguardian.com/media/2004/feb/12/broadcasting.digitalmedia.

83 Kris M. Markman, "Everything Old Is New Again: Podcasting as Radio's Revival," *Journal of Radio and Audio Media* 22, no. 2 (2015): 241.

84 Théberge, "'Plugged In': Technology and Popular Music," 18. On a sidenote, the first ever music CD album to be pressed was ABBA's *The Visitors* in 1982.

85 IFPI, *Recording Industry in Numbers 2008, the Definitive Source of Global Music Market Information* (United Kingdom: IFPI, 2008); Ethan Smith, "Music Sales Decline for Seventh Time in Eight Years: Digital Downloads Can't Offset 20% in CD Sales," *Wall Street Journal*, January 2, 2009, https://www.wsj.com/articles/SB123075988836646491.

86 The most sold CD of all time is The Eagles' 1976 album *Greatest Hits,* which sold over thirty-six million copies (Travis Clark and John Lynch, "The 50 Best Selling Albums of All Time," *Business Insider*, April 23, 2019, https://www.businessinsider.com/50-best-selling-albums-all-time-2016-9?r=US&IR=T.)

87 Zeke Graves, "When MiniDiscs Recorded the Earth," *Duke University*, April 7, 2015, https://blogs.library.duke.edu/bitstreams/2015/04/07/when-minidiscs-recorded-the-earth/.

88 Joey Faulkner, "MiniDisc, the Forgotten Format," *The Guardian*, September 28, 2012, https://www.theguardian.com/music/musicblog/2012/sep/24/sony-minidisc-20-years.

89 Katz, *Capturing Sound*, 160.

90 John S. W. MacDonald, "Suzanne Vega Is the 'Mother of the MP3,'" *The Observer*, September 25, 2008, https://observer.com/2008/09/suzanne-vega-is-the-mother-of-the-mp3/. It should also be noted that the first song to be posted online (but not as an MP3) was by Aerosmith on CompuServe as a Windows WAV format, and it would take thirty minutes to download (Peter Fabris, "Funky Music: This Year, Music Fans Don't Have to Go to a Record Store to Buy a CD. Next Year, They Won't Have to Buy a CD," *CIO WebBusiness*, December 1, 1997, 76).

91 Brett Atwood, "David Bowie Single Exclusive to Internet," *Billboard*, September 21, 1996, 58.

92 Brett Atwood, "The History of the Music Industry's First-Ever Digital Single for Sale, 20 Years After Its Release," *Billboard*, September 9, 2017, https://www.billboard.com/articles/business/7964771/history-music-industry-first-ever-digital-single-20-years-later.

93 Blake, *Popular Music: The Age of the Multimedia,* 39.

94 Leander Kahney, "Inside Look at the Birth of the iPod," *Wired*, July 21, 2004, https://www.wired.com/2004/07/inside-look-at-birth-of-the-ipod/.

95 Bull, *Sound Moves: iPod Culture and Urban Experience.*

96 iTunes library has been replaced by the Apple Music App and streaming service. See Alex Fitzpatrick, "Apple Is Pulling the Plug on iTunes. So What

Happens to All Your Music?" *Time*, June 4, 2019, https://time.com/5600502/apple-itunes-app-music/.

97 Founded by Daniel Ek and Martin Lorentzon in 2006.

98 Robert Prey, "Nothing Personal: Algorithmic Individuation on Music Streaming Platforms," *Media, Culture and Society* 40, no. 7 (2018): 1086–100.

99 Spotify offers a download feature but the music will be removed once the subscription ends.

100 Patrik Wikstrom, *The Music Industry: Music in the Cloud* (Cambridge: Polity Press, 2009).

101 Simon Frith, "Towards an Aesthetic of Popular Music," in *Music and Society: The Politics of Composition, Performance and Reception*, ed. Richard Leppert and Susan McClary (Cambridge: Cambridge University Press, 1987), 139.

102 Priya Ganapati, "Dec. 23, 1947: Transistor Opens Door to Digital Future," *Wired*, December 23, 2009, https://www.wired.com/2009/12/1223shockley-bardeen-brattain-transistor/.

103 Merrill Farby, "The Story Behind America's First Commercial Computer," *Time*, March 31, 2016, https://time.com/4271506/census-bureau-computer-history/.

104 Anon, "8-Foot 'Genius' Dedicated; UNIVAC Will Go to Work on Census Bureau's Data," *New York Times*, June 15, 1951, https://www.nytimes.com/1951/06/15/archives/8foot-genius-dedicated-univac-will-go-to-work-on-census-bureaus.html.

105 Helen Brockwell, "Forgotten Genius: The Man Who Made a Working VR Machine in 1957," *Techradar*, April 3, 2016, https://www.techradar.com/uk/news/wearables/forgotten-genius-the-man-who-made-a-working-vr-machine-in-1957-1318253.

106 Sutherland (1963) in Ken Hillis, "A Geography of the Eye: The Technologies of Virtual Reality," in *Culture of the Internet: Virtual Spaces, Real History, Living Bodies*, ed. Rob Shields (Sage: London, 1996), 80.

107 A. Michael Noll, *Principles of Modern Communications Technology* (Boston and London: Artech House, 2001), 223.

108 Tom Sito, *Moving Innovation: A History of Computer Animation* (Cambridge, MA: The MIT Press, 2013), 58.

109 Cade Metz, "Larry Roberts Calls Himself the Founder of the Internet. Who Are You to Argue," *Wired*, September 24, 2012, https://www.wired.com/2012/09/larry-roberts/.

110 Sarah Left, "Technology: Email Timeline," *The Guardian*, March 13, 2002, https://www.theguardian.com/technology/2002/mar/13/internetnews. Interesting fact: Queen Elizabeth II was an ARPANET user and was the first head of state to send an email in 1976. Also, Hotmail was one of the first companies to offer free email services in 1996.

111 Anon, "Console Portraits: A 40-Year Pictorial History of Gaming," *Wired*, June 15, 2007, https://www.wired.com/2007/06/gallery-game-history/.

112   "2011 National Film Registry—More Than a Box of Chocolates," Library of Congress, accessed May 21, 2018, https://www.loc.gov/item/prn-11-240/

113   Catmull later co-founded Pixar Animation Studios—responsible for computer-generated films such as *Toy Story* and *The Incredibles*.

114   Sito, *Moving Innovation: A History of Computer Animation*, 205. Interesting fact: Gary Demos and John Whitney Jr., owners of *Digital Productions*, were also known for creating CG effects in *The Last Starfighter* (1984) and *Labyrinth* (1986).

115   Paul Atkinson, "Man in a Briefcase: The Social Construction of the Laptop Computer and the Emergence of a Type Form," *Journal of Design History*, 18, no. 2 (2005): 8.

116   Richard Trenholm, "Britain's First Mobile-Phone Call Was Made 30 Years Ago," *CNET*, December 27, 2014, https://www.cnet.com/news/britains-first-mobile-phone-call-was-made-30-years-ago/.

117   "A Short History of the Web," CERN, accessed May 22, 2018, https://home.cern/science/computing/birth-web/short-history-web.

118   Rosie Murray-West, "From 1876 to Today: How the UK Got Connected," *The Telegraph*, October 28, 2016, https://www.telegraph.co.uk/technology/connecting-britain/timeline-how-uk-got-connected.

119   Doug Aamoth, "First Smartphone Turns 20: Fun Facts About Simon," *Time*, August 18, 2014, https://time.com/3137005/first-smartphone-ibm-simon/.

120   danah m. boyd and Nicole B. Ellison, "Social Network Sites: Definition, History, and Scholarship," *Journal of Computer-Mediated Communication*, 13 (2008): 214.

121   Julia Kollewe, "Google Timeline: A 10 Year Anniversary," *The Guardian*, September 5, 2008, https://www.theguardian.com/business/2008/sep/05/google.google.

122   "The History of the Bluetooth SIG," Bluetooth, accessed May 22, 2018, https://www.bluetooth.com/about-us/our-history/. It should be added that Bluetooth can be found in various digital media devices such as smartphones, iPads, Fitbit/Applewatch, car radio, etc. Interestingly, the origin of the name is based on a tenth-century Danish Viking, King Harald Blåtand (the surname translates to Bluetooth).

123   Kate Youde, "Broadband: The First Decade," *The Independent*, March 28, 2010, https://www.independent.co.uk/life-style/gadgets-and-tech/news/broadband-the-first-decade-1929515.html. The initial speed in 2000 was around 512 kilobits per second. Today, we can expect up to 1 gigabit (1000Mbps).

124   Skype was designed by Niklas Zennstrom of Sweden and Janus Friis of Denmark. Skype was bought by Microsoft in 2011. Doug Aamoth, "A Brief History of Skype," *Time*, May 10, 2011, https://techland.time.com/2011/05/10/a-brief-history-of-skype/.

125   Jennifer Stromer-Galley and Rosa Mikeal Martey, "Visual Spaces, Norm Governed Places: The Influence of Spatial Context Online," *New Media and Society*, 11, no. 6 (2009): 1051.

126 Don E. Descy, "All Aboard the Internet: Second Life," *Tech Trends* 52, no. 1 (2008): 5; *Wonderland*, "Virtual Adultery and Cyberspace Love" produced by Fergus O'Brien, aired January 30, 2008, on BBC Two; "What Is Second Life?," Second Life, accessed March 16, 2018, http://secondlife.com/whatis/?lang=en-US.

127 For further reading on music in Second Life, see Justin Gagen and Nicholas Cook's "Performing Live in Second Life," in *The Oxford Handbook of Music and Virtuality*. Another famous example of a virtual world game is World of Warcraft.

128 YouTube was created by Steve Chen, Chad Hurley, and Jawed Karim. The company was bought by Google in 2006. Tony Long, "YouTube and Your 15 Minutes of Fame," *Wired*, February 15, 2011, https://www.wired.com/2011/02/0215youtube-launched/.

129 In 2014, the music video "Gangnam Style" by South Korean artist, Psy, exceeded YouTube's view limit, therefore the site had to upgrade its counter. See BBC, "Gangnam Style Music Video 'Broke' YouTube View Limit," BBC News, December 4, 2014, https://www.bbc.co.uk/news/world-asia-30288542.

130 Bobbie Johnson and Lee Glendinning, "Apple Proclaims Its Revolution: A Camera, an iPod . . . oh, and a Phone," *The Guardian*, January 10, 2007, https://www.theguardian.com/technology/2007/jan/10/news.business.

131 The iPhone was designed by Jonathan Ive.

132 Steve Jobs cited in Rory Cellan-Jones, "Apple Unveils Apple iPad Tablet Device," January 27, 2010, http://news.bbc.co.uk/1/hi/technology/8483654.stm.

133 Erik Gregerson, "Bitcoin," *Britannica*, ND, https://www.britannica.com/topic/Bitcoin. Bitcoin was not the first digital currency.

134 VR, AR, and MR were gradual developments and experiments over the last fifty years and it's only now that it has really taken effect in the digital era.

135 German Lopez, "Pokémon Go, Explained," Vox, August 5, 2016, https://www.vox.com/2016/7/11/12129162/pokemon-go-android-ios-game.

136 Another example would be Bastille's concert at Birmingham New Street railway station—the first to be streamed in AR on a 5G network in 2019 (it was also used to promote an EE advert).

137 An example of MR technology is Microsoft HaloLens. This expensive device (starting price, $3500/£2500) consists of a sensory headset in which users can view their actual environment ("real world") combined with interactive digital virtual (holographic) objects. For further information, visit https://www.microsoft.com/en-us/hololens.

Chapter 2

1 Umberto Eco, *Turning Back the Clock*, trans. Alastair McEwen (London: Harvill Secker, 2007), 105.

2 Martin Heidegger, *The Question Concerning Technology and Other Essays*, trans. William Lovitt (New York and London: Garland Publishing Inc., 1977), 12.

3 Walter Benjamin, *The Work of Art in the Age of Mechanical Reproduction* (London: Penguin Books, 2008), 7.

4 Ibid., 6.

5 The term "intertexuality" was coined by Julia Kristeva and as a translation of Bakhtin's "dialogic" in 1969. See Anthony McGowan, "Names and Terms," in *The Routledge Companion to Postmodernism*, ed. Stuart Sim (London: Routledge, 2005), 244–5.

6 Serge Lacasse, "Intertextuality and Hypertextuality in Recorded Popular Music," in *The Musical Work: Reality or Invention?*, ed. Michael Talbot (Liverpool: University of Liverpool, 2000), 57; Derek B. Scott, *The Ashgate Research Companion to Popular Musicology* (Hampshire: Ashgate 2009), 10; Rambarran, "Innovations in Contemporary Popular Music and Digital Media, and Reconstructions of the Music Industry in the 21st Century" (PhD diss., University of Salford).

7 Nicolas Bourriaud, *Postproduction* (Berlin and New York: Sternberg, 2002).

8 Ibid., 19.

9 *Merriam-Webster.com Dictionary*, s.v. "virtual," accessed July 9, 2020, https://www.merriam-webster.com/dictionary/virtual.

10 Charles S. Peirce, "Virtual," *Dictionary of Philosophy and Psychology*, ed. James Mark Baldwin (New York: Macmillan, 1902), 763.

11 Shields, *The Virtual*, 2.

12 Ibid., 6.

13 Sean Griffiths, "Names and Terms," in *The Routledge Companion to Postmodernism*, ed. Stuart Sim (London: Routledge, 2005), 321.

14 Ken Jordan and Paul D. Miller, "Freeze Frame: Audio, Aesthetics, Sampling and Contemporary Media," in *Sound Unbound: Sampling Digital Music and Culture*, ed. Paul D. Miller (Cambridge, MA and London: MIT Press), 99.

15 Antonin Artaud, *The Theatre and Its Double*, trans. Mary Caroline Richards (New York: Grove Press, 1958), 49.

16 Jaron Lanier in Adam Heilbrun, "An Interview with Jaron Lanier," *Whole World Review*, 64 (1989): 110.

17 Brian Massumi, *Parables for the Virtual: Movement, Affect, Sensation* (Durham and London: Duke University Press, 2002), 21.

18 Marshall McLuhan, *Understanding the Media: The Extensions of Man* (New York: McGraw Hill Education, 1964). It should be noted that McCluhan was also referring to "electric" media that was evolving at the time, for example, television.

19 Shields, *The Virtual*, 47.

20 Paul Virilio, "Cyberwar, God and Television: Interview with Paul Virilio," interview by Louise Wilson, *CTHEORY*, December 1, 1994, transcript, http://www.ctheory.net.

21 Jean-François Lyotard, 1984. *The Postmodern Condition: A Report on Knowledge,* trans. Geoff Bennington and Brian Massumi (Manchester: Manchester University Press, 1986).

22 Jean Baudrillard. *Symbolic Exchange and Death*, trans. Iain Hamilton Grant (London: Sage Publications, 1993), 51.

23 This concept has been covered a few times; see Mark Poster, *The Mode of Information: Poststructuralism and Social Context* (Chicago: University of Chicago, 1990) and Simon Frith, *Performing Rites: Evaluating Popular Music* (Oxford and New York: Oxford University Press, 1996); Rambarran, "'DJ Hit That Button': Amateur Laptop Musicians in Contemporary Music and Society."

24 Umberto Eco, *Faith in Flakes* (London: Vintage, 1998), 40.

25 Jean Baudrillard, *America* (London: Verso, 1988), 127.

26 For an audiovisual interpretation of this concept, see the music video, The Weeknd's "Blinding Lights" (2019). Here, the video exposes The Weeknd to the hyperreal city of Las Vegas, where he is joyfully absorbing the bright lights, attractive buildings, and cityscape. He indulges in his short-lived luxurious lifestyle by joyriding in a stolen Mercedes-AMG GT Roadster, as well as visiting a casino, and seducing an attractive woman. The Weeknd's hyperreal (and delusional) experience suddenly vanishes, and is brought back to reality, when he gets beaten up by security guards, and ends up hitchhiking on the freeway (the story continues in the video's sequel, "Heartless," 2020). Also consider Manic Street Preacher's "Motorcycle Emptiness" (1992) and A$AP Rocky's "L$D (Love, $ex, Dreams)" (2015), even though both videos are set in Japan (specifically Tokyo and Yokohama).

27 Alternative terms include "post-postmodernism," "hypermodernism," "ultramodernism," "supermodernism," "altermodernism," "digimodernism," and "metamodernism." See Daniel O'Gorman and Robert Eaglestone, eds., *The Routledge Companion to Twenty-First Century Literary Fiction* (Oxon: Routledge, 2019).

28 Rambarran, "Innovations in Contemporary Popular Music and Digital Media, and Reconstructions of the Music Industry in the 21st Century," 33.

29 Walter Truett Anderson, ed., *The Truth About the Truth: De-fusing and Re-constructing the Postmodern World* (New York: Penguin, 1995), 7.

30 Dominic Strinati, *An Introduction to the Theories of Popular Culture* (London and New York: Routledge, 2004), 208.

31 Jacques Derrida, *Specters of Marx: The State of the Debt, the Work of Mourning and the New International,* trans. Peggy Kamuf (New York and London: Routledge, 1994), 202.

32 Colin Davis, "Ét at Présent: Hauntology, Specters and Phantoms," *French Studies* LIX, no. 3 (July 2005): 373.

33 Mark Fisher, "What Is Hauntology?" *Film Quarterly* 66, no. 1 (Fall 2012): 16.

34 Ibid.

35 Simon Reynolds, *Retromania: Pop Culture's Addiction to Its Own Past* (London: Faber and Faber, 2011).

36 Brian Latour, *Reassembling the Social: An Introduction to Actor Network Theory* (Oxford: Oxford University Press, 2005), 46.

37 Simon Zagorski-Thomas, *The Musicology of Record Production* (Cambridge: Cambridge University Press, 2014), 92.

Chapter 3

1 See Franco Fabbri's "How Genres Are Born, Change, Die: Conventions, Communities and Diachronic Processes," in *Critical Musicological Reflections*, ed. Stan Hawkins (Aldershot: Ashgate, 2012), 179–91; Simon Frith's *Performing Rites: Evaluating Popular Music*.

2 It should be mentioned here that a major feature that connects the mentioned genres/styles is the use of sound effects, where the audio signals are manipulated. In this chapter the following will be mentioned: Fuzz (a type of distortion where harmonics control the signal almost creating a buzzing sound); Distortion (the alteration of a signal resulting in a harsher and rougher sound); Flanger (a signal manipulated with delay and feedback producing a sweeping sound); Delay (not to be confused with echo, it is a signal that is delayed before it is released and the sound is repeated); Reverse Delay (same as delay but the sound is played backward); Echo (a repeated sound but which diminishes in volume); Phaser (where a signal divides into two, and time shifts fostering a swirling effect and a hint of an electronic sound regardless of the type of instrument used); Reverb (short for reverberation where the signal's echo reflects back from acoustics and surrounding sources, which recreates the ambience of a set space, e.g., a concert hall); Spring Reverb (creates the illusion of reverberation by feeding the signal through springs creating a distinctive metallic echo effect); and Thunderclap (a crash of thunder sounds).

3 Jennie Gottschalk, *Experimental Music Since 1970* (New York and London: Bloomsbury, 2016), 1.

4 Christoph Cox and Daniel Warner, *Audio Culture: Readings in Modern Music*. Rev. ed. (New York and London: Bloomsbury, 2017), 607.

5 Brian Eno, *Music for Airports/Ambient 1*, inner sleeve, 1978, Ambient Label (AMB001) PVC 7908.

6 Marmite is a British savory spread made of yeast and vegetable extracts. The product is known for its famous slogan "love it or hate it" because of its very distinctive salty flavor.

7 David Nicholls, *John Cage* (Illinois: University of Illinois, 2007); David Grubbs, *Records Ruin the Landscape: John Cage, the Sixties, Sound Recording* (Durham, NC: Duke University Press, 2014).

8 Cox and Warner, ed. *Audio Culture: Readings in Modern Music*, 610.

9   Brian Kane, *Pierre Schaeffer, Sound Unseen: Acousmatic Sound in Theory and Practice* (New York: Oxford University Press, 2014), 28.

10 Pierre Schaeffer, *In Search of a Concrete Music*, trans. Christine North and John Dack (Berkeley: University of California Press, 2012), 47.

11 Simon Emmerson, *Live Electronic Music* (Oxon: Routledge), 75.

12 Pierre Schaffer, *La Musique Concrète* (Paris: Presses Universitaires de France), 22.

13 I based this concept on David Nicholl's convincing take on the "virtual opera." David Nicholls, "Virtual Opera or Opera between the Ears," *Journal of the Royal Musical Association*, 129, no. 1 (2004): 105.

14 Choreographed by Maurice Béjart. The ballet consisted of eleven movements.

15 Based on twelve movements.

16 Composed between 1955 and 1956.

17 Thomas B. Holmes, *Electronic and Experimental Music: Foundations of New Music and New Listening* (New York and London: Routledge, 2002), 131.

18 Robert Worby, "Stockhausen's Gesang de Jünglinge," *BBC*, October 17, 2013, https://www.bbc.co.uk/blogs/radio3/entries/9ddca641-f42b-3298-a657-578 09377e0a5

19 Written in a letter of invitation to Luigi Nono, May 1956 (Stockhausen/K 56-05-01/02 m, ALN), cited in Carola Nielinger-Vakil, *Luigi Nono: A Composer in Context* (Cambridge: Cambridge University Press, 2015), 87.

20 For more information on the BBC Radiophonic Workshop, visit https://ww w.bbc.com/historyofthebbc/anniversaries/april/bbc-radiophonic-workshop.

21 After the Second World War, Germany was divided into East and West Germany. For more details on its history, see https://www.britannica.com/pla ce/Germany/The-era-of-partition.

22 Timothy Scott Brown, "In Search of Space: The Trope of Escape in German Electronic Music around 1968," *Contemporary European History* 26, no. 2 (2017): 352 [339–52].

23 Simon Reynolds, "Krautrock: Kosmik Dance: Krautrock and Its Legacy," in *Modulations, A History of Electronic Music: Throbbing Words on Sound*, ed. Peter Shapiro (New York: Caipirinha Productions, 2000), 33.

24 *Krautrock: The Rebirth of Germany*, produced by Ben Whalley, aired October 23, 2009, on BBC Four.

25 *Idris Elba's How Clubbing Changed the World.*

26 Minimalism originated in the 1960s. Musical characteristics include ostinato, melodic cells (see next footnote), layered textures, and diatonic harmony. Famous composers include Philip Glass, Steve Reich, and Terry Riley.

27 A cell (a tiny melodic phrase) is a more preferable term to use (other than a riff or hook) when composing minimalism.

28 There are too many artists/groups to mention but examples include David Bowie, Afrika Bambaataa, New Order, Radiohead, and Elbow, and various genres and styles such as hip-hop, Chicago house, and techno.

29 Moby in *Idris Elba's How Clubbing Changed the World.*

30 *Merriam-Webster,* s.v. "Psychedelic," accessed May 19, 2018, https://www.merriam-webster.com/dictionary/psychedelic.

31 For a detailed insight into psychedelic rock and its sociocultural and musical features, read Sheila Whiteley, "Progressive Rock and Psychedelic Coding in the Work of Jimi Hendrix," *Popular Music,* 9 (1990): 37–60, and *The Space between the Notes* (London: Routledge, 1992); Allan F. Moore, *Rock: The Primary Text—Developing a Musicology of Rock* (Oxon: Ashgate, 2001); Michael Goddard, Benjamin Halligan, and Nicola Spelman, *Resonances: Noise and Contemporary Music* (New York and London: Bloomsbury, 2013); Andy Bennett, *Cultures of Popular Music* (Berkshire: Open University Press, 2001); Simon Frith, "'The Magic That Can Set You Free': The Ideology of Folk and the Myth of the Rock Community," in *Popular Music,* 1 (1981): 159–68; Richard Middleton and John Muncie, *Pop Culture, Pop Music, and Post-War Youth: Counter-Cultures* (Milton Keynes: Open University Press, 1981); John Storey, "Rockin' Hegemony: West Coast Rock and Amerika's War in Vietnam," in *Tell Me Lies About Vietnam*, ed. Alf Louvre and Jeffrey Walsh (Milton Keynes: Open University Press, 1988): 181–97; John Shepherd, *Music as Social Text* (Cambridge: Polity, 1991).

32 Typical sound effects featured in psychedelic music include fuzz (distorted), echo, reverb, phasing, delay, reverse (backward tapes, for example)—see earlier endnote.

33 Sheila Whiteley, *The Space between the Notes* (London: Routledge, 1992), 25.

34 This experience can obviously be enhanced when the listener decodes the lyrics (if applicable), for example, the works of the Beatles, Jimi Hendrix, Grateful Dead, George Clinton, Pink Floyd, and many more.

35 Jonathyne Briggs, *Sounds French: Globalization, Cultural Communities, and Pop Music, 1958-1980* (New York: Oxford University Press), 107.

36 Pierre Henry's *Variation* includes remixes by artists such as Fatboy Slim and Area 21 (released in 2000, Philips).

37 Timothy D. Taylor, *Strange Sounds: Music, Technology and Culture* (New York and London: Routledge, 2001), 94.

38 David Toop, "Dub," *Mixmag,* 2, no. 19 (December 1992): 32 [32–6].

39 Hillegonda C. Rietveld, *This Is Our House: House Music, Cultural Spaces, and Technologies* (London and New York: Routledge, 1998).

40 Dick Hebdige, *Cut 'n' Mix: Culture, Identity and Caribbean Music* (London and New York: Comedia, 1987), 83.

41 An equalizer is a mixing device that enables the user to manipulate the sound source's tonality by increasing or reducing its (filter) frequency. A filter is an electronic circuit that facilitates in reducing the frequency (usually of a high/low/band pass filter).

42 For example, King Tubby would later invite toasters such as U-Roy (real name Ewart Beckford) to "talk over" (chat) or briefly sing over the remixed works or "versions."

43 Michael E. Veal, *Dub: Soundscapes and Shattered Sings in Jamaican Reggae* (Middletown: Wesleyan University Press, 2007); *Dub Echoes,* directed by Bruno Natal (Soul Jazz Films, 2009); Shara Rambarran, "'You've Got No Time for Me': Martin 'Sugar' Merchant, British Caribbean Musical Identity and the Media,'" in *Reggae from Yaad: Traditional and Emerging Themes in Jamaican Popular Music,* ed. Donna P. Hope (Kingston, Jamaica: Ian Randle Publishers, 2015); Christopher Partridge, *Dub in Babylon: Understanding the Evolution and Significance of Dub Reggae in Jamaica and Britain* (London: Equinox Publishing, 2010).

44 It is better to hear dub on sound systems, so that the listener can gain a full and emotional experience of the music.

45 Hillegonda C. Rietveld, "The Residual Soul Sonic Force of the 12 Vinyl Dance Single," in *Residual Media*, ed. Charles R. Acland (Minneapolis: University of Minnesota Press, 2007), 104.

46 Veal, *Dub: Soundscapes and Shattered Sings in Jamaican Reggae*, 64. For an in-depth account of Dub music, read Michael E. Veal and see *Dub Echoes*.

47 Julian Henriques, 2011:xx in Julian Henriques and Hillegonda Rietveld, "Echo," in *The Routledge Companion to Sound Studies,* ed. Michael Bull (Oxon and New York, 2019), 278; Julian Henriques, *Sonic Bodies: Reggae Sound Systems, Performance Techniques and Ways of Knowing* (London: Continuum, 2011), XX.

48 Julian Henriques, "Sonic Diaspora, Vibrations and Rhythm: Thinking Through the Sounding of the Jamaican Dancehall Session," *African and Black Diaspora* 1, no. 2 (2008): 219.

49 A reggae rockers drumbeat consists of the kick drum on beats 1 and 3, and the snare on beats 2 and 4.

50 The cross stick is a technique played on the rim of the snare creating a knocking sound.

51 The steppers consist of the kick playing on every beat (the reggae term for "four to the floor"), and allows room for the upper kit to fill in rhythms.

52 "Waterhouse" is a reference to the name of King Tubby's recording studio in the Waterhouse district in Kingston, Jamaica.

53 Smith in *Dub Echoes*.

54 Hebdige, *Cut 'n' Mix: Culture, Identity and Caribbean Music*, 62; David Sanjek, "'Don't Have to DJ No More': Sampling and the 'Autonomous' Creator," *Cardozo Arts and Entertainment Law Journal* 10 (1992): 611 [607–24].

55 The term "turntablism" was coined by DJ Babu (Chris Oroc) of Beat Junkies and Dilated Peoples—see music documentary *Scratch*, directed by Doug Pray (Palm, 2001).

56 Turntablism is mainly connected with hip-hop. It is, however, traced back to early-twentieth-century music when the turntable was used as an instrument. Examples include Stefan Wolfe performing a piece of music using eight gramophones (as instruments), all playing at different speeds; and Darius Milhaud creating a

montage of sounds using phonographs playing at different speeds. Perhaps the most famous example is John Cage's *Imaginary Landscape No1* consisting of a pianist, a cymbalist, and two turntablists playing Victorian frequency records. For further details, see Eshun, *More Brilliant than the Sun: Adventures in Sonic Fiction,* 19; Katz, *Capturing Sound,* 160; Peter Shapiro, "Deck Wreckers, the Turntable as Instrument," in *Undercurrents, the Hidden Wiring of Modern Music,* ed. Rob Young (London: Continuum, 2002), 164; Chris Cutler, "Plunderphonics," in *Sounding Off! Music as Subversion/ Resistance/Revolution*, ed. Ron Sakolsky and Fred Wei-Han Ho (Brooklyn, NY: Autonomedia, 1995), 67–86; Kembrew McLeod and Peter DiCola, *Creative License: The Law and Culture of Digital Sampling* (Durham and London: Duke University Press, 2011).

57 Joseph G. Schloss, *Making Beats: The Art of Sample-Based Hip-Hop* (Middletown, CT: Wesleyan University Press, 2004), 32; Shapiro, "Deck Wreckers, the Turntable as Instrument," 165.

58 Grandmaster Flash released his critically acclaimed turntablist album titled *The Adventures of Grandmaster Flash on the Wheels of Steel* in 1980.

59 Grand Wizzard Theodore explained how he discovered scratching: "This particular day when I came home from school and usually go home and practice and I was playing music and it would be too loud, and my mom came and banging at my door [and said]: 'if you don't cut that music down, you're gonna have to cut it off' . . . I was still rubbing a record—rubbing it back and forth. When she left, I was like, hmm, that's a pretty good idea. . . . I spurned with it a couple of months, couple of weeks, and when I was ready, we gave a party and that's when I first introduced the scratch." Interview in *Scratch*, directed by Doug Pray (Palm, 2001), DVD.

60 Eshun, *More Brilliant than the Sun: Adventures in Sonic Fiction*, 17.

61 Popular breakbeat samples include the late James Brown's drummer Clyde Stubblefield, whose "Funky Drummer" has been sampled many times in the music of Eric B. and Rakim, Public Enemy, and George Michael and many others. Schloss, *Making Beats: The Art of Sample-Based Hip-Hop*, 36; Kembrew McLeod, *Freedom of Expression: Resistance and Repression in the Age of Intellectual Property* (Minneapolis: University of Minnesota Press, 2007), 102.

62 Examples include Biz Markie v. Gilbert O'Sullivan (track "Alone Again," 1991); Vanilla Ice v. Queen and David Bowie (track "Ice Ice Baby," 1990); and Lana Del Ray v. Radiohead (track, "Get Free," 2017).

63 Cited in Kembrew McLeod, "How Copyright Law Changed Hip-Hop: An Interview with Public Enemy's Chuck D and Hank Shocklee," *Stay Free*, 2002, http://www.ibiblio.org/pub/electronic-publications/stay-free/achieves/20/pu blic_enemy.html

64 Katz calls this a performative quotation "that recreates all the details of timbre and timing evoking a unique sound event," in *Capturing Sound*, 141.

65 The term "crate digging" is used when DJs search for vinyl records in record shops/fairs/markets to sample in their compositions.

66 Andrew Mason, "Madlib in Scratch Magazine," *Stones Throw*, May 8, 2005, https://www.stonesthrow.com/news/mad-skills/.

67 Taken from the album Waldir Calmon, *E Sus Multisons*, Copacabana, 1970. It should be noted that this track is a cover version of Alfred Newman's "Airport's Love Theme" for the film *Airport* (1970).

68 A Wurlitzer is a large organ/keyboard used for theater and film. Later, portable keyboard versions were manufactured.

69 Brian Eno, *Music for Airports/Ambient 1*, inner sleeve, 1978, Ambient Label (AMB001) PVC 7908.

70 John T. Lysaker, *Brian Eno's Ambient 1: Music for Airports* (New York: Oxford University Press, 2018), 90.

71 Oblique Strategies was based on a card game created by Brian Eno and Peter Schmidt. Each card carried instructions to motivate the creator in creative situations. See Rupert Till, "Ambient Music," in *Bloomsbury Handbook for Religion and Popular Music*, ed., Christopher Partridge and Marcus Morberg (London: Bloomsbury 2017), 331; David Pattie, "Taking the Studio by Strategy," in *Brian Eno: Oblique Music*, ed. Sean Albiez and David Pattie (London: Bloomsbury, 2016), 59.

72 Shara Rambarran, "'The Time Has Come, Exodus!': Congo Natty and the Jungle (R)evolution," in *Beatified Beats: Exploring the Spiritual in Popular Music*, ed. Mike Dines and Georgina Gregory (London: Bloomsbury, forthcoming).

73 Will Straw, "Dance Music," in *The Cambridge Companion to Pop and Rock*," 174.

74 Examples of the Amen Break in jungle music include UK Apache and Shy FX's "Original Nutter" (1994), Baby D's "Let Me Be Your Fantasy" (1992), LTJ Bukem's "Demon's Theme" (1992), The Prodigy's "Evil Minds" (1992), Shy FX's "Gangster Kid" (1992), Rebel MC's "Comin' On Strong" (1991), and DJ Rap's "Digable Bass" (1994).

75 Rambarran's "'The Time Has Come, Exodus!': Congo Natty and the Jungle (R)evolution"; Christodoulou, "Rumble in the Jungle: City, Place, and Uncanny Bass."

76 Shara Rambarran, "'99 Problems' but Danger Mouse Ain't One: The Creative and Legal Difficulties of Brian Burton, 'Author' of the Grey Album," *Popular Musicology Online*, 2013.

77 It is best to hear "Clear Cut" with subwoofers or sound system to "feel" the bass line.

78 Note that there is no lyrical comparison here as the topics in "O Superman" and "Clear Cut" are thematically different.

79 I would like to thank Gareth Dylan Smith for his helpful comments on this chapter.

Chapter 4

1 Danger Mouse in Stuart Kirkman, "When in Rome: Danger Mouse and Daniele Luppi Interviewed," *The Quietus*, May 17, 2011. https://thequietus.com/articles/06268-danger-mouse-daniele-luppi-interview-rome.

2 I want to thank my friends, comrades, and the Art of Record Production family who have put up with my passion for researching on Danger Mouse's works over the last eighteen years—you know who you are!

3 Simon Reynolds, "Versus: The Science of Remixology," *Pulse!* May, 1996.

4 Eshun, 74, 1999.

5 Jacques Attali, *Noise: The Political Economy of Music,* trans. Brian Massumi (Minnesota: University of Minnesota Press, 1985), 133.

6 Margie Borschke, *This Is Not a Remix: Piracy, Authenticity and Popular Music* (New York and London: Bloomsbury, 2017), 7.

7 Lawrence Lessig, *Free Culture* (New York: Penguin, 2004), 24.

8 Eduardo Navas, *Remix Theory* (Springer: Vienna, 2012), 65.

9 For a fuller account, see Katz, *Capturing Sound*, 140.

10 McLeod and DiCola, *Creative License: The Law and Culture of Digital Sampling*, 58.

11 Paul Morley, *Words and Music: A History of Pop in the Shape of a City* (London: Bloomsbury, 2004), 205.

12 David J. Gunkel, "Rethinking the Digital Remix: Mash-Ups and the Metaphysics of Sound Recording," *Popular Music and Society,* 31 (2008): 489–510. The mash-up became more known as a creative practice in various mediums (such as videos).

13 For an in-depth discussion on the following sections based on *The Grey Album*, please see Rambarran, "'99 Problems' but Danger Mouse Ain't One: The Creative and Legal Difficulties of Brian Burton, 'Author' of the Grey Album."

14 Chris Klosterman, "The DJ Auteur," *The New York Times*, June 18, 2006, http://www.nytimes.com/2006/06/18/magazine/18barkley.html?ei=5090&en=d69638926b798ed5&ex=

15 United Press, "EMI Halts Beatles Remix Album," *United Press International*, February 16, 2004, http://web.lexis-nexis.com/executive/.

16 EMI and Capitol Records are the sound recording owners of *The White Album*.

17 "Grey Tuesday" took place on Tuesday, February 24, 2004.

18 Downhill Battle, *Downhill Battle Press Release*, 2004, http://downhillbattle.org/pressrelease/greyalbum_21104.html.

19 Michael D. Ayers, "The Cyberactivism of a Dangermouse," in *Cybersounds: Essays on Visual Music Culture (Digital Formations)*, ed. Michael D. Ayers (New York: Peter Lang Publishing, 2006), 131.

20 Other signs of online support included turning of the participants' website to the color grey for the day to symbolize the album.

21 The Digital Millennium Copyright Act (DMCA), embedded in section 1201 of the Copyright Act, was introduced in October 1998 by Congress with the aim of halting copyright infringement on the internet and other forms of digital media such as computer software, digital music formats, and DVDs.

22 Sony Music and ATV Publishing are the publishing owners of *The White Album*.

23 Joseph Patel, "Online Grey Tuesday Group Says 100,000 Downloaded Jay-Z/ Beatles Mix," *Music Television*, April 3, 2004, http://www.mtv.com/news/articl es/1485593/20040305/story.jhtml; A list of websites that participated in "Grey Tuesday" can be accessed at: http://techlawadvisor.com/blog/2004/02/grey_t uesday.htm.

24 Fredrich N. Lim, "Grey Tuesday Leads to Blue Monday?: Digital Sampling of Sound Recordings after The Grey Album," *Journal of Law, Technology and Policy*, III (2004): 372.

25 EMI in the UK could have legally challenged Burton as the recording was copyright-protected at the time.

26 See Lim, "Grey Tuesday Leads to Blue Monday?: Digital Sampling of Sound Recordings after The Grey Album"; Rambarran, "'99 Problems' but Danger Mouse Ain't One: The Creative and Legal Difficulties of Brian Burton, 'Author' of the Grey Album."

27 *Sgt. Pepper* received an Arts Council award, and Professor Wilfrid Mellers of the University of York championed their music.

28 Kembrew McLeod, "Confessions of an Intellectual (Property): Danger Mouse, Mickey Mouse, Sonny Bono, and My Long and Winding Path as a Copyright Activist-Academic," *Journal of Popular Music and Society*, 28, no. 1 (2005): 83.

29 Rambarran, "'99 Problems' but Danger Mouse Ain't One: The Creative and Legal Difficulties of Brian Burton, 'Author' of the Grey Album." Examples of famous mash-up songs include Mark Vidler's "Rapture Riders" (2005) (based on The Doors' "Riders on the Storm" (1971) and Blondie's "Rapture" (1980)), Kurtis Rush's "Can't Get Blue Monday Out of My Head" (2002) (based on Kylie Minogue's "Can't Get You Out of My Head" (2001) and New Order's "Blue Monday" (1983)), and anything by Girl Talk.

30 Sasha Frere-Jones, "1+1+1=1: The New Math of Mashups," *The New Yorker* 80, no. 42 (2005): 85.

31 Jacques Derrida, *Positions* (Continuum: London, 2004), 38.

32 Derek B. Scott, "Postmodernism and Music," in *The Routledge Companion to Postmodernism*, ed. Stuart Sim, 3rd ed. (London: Routledge, 2011), 192.

33 Rambarran, "'99 Problems' but Danger Mouse Ain't One: The Creative and Legal Difficulties of Brian Burton, 'Author' of the Grey Album."

34 Roland Barthes, *Image-Music-Text,* trans. Stephen Heath (London: Fontana Press, 1977), 148.

35 Michel Foucault, *The Foucault Reader* (Harmondsworth: Penguin, 1986), 107.

36 For an in-depth analysis please read, Rambarran, "'99 Problems' but Danger Mouse Ain't One: The Creative and Legal Difficulties of Brian Burton, 'Author' of the Grey Album."

37   Jay-Z's "99 Problems" is an autobiographical song. The main hook of the
     song is the chorus and it is an interpolation of Ice-T and Brother Marquis' "99
     Problems" (1993), supported by a looped heavy rock guitar riff and breakbeat
     (sampled from Billy Squier's "Big Beat" (1980)). A sample of Mountain's
     "Long Red" (1972) is also included.

38   "Helter Skelter" is a rock song with a musical setup of drums, guitars,
     bass, saxophone, trumpet, and backing vocals. Both John Lennon and Paul
     McCartney shared the lead guitar and bass parts, and McCartney's voice
     carried an aggressive tone to suit the style. Its title referred to the fairground
     slide, but the song subsequently became infamously connected with Charles
     Manson and the "Family murders" in 1969. Lennon had to testify in court
     that "Helter Skelter" was about the fairground slide and not a message to
     murder people. For more details on the socio-setting of the song, see David
     Quantick, *Revolution: The Making of the Beatles' White Album* (London:
     Unanimous Ltd., 2002); Jeff Russell, *The Beatles Album File and Complete
     Discography 1961-1982* (Dorset: Blandford Press, 1982).

39   Brian O'Connor, "M.A.S.H I.T U.P," *DJ Times Magazine*, August 17, 2004,
     http://www.djtimes.com/issues/2004/08/_features_index_08_2004.htm.

40   It took Burton 200 hours to create *The Grey Album*.

41   Ben Greenman, "The House That Remixed," *The New Yorker,* February 2,
     2004, http://www.newyorker.com/printables/talk/040209ta_talk_greenman

42   Ibid.

43   Danger Mouse, "The Grey Video," 2004. Directed by Ramon and Pedro.

44   Performances include "Tell Me Why," "If I Fell," "I Should Have Known
     Better," and "She Loves You."

45   The hysterical crowd was known as "youthquake" or "Beatlemania."

46   The Beastie Boys allegedly paid a set fee of $250,000 in sample clearances
     for *Paul's Boutique* (see Dan LeRoy, *Paul's Boutique* [London and New York:
     Continuum, 2006]). The Wu Tang Clan was approved by Apple Corps Ltd and
     the Harrison Estate to interpolate a song from the *White Album* (see James
     Montgomery, "Wu-Tang Clan's First-Ever Cleared Beatles Sample Claim Is
     Incorrect," *Music Television*, October 3, 2007, http://www.mtv.com/news/a
     rticles/1571114/20071003/wu_tang_clan.jhtml). Public Enemy was not lucky
     in seeking sampling clearance for using the music of the Beatles, and had to
     remove their track "Psycho of Greed" (2002), which included "Tomorrow
     Never Knows" (1966), from their *Revolverlution* album (2002).

47   "The Beatles and Black Music," presented by DJ Semtex, aired February 28,
     2011 on BBC Radio 1 Xtra.

48   Danger Mouse, *The Grey Album*, Self-Released, 2004 (CD sleeve); Lauren
     Gitlin, "DJ Makes Jay-Z Meets the Beatles: Danger Mouse Makes 'Black' and
     'White' Equal 'Grey,'" *Rolling Stone*, February 5, 2004, http://www.rollingst
     one.com/news/story/5937152/dj_makes_jayz_meet_beatles.

49   Special thanks to Mark Whelan for his comments on my research on Gnarls
     Barkley.

50 The television advert can be viewed here: https://www.youtube.com/watch?
    v=9Xx52xq3vM8

51 The song "Crazy" was also the first MP3 to be eligible for the charts. The
    song stayed at number one for nine weeks in the UK. Gnarls Barkley and their
    record label requested that the single be removed from music stores. They did
    not want the public to get fed up of hearing the song, and more importantly,
    they wanted to release new material.

52 Cee-Lo Green (real name Thomas Callaway) was a former member of Goodie
    Mob, and is now a famous pop/soul singer and celebrity (thanks mostly to the
    success of "Crazy").

53 Spaghetti western originated from the American film genre, the "western."
    It should be noted, however, that the work of pioneering spaghetti western
    director Sergio Leone and composer Ennio Morricone (who scored many
    of Leone's films) has inspired countless directors and composers to create
    similar films and music (and also to imitate popular heroic/cowboy figures).
    Director Sergio Corbucci, for example, based his film *Django* (1966) on
    Leone's famous character "The Stranger" or the "the man with no name."
    The character *Django* was further imitated by other film directors, such as
    Ferdinando Baldi in the aforementioned *Preparati la Bara!*

54 The soundtrack was composed by Gianfranco and Gianpiero Reverberi. This
    is not the first time that listeners hear songs based on samples such as Craig
    David's "Hot Stuff" (2007), in which the sample is based on David Bowie's
    "Let's Dance" (1983); Mutya Buena's "Real Girl" (2007), based on Lenny
    Kravitz's "It Ain't Over 'Til It's Over," (1991); and, Madonna's "Hung up"
    (2005), based on ABBA's "Gimme! Gimme! Gimme!" (1979). The main
    difference between the examples and Gnarls Barkley is that the samples used
    in "Crazy" are not immediately recognizable to the listener who is unfamiliar
    with spaghetti western music.

55 For more details, see Simon Harper, "When in Rome," *The Clash* (June 2011):
    76; Marco Werman, "Danger Mouse's 'Rome' Spaghetti Western," *Public
    Radio International,* May 13, 2011, http:// www.pri.org/stories/2011-05-13/
    danger-mouses-spaghetti-western.

56 The film has been released internationally with various titles such as *Django und
    die Bande der Gehenkten* (Germany); *Get the Coffin Ready*; and *Viva Django*.

57 For further information on how leitmotif is applied in film and television, see
    Philip Tagg, and Robert Clarida, *Ten Little Title Tunes: Towards a Musicology
    of the Mass Media* (New York and Montreal: The Mass Media Music Scholar
    Press, 2003).

58 I offer a deeper reading on spaghetti western, Django's leitmotif, and "Crazy"
    in Rambarran, "Innovations in Contemporary Popular Music and Digital
    Media, and Reconstructions of the Music Industry in the 21st Century."

59 *El Degüello* ("no mercy") is usually played by a bugle or trumpet and takes
    place in the main scene—the climax of the film—where the cowboy calls the
    enemy to surrender or die.

60 The male chorus, *I Cantori Moderni* (The Modern Singers), were a major
    feature in Morricone's spaghetti western film music. They were led by

Alessandro Alessandroni. Alessandroni was also the famous whistler featured on the scores (in particular, the trilogy of *A Fist Full of Dollars*). See Elio Pirari, "Alessandro Alessandroni," *La Stampa*, July 9, 2007, http://acrhivio.last ampa.it/LaStampaArchivio/main/History/tmpl_viewObj.jsp?objid+7826191.

61 Ueli Bernays, "The Apathy and Ecstasy," *Sign and Sight,* January 22, 2010, http://www.signandsight.com/features.1981.html.

62 The hip-hop element is the included beat made by Burton.

63 For example, a solo singer (such as the female singer in Morricone's "A Fistful of Dynamite" (1971)), or a choir would sing "oohs" and "ahhs" or vocalize grunts and whistles.

64 The listener will need a good pair of headphones to hear this, even in the instrumental version.

65 Brian Burton in Robert Everett-Green, "Danger Mouse: 'I'm into Melodies That Break Your Heart a Little Bit,'" *The Globe and Mail*, May 30, 2011, http://www.theglobeandmail.com/arts/music/danger-mouse-im-into-melodie s-that-break-your-heart-a-little-bit/article581379/

66 Danger Mouse in Kirkman, "When in Rome: Danger Mouse and Daniele Luppi Interviewed."

Chapter 5

1 Chipzel, a video game music composer, is referring to her love of retro and nostalgic music in video games—as told to Jessica Curry, host, "Vinyl Special: Sound of Gaming" (podcast), April 18, 2020, accessed April 18, 2020, https://www.bbc.co.uk/sounds/play/m000hgs0.

2 Mark Austin, ed., *Music Video Games: Performance, Politics and Play* (New York and London: Bloomsbury, 2016), 3.

3 Tim Summers, *Understanding Video Game Music* (Cambridge: Cambridge University Press, 2016), 6.

4 William Cheng, *Sound Play: Video Games and the Musical Imagination* (New York: Oxford University Press, 2014), 5.

5 Karen Collins, *Game Sound: An Introduction to the History, Theory, and Practice of Video Game Music and Sound* Design (Cambridge, MA and London: The MIT Press), 3.

6 By this I mean that artists/bands are digitally embodied in "video game" style in music videos such as David Bowie's "The Nomad Soul" (1999), Red Hot Chili Peppers' "Californiacation" (1999); Dragonforce's "Operation Ground and Pound" (2005); Dave's "Revenge" (2017); Kamasi Washington's "Street Fighter Mas" (2018); Big Sean's "Jump Out of the Window" (2017); and the videos of Muse (particularly, videos from *Simulation Theory* such as "Revolt," 2018).

7 For example, Pharrell Williams (pharrellwilliams.com).

8   Austin, *Music Video Games: Performance, Politics and Play*, 12.

9   Ibid.

10   Kiri Miller, *Playing Along* (Oxford and New York: Oxford University Press, 2012), 14.

11   See Stephanie Lind, "Active Interfaces and Thematic Events in the Legend of Zelda: Ocarina of Time," in *Music Video Games: Performance, Politics and Play*, 83–106.

12   See Melanie Fritsch, "Beat It!—Playing the 'King of Pop' in Video Games," in *Music Video Games: Performance, Politics and Play,* 153–76.

13   The gamer (or the aspiring musician) gets a virtual taste of the music industry.

14   Hillegonda C. Rietveld and Marco Benoît Carbone, "Introduction: Towards a Polyphonic Approach to Game and Music Studies," *Game: The Italian Journal of Game Studies*, 6 (2017): 5.

15   Even though the video games industry was developed in the 1970s, music soundtracks back then were not significant as they are now. Chiptune has also partially influenced the formation of other styles, such as grime.

16   As heard in Atari 2600, Commodore 64, and, more significantly, Nintendo Entertainment Systems.

17   Kenneth B. McAlpine, *Bits and Pieces: A History of Chiptunes* (Oxford: Oxford University Press, 2018), 4.

18   As recommended by Andrew Shartmann, as told to Isy Suttie in "While My Guitar Gently Bleeps," produced by Ben Cordrey, aired March 25, 2017, on BBC Radio 4.

19   See McAlpine, *Bits and Pieces: A History of Chiptunes*, 7.

20   As told to Andrew Webster, "Chipzel Has Spent a Decade Making Incredible Music with Gameboys," *The Verge*, April 2019. https://www.theverge.com/2019/4/19/18484887/chipzel-game-boy-music-chiptune-interview.

21   The Little Sound DJ software is a tracker that is loaded on to the Nintendo Game Boy and the user can create music (by accessing the PSGs). It is based on four monophonic channels: two pulse channels (allowing the creation of the chiptune/chirpy/bleep melodies), one noise channel (percussion and sound effects such as explosions), and one wave channel (synthesizer sounds, kick drums, bass, samples).

22   Twitch is a fast-responsive action game designed to test the player's reaction time to potential consequential situations.

23   The triangle has to escape through the small gaps in the maze. The catch is, if the triangle keeps crashing against the "wall" (i.e., side of the hexagonal), the gamer will lose and will need to start all over again.

24   The thumbs control the game. Press the left side for the triangle to move left, and the right side for the triangle to move right.

25   The titles of the tracks are "Courtesy," "Otis," and "Focus." The music was so popular that it was released as an EP in 2015.

26   A kick drum that plays on every beat.

27 Retro signifiers are also heard in the following: Grandaddy's "A. M 180" (1997), La Roux's "Bulletproof" (2009), and JME's "Famalam" (2010).

28 Peter Maxwell, "Line Boil on the Road to Hell," *Eye: The International Review of the Graphic Design,* 24, no. 96 (Summer 2018): 101.

29 David McGowan, "*Cuphead*: Animation, the Public Domain, and Home Video Remediation," *J Pop* 52 (February 2019): 10–34.

30 Other examples include "Hell's Bells " (1929), "Betty Boop" (1930), "Swing you Sinners" (1930),"Flowers and Trees" (1932), "The Cookie Carnival" (1935), "Popeye the Sailor" (1936), and "Woody Woodpecker" (1940).

31 Other notable video games of the "run and gun" style include *Contra* (1987), *Gustar Heroes* (1993), and *Mega Man* (1987+).

32 This game is perhaps more suited to the advance gamer who can work his/her way through the levels quickly, as a lot of concentration is needed in finding solutions!

33 Jazz is an African American genre with its musical origins based on blues and ragtime. Its history is traced back to early twentieth century and New Orleans. For accessible information on Jazz, see https://www.britannica.com/art/jazz.

34 I would like to thank Paul Novotny for putting me in contact with Kris Maddigan.

35 Kristofer Maddigan, interview by author, UK and Canada, May 19, 2020.

36 Ibid.

37 Ibid.

38 An American Fotoplayer is a multi-keyboard instrument consisting of a piano roll, horns, bells, whistles, and other percussion. The instrument was used to accompany silent films.

39 See Chapter 1 for a recap on the Theremin.

40 See previous chapter for a definition of the leitmotif.

41 Maddigan, , interview by author, UK and Canada, May 19, 2020.

42 Ibid.

43 Jeremy Darby has produced for the likes of David Bowie, Lou Reed, Prince, Aretha Franklin, Alicia Keys, Herbie Hancock, and many others.

44 Maddigan, , interview by author, UK and Canada, May 19, 2020.

45 Ibid.

46 Ibid.

47 Kris Maddigan, "Historical Precedent and the Creative Process in the Music of Cuphead," talk/lecture https://www.youtube.com/watch?v=dGaYdeCvdbc&t =2183s.

48 Paul Novotny, interview by author, UK and Canada, May 13, 2020.

49 Ibid.

50 Ibid.

51 Also known as Mr. King's Dice Theme.

52 There is a virtual connection here: Cab Calloway appeared virtually as a ghost, and sang "Minnie the Moocher" in the *Betty Boop* animation in 1932—see Chapter 7.

53 Due to the great success of the game, *Cuphead* is currently being made into a cartoon series on *Netflix*.

54 With support from Radical Media and EMI.

55 Familiar listeners of this song will be aware that "Black" has been used in television dramas such as *Breaking Bad* and *Emmerdale*.

56 Thanks to Gareth Dylan Smith for confirming this drumming technique to me in 2015.

57 Shara Rambarran, "99 Problems but Danger Mouse IS One: The Evolution of the Music Producer Brian Burton" (Paper presented at the 10th Art of Record Production Conference, Drexel University, Philadelphia USA, November 6–8, 2015), www.artofrecordproduction.com.

58 This scene would represent horror movies, in particular, films set in a post-apocalyptic world such as *28 Days Later* (2002), *Mad Max* (1979), and *Akira* (1988).

59 To experience the music video game, visit www.ro.me.

Chapter 6

1 Simon Frith, *Sound Effects: Youth, Leisure, and the Politics of Rock 'n' Roll* (London: Constable, 1983); Simon Frith, "The Industrialization of Popular Music," in *Popular Music and Communication*, ed. James Lull (Newbury Park, CA: Sage, 1992), 49–74; Richard James Burgess, *The Art of Music Production: The Theory and Practice*, 4th ed. (New York: Oxford University Press, 2013); Ann Harrison, *Music: The Business*, 7th ed. (Croydon: Virgin Books, 2017); Bemuso, www.bemuso.com; M. H, "A Funny Business: The Relationship Between Musicians, Master Recordings and Record Labels," *The Economist*, July 8, 2019, https://www.economist.com/prospero/2019/07/08/the-relationship-between-musicians-master-recordings-and-record-labels; Adam Gustafson, "How Prince's Quest for Complete Artistic Control Changed the Music Industry Forever," *The Conversation,* April 22, 2016,https://theconversation.com/how-princes-quest-for-complete-artistic-control-changed-the-music-industry-forever-58267. For a hands-on guide and personal accounts of highs and lows of working in the business: https://www.theguardian.com/books/2015/jun/26/musicians-writers-choose-favourite-books-music-brian-eno-beck

2 Derek B. Scott, *Sounds of the Metropolis: The 19th Century Popular Music Revolution in London, New York, Paris, and Vienna* (New York: Oxford University Press, 2008); Shara Rambarran, "'Very' British: A Pop Musicological Approach to the Pet Shop Boys' 'Always on My Mind,'" in *Popular Musicology and Identity: Essays in Honor of Stan Hawkins*, ed. Eirik Askerøi, Kai Arne Hansen, and Freya Jarman (New York: Routledge, 2020).

3 Mike Featherstone, *Consumer Culture and Postmodernism* (London: Sage, 1991), 95–7.

4 Jock McGregor, "Madonna: Icon of Postmodernity," *Facing the Challenge* 1997, https://www.facingthechallenge.org/madonna.php; Kevin O'Donnell, *Postmodernism* (Oxford: Lion Publishing, 2003); Sam Wolfson, "Madame X: Madonna's New Album Is Both Anonymous and Well-Trodden," *The Guardian*, April 15, 2019, https://www.theguardian.com/music/2019/apr/15/madame-x-madonna-new-album-alter-ego.

5 I use the word "speculate" because we are now more aware of Madonna's personal life, thanks to the tabloid press and her social media pages (e.g., Instagram).

6 Richard Fitch, "In this Age of Grand Allusion: Bowie, Nihilism, and Meaning," in *David Bowie: Critical Perspectives*, ed. Eoin Devereux, Aileen Dillane and Martin J. Power (New York and London: Routledge, 2015), 28; Barish Ali and Heidi Wallace, "Out of This World: Ziggy Stardust and the Spatial Interplay of Lyrics, Vocals, and Performance," in *David Bowie: Critical Perspectives*, 264.

7 Christopher Welch, *David Bowie* (London: Carlton, 2018); James E. Perone's *The Words and Music of David Bowie* (Connecticut: Praeger Publishers, 2007).

8 Stan Hawkins, *Queerness in Pop Music: Aesthetics, Gender Norms, and Temporality* (London and New York: Routledge, 2016), 64.

9 Stan Hawkins, "Introduction: David Bowie (1947–2016)," *Contemporary Music Review*, 37 no. 3 (2018): 189.

10 Featherstone, *Consumer Culture and Postmodernism*, 97.

11 Oscar Wilde, *The Decay of Lying*, 1889; see *The Cambridge Companion to Oscar Wilde*, ed. Peter Raby (Cambridge: Cambridge University Press, 1997).

12 Featherstone, *Consumer Culture and Postmodernism*, 97.

13 Ibid.

14 Andrew Goodwin, "Sample and Hold: Pop Music in the Digital Age of Reproduction," *Critical Quarterly*, 30, no. 3 (1988): 34–49.

15 Allan F. Moore, "Authenticity as Authentication," *Popular Music*, 21, no. 2 (May 2002): 209–23; Stan Hawkins, *Settling the Pop Score: Pop Texts and Identity Politics* (Aldershot: Ashgate, 2002).

16 Nathan Wiseman-Trowse, *Performing Class in British Popular Music* (Hampshire: Palgrave Macmillan, 2008).

17 Andrew Herman and John M. Sloop, "The Politics of Authenticity in Postmodern Rock Culture: The Case of Negativland and the Letter 'U' and the Numeral '2,'" *Critical Studies in Mass Communication*, 15, no. 1 (1998): 13–14.

18 Moore, "Authenticity as Authentication."

19 Lawrence Grossberg, "'You (Still) Have to Fight for Your Right to Party': Music Television as Billboards of Post-modern Difference," *Popular Music*, 7, no. 3 (1988): 326.

20 Lawrence Grossberg, "The Media Economy of Rock Culture: Cinema, Postmodernity and Authenticity," in *Sound and Vision: The Music Video*

Reader, ed. Simon Frith, Andrew Goodwin, and Lawrence Grossberg (London: Routledge, 1993): 205–6.

21 Simon Reynolds, *Shock and Awe: Glam Rock and Its Legacy* (London: Faber and Faber 2016); Roxanne Gay, "Madonna's Spring Awakening," *Harper's Bazaar*, January 10, 2017, https://www.harpersbazaar.com/culture/features/a19761/madonna-interview/

22 Grossberg, "The Media Economy of Rock Culture: Cinema, Postmodernity and Authenticity," 206.

23 Auslander, *Performing Glam Rock: Gender and Theatricality in Popular Music*, 13. It should be added that glam rockers, or any artist, revealing their true identities does not always work well with their fans. Kiss, as an example, removed their famous makeup in 1983, and it was a disaster (thanks to Lucinda Hawksley for pointing this out).

24 Ibid., 67.

25 Ibid., 138.

26 The actual birth year of Grace Jones has always remained a mystery for her fans and media.

27 Timothy Warner, *Pop Music—Technology and Creativity: Trevor Horn and the Digital Revolution* (Aldershot: Ashgate, 2003), 125.

28 Grace Jones has famously worked with musicians and producers such as Sly Dunbar, Robbie Shakespeare, Chris Blackwell, and Trevor Horn.

29 Michael Deangelis, "Jones, Grace," in *Routledge International Encyclopedia of Queer Culture*, ed. David A. Gerstner (New York and Oxon: Routledge, 2006), 331.

30 Sheila Whiteley, *Women and Popular Music: Sexuality, Identity and Subjectivity* (London and New York: Routledge, 2000), 125.

31 Grace Jones in Andy Warhol and André Leon Talley, "New Again," *The Interview*, 22 (October 1984): 55.

32 Grace Jones, *I'll Never Write My Memoirs* (London: Simon & Schuster, 2015), 258–9.

33 Francesca T. Royster, *Sounding Like a No-No: Queer Sounds and Eccentric Acts in the Post-Soul Era* (Ann Arbor: The University of Michigan Press, 2013), 144.

34 Jones, *I'll Never Write My Memoirs*, 259–60.

35 Steven Shaviro, *Post-Cinematic Effect* (Winchester, UK, and Washington, USA, O Books), 11.

36 Grace Jones's other music videos usually consist of surreal postmodern collages of her images, recorded performances, and artwork.

37 Grace Jones, "Love You to Life," July 19, 2014, music video, 3:46, https://youtu.be/m5EWsJQG9KE.

38 Grace Jones wrote the song for a friend who was in a coma. See Miranda Sawyer, "State of Grace," *The Guardian*, October 11, 2008, https://www.theguardian.com/music/2008/oct/12/grace-jones-hurricane.

39   Chris Levine in Liane Escorza, "Grace Jones x Chris Levine," *Dazed*, April 27, 2010, https://www.dazeddigital.com/photography/article/7418/1/grace-jones-x-chris-levine.

40   Chris Levine in Natalia Santos, "Chris Levine—Vulture Hound Interview," *Vulture Hound*, September 20, 2016, https://vulturehound.co.uk/2016/09/chris-levine-vulture-hound-interview/.

41   Chris Levine in Liane Escorza, "Grace Jones x Chris Levine."

42   Kai Arne Hansen, "It's a Dark Philosophy: The Weeknd's Intermedial Aestheticization of Violence," in *On Popular Music and Its Unruly Entanglements*, ed. Nick Braae and Kai Arne Hansen (Cham, Switzerland: Palgrave Macmillan, 2019), 243–4; Frederik Dhaenens and Sander De Ridder, "Resistant Masculinities In Alternative R&B? Understanding Frank Ocean and The Weeknd's Representations of Gender," *European Journal of Cultural Studies*, 3, no. 18 (2015): 283–99. For further insight on hegemonic masculinity, see R. W. Cornell, *Masculinities* (Berkeley and Los Angeles: University of California Press, 2015).

43   Tasfaye in Tom Lamont, "The Weeknd: Drugs Were a Crutch for Me," *The Guardian*, December 3, 2016, https://www.theguardian.com/music/2016/dec/03/the-weeknd-abel-tesfaye-interview-music-tom-lamont.

44   Directed by Grant Singer.

45   Hansen, It's a Dark Philosophy: The Weeknd's Intermedial Aestheticization of Violence," 236.

46   From the album, *Beauty behind the Madness*.

47   The music video was directed by Grant Singer.

48   These visual traits do not apply to all of The Weeknd's videos but are arguably noticeable in most of his videos.

49   Nabil Elderkin has previously worked with The Weeknd (he shot the album cover for *Starboy*). GoPro have previously filmed The Weeknd's concert in London using Hero3+ Black edition cameras.

50   Experience the VR music video here: The Weeknd featuring Eminem, "The Hills," October 20, 2015, VR music video, 1:50, https://youtu.be/2fhjdtQDcOo.

51   The Weeknd, "Blinding Lights," in *The Late Show with Stephen Colbert*, December 7 2019, performance, 3:31, https://www.youtube.com/watch?v=sveiX_mA9A4.

52   The song is from his latest album *After Hours*, 2020. The videos based on the album carry the theme of The Weeknd being happily lost in Las Vegas, and indulging in driving, gambling, and drinking. See Chapter 2, endnote 26.

53   Synthwave (also known as retrowave and outrun) is an offshoot of synth-pop dedicated to 1980s music and film/video games with dystopian, nostalgic, and futuristic themes. "Blinding Lights" casually resembles early up-tempo and synth-ridden 1980s music such as Rod Stewart's "Young Turks" (1981); "A Flock of Seagulls," "I Ran (So Far Away)" (1982); Pat Benatar's "Love is a Battlefield" (1983); Michael Sambello's "Maniac"(1983); Laura Brannigan's

"Self-Control" (1984); and A-Ha's "Take on Me" (1984). "Blinding Lights" was produced by Max Martin, Oscar Holter, and The Weeknd.

54 The actual video for "Blinding Lights" displays the classic visual and dystopian traits of The Weeknd visual, that is, sexual encounters, voyeurism, bitter failed relationships, drugs, violence, and driving a Mercedes-AMG GT Roadster. See Chapter 2 (endnote 26) and https://www.theweeknd.com/.

 The Weeknd in Josh Eeels, "Sex, Drugs, and R&B: Inside the Weeknd's Dark Twisted Fantasy," *Rolling Stone*, October 21, 2015, https://www.rollings tone.com/music/music-news/sex-drugs-and-rb-inside-the-weeknds-dark-twi sted-fantasy-176091/.

55 The Weeknd in Josh Eeels, "Sex, Drugs, and R&B: Inside the Weeknd's Dark Twisted Fantasy," *Rolling Stone*, October 21, 2015, https://www.rollingstone.com/music/music-news/sex-drugs-and-rb-inside-the-weeknds-dark-twisted-fantasy-176091/.

Chapter 7

1 Sheila Whiteley, "Introduction," in *Music, Place and Space: Popular Music and Cultural Identity*, ed. Sheila Whiteley, Andy Bennett, and Stan Hawkins (Ashgate: Farnham, 2004), 4.

2 Jem Kelly, "Pop Music, Multimedia and Live Performance," in *Music, Sound and Multimedia: From the Live to the Virtual*, ed. Jamie Sexton (Edinburgh: Edinburgh University Press, 2007), 107.

3 Matt Stahl, "The Synthespian's Animated Prehistory: The Monkees, the Archies, Don Kirshner, and the Politics of 'Virtual Labor,'" *Television and New Media*, 12, no. 1 (2010): 3–22.

4 Paul Sanden, *Liveness in Modern Music: Musicians, Technology, and the Perception of Performance* (New York: Routledge, 2013).

5 Philip Auslander, *Liveness: Performance in a Mediatized Culture* (London: Routledge, 1999).

6 Lucy Bennett, "Music Audiences: An Introduction," in *Journal of Audience and Reception Studies,* 9. no. 2 (November 2012): 203.

7 Lucy Bennett and Pete Booth, eds., *Seeing Fans: Representations of Fandom Media and Popular Culture* (London: Bloomsbury, 2016); Mark Duffett, *Understanding Fandom: An Introduction to the Study of Media Fan Culture* (London: Bloomsbury, 2013).

8 Karen Collins, Bill Kapralos, and Holly Tessler, eds., *The Oxford Handbook of Interactive Audio* (New York: Oxford University Press, 2014); Benjamin Halligan, Kirsty Fairclough, Robert Edgar, and Nicola Spelman, eds., *The Arena Concert: Music, Media and Mass Entertainment* (New York: Bloomsbury, 2015).

9 Wikstrom, *The Music Industry: Music in the Cloud.*

10 Richard A. Peterson and Andy Bennett, "Introducing Music Scenes," in *Music Scenes: Local, Translocal, and Virtual*, ed. Richard A. Peterson and Andy Bennett (Nashville: Vanderbilt University Press, 2004), 10.

11 Chat room/live chat involves a real-time virtual communication via texting/typing.

12 R. J. Bennett, "Live Concerts and Fan Identity in the Age of the Internet," in *The Digital Evolution of Live Music,* ed. Angie Jones and Rebecca Jane Bennett (Oxford: Chandos Publishing, 2015), 10.

13 Louise H. Jackson and Mike Dines, "Vocaloids and Japanese Virtual Vocal Performance: The Cultural Heritage and Technological Futures of Vocal Puppetry," in *The Oxford Handbook of Music and Virtuality*, 103.

14 View the cartoon here: Betty Boop, "Minnie the Moocher—1932," N.D, animation, 7:54, https://www.youtube.com/watch?v=N7VUU_VPI1E

15 Starring Grace Kelly, Bing Crosby, and Frank Sinatra. View the footage here: *High Society* (1956), "Beginning & End with Louis Armstrong & His Band," November 23, 2010, film excerpt, 3:17, https://www.youtube.com/watch?v=FtfxSAnOgoU.

16 Thomas Conner, "Hatsune Miku, 2.0Pac, and Beyond: Rewinding and Fast-Forwarding the Virtual Pop Star," in *The Oxford Handbook of Music and Virtuality*, 129–47.

17 There are too many virtual bands to mention! The internet is always a useful starting point to research when, where, and how many of these bands exist. For scholarly articles, see Conner's "Hatsune Miku, 2.0Pac, and Beyond: Rewinding and Fast-Forwarding the Virtual Pop Star," and John Richardson's *An Eye for Music: Popular Music and the Audiovisual Surreal* (New York: Oxford University Press, 2012).

18 E. Ann Kaplan, *Rocking Around the Clock: Music Television, Postmodernism, and Consumer Culture* (New York and London: Methuen, 1987); Andrew Goodwin, *Music Television and Popular Culture: Dancing in the Distraction Factory* (London: Routledge, 1993); Carol Vernallis, *Experiencing Music Video: Aesthetics and Cultural Context* (New York: Columbia University Press, 2004); Carol Vernallis, *Unruly Media: YouTube, Music Video, and the New Digital Cinema* (Oxford: Oxford University Press, 2013); John Richardson, Claudia Gorban, and Carol Vernallis, eds., *The Oxford Handbook of New Audiovisual Aesthetics* (New York: Oxford University Press, 2013).

19 For more information on the programming of music video on television, see Gina Arnold, Daniel Cookney, Kirsty Fairclough, and Michael Goddard's *Music/Video: Histories, Aesthetics, Media* (New York: Bloomsbury, 2017).

20 Sunil Manghani, "The Pleasures of (Music) Video," in *Music/Video: Histories, Aesthetics, Media*, 39.

21 Cyborg stands for cybernetic organism and is a being that is part-human and part-machine.

22 Donna Haraway, *A Cyborg Manifesto: Science, Technology, and Socialist-Feminism in the Late Twentieth Century* (Minneapolis: University of Minnesota Press, 2006), 6.

23 Anne Balsamo, "Reading Cyborgs, Writing Feminism," in *Cybersexualities: A Reader on Feminist Theory, Cyborgs and Cyberspace*, ed. Jenny Wolmack (Edinburgh: Edinburgh University Press, 1999), 145–56.

24 Haraway, *A Cyborg Manifesto*, 9.

25 Richardson, Gorban, and Vernallis, eds., *The Oxford Handbook of New Audiovisual Aesthetics*, 8.

26 Successful artists/groups who were discovered on the internet include The Arctic Monkeys (MySpace), Justin Bieber (YouTube), Shawn Mendes (Vine), Lil Nas X (TikTok/Twitter), and Chance the Rapper (SoundCloud).

27 Musical collaborations on Phase 6 include Tony Allen, Skepta, and Peter Hook.

28 As the Gorillaz project developed, Remi Kabaka Jr. became part of the creative collective (he is also the drummer for the group, i.e., in live and recording sessions).

29 Blur are a famous Britpop group. See John Harris, *The Last Party: Britpop, Blair and the Demise of English Rock* (London: Harper Perennial, 2004); Michael Bracewell, *The Nineties: When Surface Was Depth* (London: Flamingo, 2003); Martin Cloonan, *Popular Music and the State in the UK: Culture, Trade, or Industry?* (Oxon and New York: Routledge, 2016); Andy Bennett and Jon Stratton eds., *Introduction to Britpop and the English Music Tradition* (Farnham: Ashgate, 2010); Christian Lloyd and Shara Rambarran, "'Brand New You're Retro': Tricky as Engpop Dissident," in *Mad Dogs and Englishness: Popular Music and English Identities*, ed. Lee Brooks, Mark Donnelly, and Richard Mills (Bloomsbury: London, 2017), 162–73; Rambarran, "'You've Got No Time for Me': Martin 'Sugar' Merchant, British Caribbean Musical Identity and the Media." Also, these sources offer more insight on the highs and lows of Britpop music and its (mis)representation in British culture and society.

30 Conner, "Hatsune Miku, 2.0Pac, and Beyond: Rewinding and Fast-Forwarding the Virtual Pop Star"; Richardson, *An Eye for Music: Popular Music and the Audiovisual Surreal*; Shara Rambarran, "Reality vs. Hyperreality: Feel Good with the Gorillaz and Reject False Icons" (Paper presented at Engaging Baudrillard: International Conference, University of Swansea, UK, September 5–7, 2006).

31 Rambarran, "'Feel Good' with Gorillaz and 'Reject False Icons': The Fantasy Worlds of the Virtual Group and Their Creators," 150.

32 Examples of J-pop culture include *Battle Royale* and Hayao Miyazaki films. For further insight on Gorillaz, see Cass Browne, *Gorillaz: The Rise of the Ogre* (New York: Riverhead Books, 2006) and *Bananaz*, directed by Ceri Levy (Bananaz Productions: UK, 2009), DVD.

33 Musical collaborations include Bootie Brown, De La Soul, MF Doom, Roots Manuva, and Shaun Ryder.

34 Musical collaborations include Snoop Dogg, Mos Def, Bobby Womack, Mark E. Smith, Mick Jones, Paul Simonon, Hypnotic Brass Ensemble, and Little Dragon, Bashy, and Kano.

35 Musical collaborations include Grace Jones, De La Soul, Popcaan, Mavis Staples, D.R.A.M, and Pusha T.

36 Musical collaborations include George Benson, Snoop Dogg, and Jamie Principle.

37   Written and produced by Daman Albarn, James Albarn, and Remi Kakaba Jr. The title is possibly a wordplay on either "transcendence" (the notion of feeling superior or going beyond normal limits) or "trance" as the music carries elements of that style such as the hypnotic beats and psychedelic synth hooks (and is enhanced by the music video). The video was created by Jamie Hewlett, Nicos Livesy, Blinkink, and Eddy. Video link: Gorillaz, "Tranz (Official Video)," September 13, 2018, music video, 2:54, https://www.you tube.com/watch?v=E2Q52cVx7Bo.

38   2D and Murdoc are known to clash a lot.

39   The backdrop of the visuals is reminiscent of the performance stage on *The Word*, a 1990s British youth program on television Channel 4 (presented by Terry Christian).

40   The term "shoegazing" is a reference to 1990s British (northern/Manchester) indie rock music where the guitarists would perform by "staring" downward toward their shoes.

41   Timothy Warner, "The Song of the Hydra: Multiple Lead Vocals in Modern Pop Recordings," in *Art of Record Production Conference Proceedings* (London: University of Westminster, 2005).

42   Used for film and video production, a green screen is a green background where moving subjects are filmed in front (e.g., people). In the editing stage, the green screen is replaced by a visual of some sort (say a forest or an office) that blends with the moving subject, giving a realistic impression that the scene is real.

43   As told to Simon Vorzick-Levinson, "Damon Albarn Is Living in the Now," *Rolling Stone*, September 25, 2018, https://www.rollingstone.com/music/music -features/damon-albarn-gorillaz-blur-tour-interview-727984/.

44   As told to Craig Jenkins, "Damon Albarn Is Unfortunately Really Good at Predicting the Future," *Vulture*, November 8, 2017, https://www.vulture.com/2 017/11/interview-damon-albarn.html.

45   The vocals are provided by Saki Fujita.

46   Jackson and Dines, "Vocaloids and Japanese Virtual Vocal Performance: The Cultural Heritage and Technological Futures of Vocal Puppetry"; Ragnhild Brøvig-Hannsen and Anne Danielsen, *Digital Signatures: The Impact of Digitalization on Popular Music Sound* (Cambridge, MA: MIT Press, 2016).

47   In Japan, users would share their music and visual creations of Hatsune Miku on the digital video platform, Nico Nico Douga.

48   It is thought that at least 100,000 songs have been created by fans. It should also be stated that while fans have the freedom of creating music and recreating the image of Hatsune Miku, it is for noncommercial use only— the virtual idol is a brand after all and is owned by Crypton Future Media. However, there are some exceptions, such as the group Supercell who shared their Vocaloid compositions on Nico Nico Douga and caught the attention of Crypton Future Media, and were later signed by Sony Music.

49   A cutismo is a Japanese girl or woman displaying innocent signs of cuteness.

50   "Uncanny Valley" is a term invented by Masahiro Mori in 1970. The term is
     used to describe the acceptance of a replicated nonhuman being (e.g., robot)
     until a point where we start to feel uneasy upon discovering certain features
     that are nonhuman like (e.g., actions, expressions, voice). See Masahiro Mori,
     "The Uncanny Valley," *Energy*, 7, no. 4 (1970): 33–5.

51   Suzanne Livingston, "What Makes Us Human?//Unpacking the Themes Behind
     AI: More than Human," Barbican Centre, May 17, 2019, https://www.you
     tube.com/watch?v=VoDAdiNDxF8.

52   Yuji Sone, *Japanese Robot Culture: Performance, Imagination, and Modernity*
     (New York: Palgrave Macmillan, 2017).

53   Kate Hutchinson, "Hatsune Miku: Japan's Holographic Pop Star Might Be the
     Future of Music," *The Guardian*, December 5, 2014, https://www.theguardian.
     com/music/2014/dec/05/hatsune-miku-japan-hologram-pop-star#maincontent.

54   Jackson and Dines, "Vocaloids and Japanese Virtual Vocal Performance:
     The Cultural Heritage and Technological Futures of Vocal Puppetry"; Rafal
     Zaborowski, "Hatsune Miku and Japanese Virtual Idols," in *The Oxford
     Handbook of Music and Virtuality,* 111–28.

55   Before one judges this story, do read the following emotional article: Stephanie
     Hegarty, "Why I Married a Cartoon Character," *BBC News*, August 17, 2019,
     https://www.bbc.co.uk/news/stories-49343280.

56   Cosplay is the practice of dressing up as characters based on J-pop culture
     (such as a film, book, anime, manga, comic, etc.).

57   View the concert here: Miku, "Expo Europe Tour 2020—Brixton 02 London,"
     January 13, 2020, video, 1:42:16, https://www.youtube.com/watch?v=1jD
     gd2-IrPg.

58   Other virtual performers include Rin Kagamine, Len Kagamine, Kaito, and
     Luka.

59   Jean Baudrillard, "Objects, Images, and the Possibilities of Aesthetic Illusion,"
     in *Jean Baudrillard: Art and Artefact,* ed. Nicholas Zurbrugg (London: Sage,
     1997), 12.

60   See Miquela's Instagram page, https://www.instagram.com/lilmiquela.

61   Melissa Chan, "The 25 Most Influential People of the Internet," *Time*, June 30,
     2018, https://time.com/5324130/most-influential-internet/.

62   Minna Fingerhood, "Lil Miquela, Postmodernism, and a Cynicism Towards
     Truth in American Society," *Medium*, August 20, 2019, https://medium.com/
     swlh/lil-miquela-postmodernism-and-a-cynicism-towards-truth-in-american
     -society-6f42b1434ce4.

63   As a reminder to the reader: Gorillaz was created as a response to the
     commodified music industry and celebrity culture. Hatsune Miku was created
     to allow fans to create her music, visuals, and communities.

64   Steff Yotka, "Go Viral, Post #Spon, Get #Canceled: How Social Media
     Transformed Fashion in the 2010s," *Vogue*, July 18, 2019, https://www.vog
     ue.com/article/2010s-fashion-social-media-impact.

65   View the video here: Miquela, "Money," 2019, music video, 3:41, https://ww
     w.youtube.com/watch?v=2gnHYLRtCGk.

66   Visit www.minecraft.net.

67   Zack O'Malley Greenburg, "Forbes 30 Under 30 Cover Story: How
     Marshmello Became a $44 Million DJ," *Forbes*, November 7, 2018, https
     ://www.forbes.com/sites/zackomalleygreenburg/2018/11/07/forbes-30-unde
     r-30-cover-story-how-marshmello-became-a-44-million-dj/#6d5cb046618b.
     Of course, this is not the first time that artists have practiced concealing
     their identities in live settings, for example, Danger Mouse, Gnarls Barkley,
     Deadmau5, Daft Punk, and Gorillaz.

68   The online video game Fortnite, developed by Epic Games, is available in
     three modes: "Save the World" (a survival game where the players have to
     face challenges so that they will not "die"/lose); "Battle Royale" (a multiple
     player game that has similar features to the survival genre but with many
     virtual players involved); "Creative" (a sandbox game where the players can
     create, destroy, and modify their virtual environment). For more information,
     visit: www.epicgames.com/fortnite. It is also worth mentioning that the game
     is mainly aimed at a young audience, and it's estimated that it has 250 million
     registered users and 80 million monthly players, making it a very popular
     game.

69   Katherine Isbister, *How Games Move Us: Emotions by Design* (Cambridge,
     MA: The MIT Press, 2017), 53.

70   View it here: Marshmello, "Marshmello Holds First Ever Fortnite Concert
     Live at Pleasant Park," February 2, 2019, video, 10:17, https://www.youtube.
     com/watch?v=NBsCzN-jfvA

71   Sammy Andrews in Tim Ingham, "Marshmello Just Played a Live Set to
     10 Million People in Video Game Fortnite—And That Wasn't the Most
     Interesting Move He Made This Weekend," *Music Business Worldwide*,
     February 3, 2019, https://www.musicbusinessworldwide.com/marshmello-just-
     played-a-live-set-to-10m-people-in-video-game-fortnite-and-that-wasnt-even-
     the-most-interesting-move-he-made-this-weekend/.

72   Marshmello and Epic/Fortnite made a healthy profit from these concerts
     through merchandise, music and game subscribers. Marshmello's merchandise
     included his avatar's skin, emote and glider skin in digital form. Physical items
     included clothing (e.g., hoodies). The high intake of sales proves that this
     concert was a tremendous success and a game changer in terms of expanding
     avenues (Sarah E. Needleman and Anne Steele, "Fortnite—Marshmello Mashup
     Showcases New Avenues for Games, Music," *The Wall Street Journal*, February
     9, 2019, https://www.wsj.com/articles/a-glimpse-of-fortnites-future-music-
     and-dancing-without-the-guns-11549720800.), and revenues in the music and
     creative industries. Furthermore, immediately after the concert, music streams
     of Marshmello's songs rapidly increased, according to Nielsen Music (Tatiana
     Cirisano, "Marshmello's Virtual 'Fortnite' Concert Drove Major Streaming,
     Sales Gains," *Billboard*, February 7, 2019, https://www.billboard.com/articles/
     business/8497184/marshmello-fortnite-concert-streaming-sales-gains).

73 MelodyVR has partnerships with major record labels (Warner, Universal, and Sony) as well as independent labels.

74 Steven Hancock in James Hanley, "Melody VR's Steven Hancock on How Virtual Reality is Transforming the Music Biz," *Music Week*, September 26, 2018, https://www.musicweek.com/digital/read/melody-vr-s-steven-hancock -on-how-virtual-reality-is-transforming-the-music-biz/073936.

75 A full concert would range from £7/$9–£12/$15, or £1.99/$2.60 per song/footage. There are plans to move it to a subscription-based model in the future.

76 However, it is worth noting that the number of jump spots varies, which will affect the price.

Chapter 8

1 Bowie on the evolution of the internet as told to Jeremy Paxman, *BBC Newsnight*, 1999.

2 An example of a successful (online) DIY artist is Odd Future's Tyler the Creator (Tyler Okonma), who became popular with "horrorcore" rap.

3 Online interactivity between the artist and fan has not always worked. Take, for example, U2's disastrous marketing attempt at distributing their *Songs of Innocence* album (2014) directly on Apple users' devices without permission.

4 Nicola Dibben, *Björk's Biophilia* (New York: Bloomsbury, 2014).

5 Samantha Bennett, "The Listener as Remixer: Mix Stems in Online Fan Community and Competition Contexts," in *The Oxford Handbook of Music and Virtuality*, ed. Sheila Whiteley and Shara Rambarran (New York: Oxford University Press, 2016), 355–76.

6 This was exclusively designed for the *AI: More than Human* exhibition at London's Barbican Center in 2019.

7 Justin A. Williams and Ross Wilson's "Music and Crowdfunded Websites: Digital Patronage and Artist-Fan Interactivity," in *The Oxford Handbook of Music and Virtuality*, 593–612.

8 Whiteley and Rambarran, *The Oxford Handbook of Music and Virtuality*, 554.

9 Nancy K. Baym, *Playing to the Crowd: Musicians, Audiences, and the Intimate Work of Connection* (New York: New York University Press, 2018), 79–80.

10 The purpose of the apps depends on what the user's needs are and what is available, such as food shopping, health check, banking, maps, drawing, playing games, and, more significantly, for music purposes (e.g., albums; see also other examples in this chapter).

11 The interview can be viewed here: "Bowie Talks to Paxman about Music, Drugs, and the Internet," January 11, 2016, video, https://www.bbc.co.uk/new s/av/entertainment-arts-35286749/bowie-talks-to-paxman-about-music-dru gs-and-the-internet.

12 A CD ROM is a compact disc having "read only memory" with installed data (e.g., text/graphics) that can only be "read" by a computer.

13 BowieNet ended up as a server in 2006 and became used for fans to communicate until 2012.

14 The event was judged by David Bowie and famous mash-up DJ Mark Vidler (aka Go Home Productions). The competition was won by David Choi and his track "Big Shaken Car"—a mashup of "She'll Drive the Big Car" (from the *Reality* album) and "Shake It" (from the 1983 album *Let's Dance*).

15 A stem is a specific recorded part of a track such as bass, voice, guitar, etc.

16 Christopher Moore, "2004 (Bowie vs Mashup)," in *Enchanting David Bowie: Space/Time/Body/Memory*, ed. Tolja Cinque, Christopher Moore, and Sean Redmond (New York: Bloomsbury, 2015). Vidler's mashup was based on the tracks "Rebel Rebel" (from *Diamond Dogs*, 1974) and "Never Get Old" (*Reality* album, 2004).

17 Quoted in Craig McLean, "Caught in a Flash," *The Observer*, December 9, 2007, https://www.theguardian.com/music/2007/dec/09/popandrock.radiohead3.

18 www.Radiohead.com.

19 It was estimated that 62 percent paid nothing for the download and the average amount paid was £1.29.

20 Thom Yorke, "Web-Only Album 'Mad' Says Yorke," *BBC News*, January 2, 2008, http://news.bbc.co.uk/1/hi/entertainment/7167759.stm.

21 https://universaleverything.com/projects/polyfauna. You can download the app here: https://apps.apple.com/us/app/polyfauna/id919089402.

22 That is, the app we use for reading, shopping, to check travel, weather, our heart rate, etc.

23 Georgiana Bogdan, "Is the Music Album App the Next Game Changer?" *The Guardian*, August 21, 2011, https://www.theguardian.com/media-network/2013/aug/21/music-album-app.

24 Jonathan Shakhovskoy and Rob Toulson, "Future Music Formats: Evaluating the 'Album App,'" *Journal on the Art of Record Production* 10 (July 2015), https://www.arpjournal.com/asarpwp/future-music-formats-evaluating-the-album-app/

25 I interviewed the founder and developer of variPlay, Rob Toulson, about the concept of the app.

26 Toulson interview by author, UK, June 29, 2020.

27 Ibid.

28 Justin Paterson, Rob Toulson, and Russ Hepworth-Sawyer, "User-Influenced/Machine-Controlled Playback: The variPlay Music App Format for Interactive Recorded Music," *Arts*, 8, no. 3 (2019): 112.

29 Toulson, interview by author, UK, June 29, 2020.

30 Ibid.

31 Ibid.

32 Ibid.

33 Spotify enhanced the audio experience by introducing the "visual loop" in 2019, where the music is accompanied by a looped expressive visual (instead of an image of an album cover) that the listener can engage with. For details see, https://canvas.spotify.com/en-us.

34 Massive Attack originally released the app *Fantom* in 2016. Users could remix the tracks by using the moving camera, movements, heartbeat, time, and location. The other co-creators were Andrew Melchior, Robert Thomas, and Yair Szarf.

35 For more information see, https://fantom.live/.

36 Robert Del Naja quoted in Laura Stavropoulos, "Massive Attack's App Lets Fans Remix their Album 'Mezzanine,'" *U Discover Music*, December 7, 2018, https://www.udiscovermusic.com/news/massive-attacks-app-lets-fans-remix-their-album/.

37 There is an "option" function where you can customize the app and read the credits.

38 If the reader is eager to remix a famous song without having to commit to purchasing or downloading apps, etc. then check this out: "The Rick Astley Remixer," http://dinahmoelabs.com/rickastley.

Chapter 9

1   Lil Nas X on his thoughts on virality and online communities. As told to Andrew R. Chow, "'It Feels Like I'm Chosen to Do This.' Inside the Record-Breaking Rise of Lil Nas X," *Time*, August 15, 2019, https://time.com/5652803/lil-nas-x/.

2   To be fair, those who wanted to work in the music industry would see this as one of the many ways of gaining future work in music.

3   Whiteley and Rambarran, eds., *The Oxford Handbook of Music and Virtuality*, 327.

4   Baym, *Playing to the Crowd: Musicians, Audiences, and the Intimate Work of Connection.*

5   Leah A. Lievrouw, *Alternative and Activist New Media* (Cambridge: Polity, 2011), 2.

6   It must be stated that there are now YouTube subscriptions that users could buy to watch videos without advertisements.

7   Founded in 2007.

8   Founded in 2006.

9   Founded in 2004.

10 Founded in 2010.

11 Instagram is also used for music shout-outs/promotion from famous artists, where they post an audiovisual of a song they like and mention the artist in

the post. This guarantees many "likes" and new followers for both artists in question.

12   Karine Nahon and Jeff Hemsley, *Going Viral* (Cambridge: Polity, 2013), 16.

13   Ibid.

14   The first viral video, shared by email, was known as "badday.mpg'" involving an angry man smashing a computer in his office.

15   Based on Jonah Berger's "STEPPS" formula (Social Currency, Trigger, Emotion, Public, Practical Value, and Stories) in *Contagious: Why Things Catch On* (New York: Simon and Schuster, 2013).

16   Examples of viral music videos include Ok Go's "Here it goes again" (2006); Rebecca Black's "Friday" (2011); The Chainsmoker's "#SELFIE" (2013); Pharrell Williams's "Happy" (2014); Psy's "Gangnam Style" (2012); and Luis Fonsi and Daddy Yankee's "Despacito" (2019) (featuring Justin Bieber) (2019).

17   Directed by Director X (Julien Christian Lutz). View the video here: https://www.youtube.com/watch?v=uxpDa-c-4Mc.

18   The Weeknd was at Number One with "The Hills."

19   His real name is Harry Bauer Rodrigues.

20   "Harlem Shake" went to number one in the Billboard Hot music charts in 2013.

21   Hilde Van den Bulck and Anders Olof Larsson, "'There's a Starman Waiting in the Sky': Mourning David #Bowie on Twitter," *Convergence: The International Journal of Research into New Media Technologies,* 25, no. 2 (2019): 307–23.

22   Nathalie Claessens and Hilde Van den Bulck, "Parasocial Relationships with Audiences' Favourite Celebrities: The Role of Audience and Celebrity Characteristics in a Representative Flemish Sample," *Communications,* 40, no. 1 (2015): 43–56; P. David Marshall, ed., *The Celebrity Culture Reader* (London: Routledge, 2006).

23   Van den Bulck and Larsson, "'There's a Starman Waiting in the Sky': Mourning David #Bowie on Twitter," 310

24   Ibid.

25   Introduced by biologist Richard Dawkins in his 1976 research, *The Selfish Gene.* The first nonmusical meme was the "dancing baby" in 1996, created on *Character Studio* software, and it went viral on websites and television programs. A famous musical meme is the "Rick Rolled" prank and clickbait, where the user clicks on a web link and is redirected to Rick Astley's "Never Gonna Give You Up."

26   Music memes include Migos featuring Lil Uzi Vert—"Bad and Boujee" (2016); Arianna Grande's *My Everything* stool challenge (2014).

27   Lil Nas X prefers to describe the song as country trap. Trap music is an offshoot of hip-hop that musically relies on machines (e.g., TR-808 kick drums and bass synthesized sounds) to portray melodic but melancholic sounds. The song was based on a prerecorded rhythm track, by Dutch producer YoungKio

(Kiowa Roukema). The track includes a Nine Inch Nails' sample, "34 Ghosts IV" consisting of a steel guitar melody blended with YoungKio's trap twist of drum and bass.

28 The term was coined by Bri Malandro, "'One In Four Cowboys Are Black': The YeeHaw Agenda's Founder on the Politics of Cowboy Style," *The Guardian,* February 21, 2020, https://www.theguardian.com/fashion/2020/feb/21/one-in-four-cowboys-were-black-the-yee-haw-agendas-founder-on-the-politics-of-cowboy-style.

29 Chow, "'It Feels Like I'm Chosen to Do This.' Inside the Record-Breaking Rise of Lil Nas X."

30 Lil Nas X in Brittany Spanos, "How Lil Nas X and 'Old Town Road' Defy Categorization," *Smithsonian Magazine,* December 2019, https://www.smithsonianmag.com/arts-culture/lil-nas-x-old-town-road-american-ingenuity-180973492/.

31 TikTok was formally known as "Musical.ly" created by Alex Zhu and Luyu Yang in 2014.

32 The song was removed from the number one spot in the Billboard Hot Country chart with the claim that it did not sound "country" enough . . . hmm. If you research the history of Country Music, you can make up your own mind on this matter. Hootie and the Blowfish anyone (and it's the only country band that I like!)?

33 As told to Ben Homewood, "On the Radar Lil Nas X," *Music Week,* May 6, 2019, 11.

Conclusion

1 Not forgetting the staff and other businesses that help to make the live performance happen, for example, ticketing, transportation, catering, hospitality, technicians, sound engineers, and so forth.

2 For example, there are rumors that there could be virtual performances by Amy Winehouse and Roy Orbison in the future.

3 Popular posthumous albums include the works of Marvin Gaye, Janis Joplin, Otis Redding, Ray Charles, Jimi Hendrix, Joy Division, Prince, John Lennon, Jeff Buckley, Mac Miller, and Juice WRLD. Estates of the following artists that raised their concerns and disapproval in releasing posthumous material include Aaliyah, Amy Winehouse (in this case, Universal's Chief Executive made the decision to destroy copies of her later demos), and Chris Cornell (Soundgarden).

4 A respectable collaboration would be Natalie Cole's duet with her father, Nat King Cole, on the song "Unforgettable" (1991), and Stephen Marley's *Bob Marley: Chant Down Babylon* (that features Lauryn Hill, Erykah Badu, Rakim, and Chuck D). A questionable collaboration would be Tony Bennett's virtual duet with Billie Holiday's "God Bless this Child" (1997).

5 Oculus, "'Tim' by Avicii: A VR Experience," June 6, 2019, https://www.oculus.com/experiences/event/398766307379450/?intern_source=blog&intern_conten

t=experience-the-world-premiere-of-aviciis-posthumous-album-tim-in-oculus-v
enues.

6 View the performance here: Jimmy Kimmel Live, "Gorillaz—Aries," May 20,
   2020, video, https://www.youtube.com/watch?v=HLm8zvM7cwM.

7 Arjun Appadurai, "Futures in the Making," in *The Future Starts Here*, ed. Rory
   Hyde, Mariana Pestana, and Kieran Long (London: V&A Publishing, 2018),
   155.

8 AI in music is not a new concept, but it is a rapid development. Despite the
   obvious links with virtual music and digital technology, I have not touched on
   AI music mainly because it has its own history (that dates back to the twentieth
   century) and various areas of discussion. However, it is worth mentioning that
   in 1995 David Bowie launched an app, "Verbasizer," that randomized and
   structured words which he later used as lyrics. Current types of AI software
   include AMPER that generates compositions based on mood and genres
   resulting in artists such as Taryn Southern and her album *I AM AI* (2017);
   bots (robots) that automate tasks on the internet, such as Dadabots, a neural
   network that generates automated metal music 24/7 on YouTube; and music
   recognition software such as Shazam where it can detect, identify, and provide
   information on songs instantly to the user.

9 Jaron Lanier in Peter Rubin, "A Conversation with Jaron Lanier, VR
   Juggernaut," *Wired*, November 21, 2017, https://www.wired.com/story/jaron-l
   anier-vr-interview/.

BIBLIOGRAPHY

Aamoth, Doug. "A Brief History of Skype." *Time*, May 10, 2011. https://techlan
d.time.com/2011/05/10/a-brief-history-of-skype/.

Aamoth, Doug. "First Smartphone Turns 20: Fun Facts About Simon." *Time*,
August 18, 2014. https://time.com/3137005/first-smartphone-ibm-simon/.

Acland, Charles R, ed. *Residual Media*. Minneapolis: University of Minnesota,
1998.

Aitken, Hugh G. J. *The Origins of Radio*. Princeton: Princeton University Press,
1985.

Albiez, Sean and David Pattie, eds. *Brian Eno: Oblique Music*. London:
Bloomsbury, 2016.

Ali, Barish and Heidi Wallace. "Out of This World: Ziggy Stardust and the
Spatial Interplay of Lyrics, Vocals, and Performance." In *David Bowie: Critical
Perspectives*, edited by Eoin Devereux, Aileen Dillane, and Martin J. Power,
263–79. New York and London: Routledge, 2015.

Anderson, Tim. *Popular Music in a Digital Music Economy: Problems and
Practices for an Emerging Service Industry*. New York: Routledge, 2014.

Anderson, Walter Truett, ed. *The Truth About the Truth: De-fusing and Re-
constructing the Postmodern World*. New York: Penguin, 1995.

Anon. "8-Foot 'Genius' Dedicated; UNIVAC Will Go to Work on Census Bureau's
Data." *New York Times*, June 15, 1951. https://www.nytimes.com/1951/06/15/
archives/8foot-genius-dedicated-univac-will-go-to-work-on-census-bureaus.ht
ml.

Anon. "Console Portraits: A 40-Year Pictorial History of Gaming." *Wired*, June 15,
2007. https://www.wired.com/2007/06/gallery-game-history/.

Appadurai, Arjun. *Modernity at Large: Cultural Dimensions of Globalization*.
Minneapolis: University of Minnesota Press, 1996.

Appadurai, Arjun. "Futures in the Making." In *The Future Starts Here*, edited
by Rory Hyde, Mariana Pestana, and Kieran Long, 154–5. London: V&A
Publishing, 2018.

Arditi, David. *iTake-Over: The Recording Industry in the Digital Era*. London:
Rowman and Littlefield, 2017.

Arnold, Gina, Daniel Cookney, Kirsty Fairclough, and Michael Goddard, eds.
Music/Video: Histories, Aesthetics, Media. New York: Bloomsbury, 2017.

Artaud, Antonin. *The Theatre and Its Double*, trans. Mary Caroline Richards. New
York: Grove Press, 1958.

Askerøi, Eirik, Kai Arne Hansen, and Freya Jarman, eds. *Popular Musicology and
Identity: Essays in Honor of Stan Hawkins*. New York: Routledge, 2020.

Atkinson, Paul. "Man in a Briefcase: The Social Construction of the Laptop
    Computer and the Emergence of a Type Form." *Journal of Design History*, 18,
    no. 2 (2005): 8.
Attali, Jacques. *Noise: The Political Economy of Music*. Translated by Brian
    Massumi. Minnesota: University of Minnesota Press, 1985.
Atwood, Brett. "David Bowie Single Exclusive to Internet." *Billboard*, September
    21, 1996.
Atwood, Brett. "The History of the Music Industry's First-Ever Digital Single for
    Sale, 20 Years After Its Release." *Billboard*, September 9, 2017. https://www.bil
    lboard.com/articles/business/7964771/history-music-industry-first-ever-digital-s
    ingle-20-years-later.
Auslander, Philip. *Liveness: Performance in a Mediatized Culture*. London:
    Routledge, 1999.
Auslander, Philip. *Performing Glam Rock: Gender and Theatricality in Popular
    Music*. Michigan: The University of Michigan Press, 2006.
Austin, Mark, ed. *Music Video Games: Performance, Politics and Play*. New York
    and London, Bloomsbury, 2016.
Ayers, Michael D., ed. *Cybersounds: Essays on Visual Music Culture (Digital
    Formations)*. New York: Peter Lang Publishing, 2006.
Ayers, Michael D. "The Cyberactivism of a Dangermouse." In *Cybersounds: Essays
    on Visual Music Culture (Digital Formations)*, edited by Michael D. Ayers,
    127–36. New York: Peter Lang Publishing, 2006.
Balsamo, Anne. "Reading Cyborgs, Writing Feminism." In *Cybersexualities: A
    Reader on Feminist Theory, Cyborgs and Cyberspace*, edited by Jenny Wolmack,
    145–56. Edinburgh: Edinburgh University Press, 1999.
Bananaz. Directed by Ceri Levy. Bananaz Productions: UK, 2009. DVD.
Barthes, Roland. *Image-Music-Text*. Translated by Stephen Heath. London:
    Fontana Press, 1977.
Baudrillard, Jean. *America*. London: Verso, 1988.
Baudrillard, Jean. *Symbolic Exchange and Death*. Translated by Iain Hamilton
    Grant. London: Sage Publications, 1993.
Baudrillard, Jean. *Simulacra and Simulation*. Translated by Sheila Glaser. Ann
    Arbor, MI: University of Michigan Press, 1994.
Baudrillard, Jean. "Objects, Images, and the Possibilities of Aesthetic Illusion." In
    Jean Baudrillard: Art and Artefact, edited by Nicholas Zurbrugg, 7–18. London:
    Sage, 1997.
Baym, Nancy K. *Playing to the Crowd: Musicians, Audiences, and the Intimate
    Work of Connection*. New York: New York University Press, 2018.
BBC. "Radio." Accessed May 12, 2018. https://www.bbc.co.uk/bitesize/guides/z2
    s97hv/revision/1.
BBC News. "Web-Only Album 'Mad' Says Yorke." *BBC*, January 2, 2008. http://
    news.bbc.co.uk/1/hi/entertainment/7167759.stm.
Bell, Adam Patrick. "D.I.Y. Recreational Recording as Music Making." In *The
    Oxford Handbook of Music Making and Leisure*, edited by Roger Mantie and
    Gareth Dylan Smith, 81–98. New York: Oxford University Press, 2017.
Bemuso. "Music Biz." Accessed August 1, 2018. https://www.bemuso.com.
Benjamin, Walter. *The Work of Art in the Age of Mechanical Reproduction*.
    London: Penguin Books, 2008.

Bennett, Andy. *Cultures of Popular Music*. Berkshire: Open University Press, 2001.

Bennett, Andy and Jon Stratton, eds. *Introduction to Britpop and the English Music Tradition*. Farnham: Ashgate, 2010.

Bennett, Lucy and Pete Booth, eds. *Seeing Fans: Representations of Fandom Media and Popular Culture*. London: Bloomsbury, 2016.

Bennett, R. J. "Live Concerts and Fan Identity in the Age of the Internet." In *The Digital Evolution of Live Music*, edited by Angie Jones and Rebecca Jane Bennett, 3–16. Oxford: Chandos Publishing, 2015.

Bennett, Samantha. "The Listener as Remixer: Mix Stems in Online Fan Community and Competition Contexts." In *The Oxford Handbook of Music and Virtuality*, edited by Sheila Whiteley and Shara Rambarran, 355–76. New York: Oxford University Press, 2016

Berger, Jonah. *Contagious: Why Things Catch On*. New York: Simon and Schuster, 2013.

Bernays, Ueli. "The Apathy and Ecstasy." *Sign and Sight*, January 22, 2010. http://www.signandsight.com/features.1981.html.

Blake, Andrew. *The Music Business*. London: B.T. Batsford, 1992.

Blake, Andrew. *Popular Music: The Age of the Multimedia*. London: Middlesex University Press, 2007.

"Bluetooth. The History of the Bluetooth SIG." Accessed May 22, 2018. https://www.bluetooth.com/about-us/our-history/

Bogdan, Georgiana. "Is the Music Album App the Next Game Changer?" *The Guardian*, August 21, 2011. https://www.theguardian.com/media-network/2013/aug/21/music-album-app.

Bomb the Bass. "Clear Cut." Recorded in 2001. Morr Music MM018. CD.

Borschke, Margie. *This Is Not a Remix: Piracy, Authenticity and Popular Music*. New York and London: Bloomsbury, 2017.

Bourriaud, Nicolas. *Postproduction*. Berlin and New York: Sternberg, 2002.

boyd, danah m. and Nicole B. Ellison. "Social Network Sites: Definition, History, and Scholarship." *Journal of Computer-Mediated Communication*, 13 (2008): 210–30.

Braae, Nick and Kai Arne Hansen, eds. *On Popular Music and Its Unruly Entanglements*. Cham, Switzerland: Palgrave Macmillan, 2019.

Bracewell, Michael. *The Nineties: When Surface Was Depth*. London: Flamingo, 2003.

Briggs, Jonathyne. *Sounds French: Globalization, Cultural Communities, and Pop Music, 1958–1980*. New York: Oxford University Press.

Bright, Peter. "Microsoft Buys Skype for $8.5 Billion. Why, Exactly?" *Wired*, October 5, 2011. https://www.wired.com/2011/05/microsoft-buys-skype-2/.

British Library. "Recording and Sound History: Playback and Recording Equipment." Accessed May 10, 2018. https://sounds.bl.uk/Sound-recording-history/Equipment/029M-UNCAT01XXXXX-0002V0.

Brockwell, Helen. "Forgotten Genius: The Man Who Made a Working VR Machine in 1957." *Techradar*, April 3, 2016. https://www.techradar.com/uk/news/wearables/forgotten-genius-the-man-who-made-a-working-vr-machine-in-1957-1318253.

Brooks, Lee, Mark Donnelly, and Richard Mills, eds. *Mad Dogs and Englishness: Popular Music and English Identities*. Bloomsbury: London, 2017.

Brooks, Mikey. "Money Is Not All." Recorded 1978. Fat Man. FM004, 1978. 7"
    Single.
Brøvig-Hannsen, Ragnhild and Anne Danielsen. *Digital Signatures: The Impact of
    Digitalization on Popular Music Sound*. Cambridge, MA: MIT Press, 2016.
Browne, Cass. *Gorillaz: The Rise of the Ogre*. New York: Riverhead Books, 2006.
Brown, Timothy Scott. "In Search of Space: The Trope of Escape in German
    Electronic Music Around 1968." *Contemporary European History*, 26, no. 2
    (2017): 339–52.
Bull, Michael. *Sound Moves: iPod Culture and Urban Experience*. Routledge:
    London, 2007.
Bull, Michael, ed. *The Routledge Companion to Sound Studies*. Routledge: Oxon
    and New York, 2019.
Bull, Michael and Les Back, eds. *The Auditory Culture Reader*. New York: Berg,
    2003.
Burgess, Richard James. *The Art of Music Production: The Theory and Practice*.
    4th ed. New York: Oxford University Press, 2013.
Burgess, Richard James. *The History of Music Production*. New York: Oxford
    University Press, 2014.
Calmon, Waldir. *E Sus Multisons*. Recorded 1970. Copacabana SOLP 40208. LP.
CERN. "A Short History of the Web." Accessed May 22, 2018. https://home.cern/sc
    ience/computing/birth-web/short-history-web.
Cellan-Jones, Rory. "Apple Unveils Apple iPad Tablet Device." January 27, 2010.
    http://news.bbc.co.uk/1/hi/technology/8483654.stm.
Cesarini, Paul. "I Am a DJ, I Am What I Say: The Rise of Podcasting." In *Small
    Tech: The Culture of Digital Tools*, edited Bryon Hawk, David M. Rieder, and
    Ollie Oviedo, 98–100. Minneapolis, MN: University of Minnesota Press, 2008.
Chan, Melissa. "The 25 Most Influential People of the Internet." *Time*, June 30,
    2018. https://time.com/5324130/most-influential-internet/.
Chanan, Michael. *Repeated Takes: A Short History of Recording and Its Effects on
    Music*. London and New York: Verso, 1997.
Cheng, William. *Sound Play: Video Games and the Musical Imagination*. New
    York: Oxford University Press, 2014.
Chow, Andrew R. "'It Feels Like I'm Chosen to Do This.' Inside the Record-
    Breaking Rise of Lil Nas X." *Time*, August 15, 2019. https://time.com/5652803/
    lil-nas-x/.
Christodoulou, Chris. "Rumble in the Jungle: City, Place, and Uncanny Bass."
    Dancecult: Journal of Electronic Dance Music Culture, 3, no. 1 (2001): 44–63.
Cinque, Tolja, Christopher Moore, and Sean Redmond, eds. *Enchanting David
    Bowie: Space/Time/Body/Memory*. New York: Bloomsbury, 2015.
Cirisano, Tatiana. "Marshmello's Virtual 'Fortnite' Concert Drove Major
    Streaming, Sales Gains." *Billboard*, February 7, 2019. https://www.billboar
    d.com/articles/business/8497184/marshmello-fortnite-concert-streaming-sales
    -gains.
Claessens, Nathalie and Hilde Van den Bulck. "Parasocial Relationships with
    Audiences' Favourite Celebrities: The Role of Audience and Celebrity
    Characteristics in a Representative Flemish Sample." *Communicationsm*, 40, no.
    1 (2015): 43–56.

Clark, Travis and John Lynch. "The 50 Best Selling Albums of All Time." *Business Insider*, April 23, 2019. https://www.businessinsider.com/50-best-selling-albums-all-time-2016-9?r=US&IR=T.

Cloonan, Martin. *Popular Music and the State in the UK: Culture, Trade, or Industry?* Oxon and New York: Routledge, 2016.

Collins, Karen. *Game Sound: An Introduction to the History, Theory, and Practice of Video Game Music and Sound Design.* Cambridge, MA and London: The MIT Press.

Collins, Karen, Bill Kapralos, and Holly Tessler, eds. *The Oxford Handbook of Interactive Audio.* New York: Oxford University Press, 2014.

Conner, Thomas. "Hatsune Miku, 2.0Pac, and Beyond: Rewinding and Fast-Forwarding the Virtual Pop Star." In *The Oxford Handbook of Music and Virtuality*, edited by Sheila Whiteley and Shara Rambarran, 129–47. New York: Oxford University Press, 2016.

Cook, Nicholas, David Wilson-Leech, and Eric Clarke, eds. *Cambridge Companion to Recorded Music.* Cambridge: Cambridge University Press, 2009.

Corcoran, Elizabeth. "Have You Heard DAT?" *Scientific American*, 258, no. 5 (May 1988): 30.

Cornell, R. W. *Masculinities.* Berkeley and Los Angeles: University of California Press, 2015.

Cox, Christoph and Daniel Warner, eds. *Audio Culture: Readings in Modern Music.* London: Continuum, 2004.

Cox, Christoph and Daniel Warner, eds. *Audio Culture: Readings in Modern Music.* Rev. ed. New York and London: Bloomsbury, 2017.

Csikszentmihalyi, Mihaly. *Flow: The Psychology of Optimal Experience.* New York: Harper-Perennial, 1990.

Csikszentmihalyi, Mihaly. *Finding Flow: The Psychology of Engagement with Everyday Life.* New York: Basic Books, 1997.

Cutler, Chris. "Plunderphonics." In *Sounding Off! Music as Subversion/ Resistance/ Revolution*, edited by Ron Sakolsky and Fred Wei-Han Ho. Brooklyn, NY: Autonomedia, 1995.

Danger Mouse. *The Grey Album.* Self-Released, 2004.

Davis, Colin. "Ét at Présent: Hauntology, Specters and Phantoms." *French Studies*, LIX, no. 3 (July 2005): 373–9.

Deangelis, Michael. "Jones, Grace." In *Routledge International Encyclopedia of Queer Culture*, edited by David A. Gerstner, 331. New York and Oxon: Routledge, 2006.

Demers, Joanna. *Steal This Music: How Intellectual Property Law Affects Musical Creativity.* Athens and London: The University of Georgia Press, 2006.

Derrida, Jacques. *Specters of Marx: The State of the Debt, the Work of Mourning and the New International.* Translated by Peggy Kamuf. New York and London: Routledge, 1994.

Derrida, Jacques. *Positions.* Continuum: London, 2004.

Descy, Don E. "All Aboard the Internet: Second Life." *Tech Trends*, 52, no. 1 (2008): 5–6.

Devereux, Eoin, Aileen Dillane, and Martin J. Power. *David Bowie: Critical Perspectives.* New York and London: Routledge, 2015.

Dhaenens, Frederik and Sander De Ridder. "Resistant Masculinities In Alternative R&B? Understanding Frank Ocean and The Weeknd's Representations of Gender." *European Journal of Cultural Studies*, 3, no. 18 (2015): 283–99.

Dibben, Nicola. *Björk's Biophilia*. New York: Bloomsbury, 2014.

Dines, Mike and Georgina Gregory. *Beatified Beats: Exploring the Spiritual in Popular Music*. London: Bloomsbury, forthcoming.

Downes, Kieran. "'Perfect Sound Forever': Innovation, Aesthetics, and the Re-making of Compact Disc Playback." *Technology and Culture*, 51, no. 2 (April 2010): 305–31.

Downhill Battle. *Downhill Battle Press Release*, 2004. http://downhillbattle.org/pressrelease/greyalbum_21104.html.

Draper, Paul and Frank Millard. "Music in Perpetual Beta: Composition, Remediation, and 'Closure." In *The Oxford Handbook of Music and Virtuality*, edited by Sheila Whiteley and Shara Rambarran, 248–65. New York: Oxford University Press, 2016.

du Gay, Paul, Stuart Hall, Linda Jones, High Mackay, and Keith Negus. *Doing Cultural Studies: The Story of the Sony Walkman*. London: Sage, 1997.

Dub Echoes. Directed by Bruno Natal. Soul Jazz Films, 2009. DVD.

Duckworth, William. *Virtual Music: How the Web Got Wired for Sound*. New York: Routledge, 2005.

Duffett, Mark. *Understanding Fandom: An Introduction to the Study of Media Fan Culture*. London: Bloomsbury, 2013.

Eco, Umberto. *Faith in Flakes*. London: Vintage, 1998.

Eco, Umberto. *Turning Back the Clock*. Translated by Alastair McEwen. London: Harvill Secker, 2007.

Edison, Thomas A. "The Phonograph and Its Future." *North American Review*, 126/262 (May–June 1878): 527–36.

Eeels, Josh. "Sex, Drugs, and R&B: Inside the Weeknd's Dark Twisted Fantasy." *Rolling Stone*, October 21, 2015. https://www.rollingstone.com/music/music-news/sex-drugs-and-rb-inside-the-weeknds-dark-twisted-fantasy-176091/.

Eisenberg, Evan. *The Recording Angel*. New Haven and London: Yale University Press, 2005.

EMI. "Alan Blumlein and the Invention of Stereo." Accessed May 8, 2018. https://www.www.emiarchivetrust.org//alan-blumlein-and-the-invention-of-stereo/

EMI. "History of Recorded Music Timeline." Accessed May 8, 2018. https://www.www.emiarchivetrust.org/about/history-of-recording/

Emmerson, Simon. *Live Electronic Music*. Oxon: Routledge.

Eno, Brian. *Music for Airports/Ambient 1*. Recorded 1978. Ambient Label (AMB001) PVC 7908. LP.

Escorza, Liane. "Grace Jones x Chris Levine." *Dazed*, April 27, 2010. https://www.dazeddigital.com/photography/article/7418/1/grace-jones-x-chris-levine.

Eshun, Kodwo. *More Brilliant than the Sun: Adventures in Sonic Fiction*. London: Quartet Books, 1998.

Everett-Green, Robert. "Danger Mouse: 'I'm into Melodies That Break Your Heart a Little Bit.'" *The Globe and Mail*, May 30, 2011. http://www.theglobeandmail.com/arts/music/danger-mouse-im-into-melodies-that-break-your-heart-a-little-bit/article581379/.

Fabbri, Franco. "How Genres Are Born, Change, Die: Conventions, Communities and Diachronic Processes." In *Critical Musicological Reflections*, edited by Stan Hawkins, 179–91. Aldershot: Ashgate, 2012.

Fabris, Peter. "Funky Music: This Year, Music Fans Don't Have to Go to a Record Store to Buy a CD. Next Year, They Won't Have to Buy a CD." *CIO WebBusiness*, December 1, 1997.

Farby, Merrill. "The Story Behind America's First Commercial Computer." *Time*, March 31, 2016. https://time.com/4271506/census-bureau-computer-history/.

Faulkner, Joey. "MiniDisc, the Forgotten Format." *The Guardian*, September 28, 2012. https://www.theguardian.com/music/musicblog/2012/sep/24/sony-mini disc-20-years.

Featherstone, Mike. *Consumer Culture and Postmodernism*. London: Sage, 1991.

Fingerhood, Minna. "Lil Miquela, Postmodernism, and a Cynicism Towards Truth in American Society." *Medium*, August 20, 2019. https://medium.com/swlh/lil-mi quela-postmodernism-and-a-cynicism-towards-truth-in-american-society-6f42b1 434ce4.

Finnegan, Ruth. *The Hidden Musicians: Music-Making in an English Town.* Cambridge: Cambridge University Press, 1989.

Fisher, Mark. "What Is Hauntology?"*Film Quartely*, 66, no. 1 (Fall 2012): 16–24.

Fitch, Richard. "In This Age of Grand Allusion: Bowie, Nihilism, and Meaning." In *David Bowie: Critical Perspectives*, edited by Eoin Devereux, Aileen Dillane, and Martin J. Power, 19–34. New York and London: Routledge, 2015.

Fitzpatrick, Alex. "Apple Is Pulling the Plug on iTunes. So What Happens to All Your Music?" *Time*, June 4, 2019. https://time.com/5600502/apple-itunes-ap p-music/.

Forman, Murray and Mark Anthony Neal. *That's the Joint! The Hip-Hop Studies Reader*. New York: Routledge, 2004.

Foucault, Michel. *The Foucault Reader*. Harmondsworth: Penguin, 1986.

Frere-Jones, Sasha. "1+1+1=1: The Math of Mashups." *The New Yorker*, 80, no. 42 (2005): 85.

Frith, Simon. "'The Magic That Can Set You Free': The Ideology of Folk and the Myth of the Rock Community." *Popular Music*, 1 (1981): 159–68.

Frith, Simon. *Sound Effects: Youth, Leisure, and the Politics of Rock "n" Roll*. London: Constable, 1983.

Frith, Simon. "Towards an Aesthetic of Popular Music." In *Music and Society: The Politics of Composition, Performance and Reception*, edited by Richard Leppert and Susan McClary, 133–49. Cambridge: Cambridge University Press, 1987.

Frith, Simon. "The Industrialization of Popular Music." In *Popular Music and Communication*, edited by James Lull, 49–74. Newbury Park, CA: Sage, 1992.

Frith, Simon. *Performing Rites: Evaluating Popular Music*. Oxford and New York: Oxford University Press, 1998.

Frith, Simon. "The Popular Music Industry." In *Cambridge Companion to Pop and Rock*, edited by Simon Frith, Will Straw, and John Street, 26–52. Cambridge: Cambridge University Press, 2001.

Frith, Simon, Andrew Goodwin, and Lawrence Grossberg, ed. *Sound and Vision: The Music Video Reader*. London: Routledge, 1993.

Frith, Simon, Will Straw, and John Street, eds. *Cambridge Companion to Pop and Rock*. Cambridge: Cambridge University Press, 2001

Fritsch, Melanie. "Beat It! – Playing the 'King of Pop' in Video Games." In *Music Video Games: Performance, Politics and Play*, edited by Mark Austin, 153–76. New York and London, Bloomsbury, 2016.

Gallagher, Mitch. "Insider's View of the Modern SAW." *Sweetwater Music Instruments and Pro* Audio, 2008. http://www.sweetwater.com/featyre/daw/daw:defined.php.

Ganapati, Priya. "Dec. 23, 1947: Transistor Opens Door to Digital Future." *Wired*, December 23, 2009. https://www.wired.com/2009/12/1223shockley-bardeen-brattain-transistor/.

Gay, Roxanne. "Madonna's Spring Awakening." *Harper's Bazaar*, January 10, 2017. https://www.harpersbazaar.com/culture/features/a19761/madonna-interview.

George, Nelson. "Sample This." In *That's The Joint! The Hip-Hop Studies Reader*, edited by Murray Forman and Mark Anthony Neal, 437–47. New York: Routledge, 2004.

Gerstner, David A., ed. *Routledge International Encyclopedia of Queer Culture*. New York and Oxon: Routledge, 2006.

Gitelman, Lisa. "Media, Materiality, and The Measure of the Digital; Or, the Case of Sheet Music and the Problem of Piano Rolls." In *Memory Bytes: History, Technology, and Digital Culture*, edited by Lauren Rabinovitz and Abraham Geil, 199–217. Durham, NC: Duke University Press, 2004.

Gitlin, Lauren. "DJ Makes Jay-Z Meets the Beatles: Danger Mouse Makes 'Black' and 'White' Equal 'Grey.'" *Rolling Stone*, February 5, 2004. http://www.rollingstone.com/news/story/5937152/dj_makes_jayz_meet_beatles.

Gnarls Barkley. "Crazy." Recorded 2006 on Downtown and Warner Music Group, Single.

Goddard, Michael, Benjamin Halligan, and Nicola Spelman, eds. *Resonances: Noise and Contemporary Music*. New York and London: Bloomsbury, 2013.

Goodwin, Andrew. "Sample and Hold: Pop Music in the Digital Age of Reproduction." *Critical Quarterly*, 30, no. 3 (1988): 34–49.

Goodwin, Andrew. *Music Television and Popular Culture: Dancing in the Distraction Factory*. London: Routledge, 1993.

Gottschalk Jennie. *Experimental Music since 1970*. New York and London: Bloomsbury, 2016.

Graves, Zeke. "When MiniDiscs Recorded the Earth." *Duke University*, April 7, 2015. https://blogs.library.duke.edu/bitstreams/2015/04/07/when-minidiscs-recorded-the-earth/.

Grayson, Robert. *Sony: The Company and Its Founders*. Minnesota: ABDO Publishing Company, 2013.

Greenman, Ben. "The House That Remixed." *The New Yorker*, February 2, 2004. http://www.newyorker.com/printables/talk/040209ta_talk_greenman

Gregerson, Erik. "Bitcoin." *Britannica*, ND. https://www.britannica.com/topic/Bitcoin.

Griffiths, Sean. "Names and Terms." In *The Routledge Companion to Postmodernism*, edited by Stuart Sim, 3rd ed., 321. London: Routledge, 2005.

Grimshaw, Mark, ed. *The Oxford Handbook of Virtuality*. New York: Oxford University Press, 2013.

Grossberg, Lawrence. "'You (Still) Have to Fight for Your Right to Party': Music Television as Billboards of Post-modern Difference." *Popular Music*, 7, no. 3 (1988): 315–32.

Grossberg, Lawrence. "The Media Economy of Rock Culture: Cinema, Postmodernity and Authenticity." In *Sound and Vision: The Music Video Reader*, edited by Simon Frith, Andrew Goodwin, and Lawrence Grossberg, 185–209. London: Routledge, 1993.

Grubbs, David. *Records Ruin the Landscape: John Cage, The Sixties, Sound Recording*. Durham, NC: Duke University Press, 2014.

Gunkel, David J. "Rethinking the Digital Remix: Mash-Ups and the Metaphysics of Sound Recording." *Popular Music and Society*, 31 (2008): 489–510.

Gustafson, Adam. "How Prince's Quest for Complete Artistic Control Changed the Music Industry Forever." *The Conversation*, April 22, 2016. https://theconversat ion.com/how-princes-quest-for-complete-artistic-control-changed-the-music-i ndustry-forever-58267.

Haire, Meaghan. "A Brief History of The Walkman." *Time*, July 1, 2009. http://con tent.time.com/time/nation/article/0,8599,1907884,00.html.

Halligan, Benjamin, Kirsty Fairclough, Robert Edgar, and Nicola Spelman, eds. *The Arena Concert: Music, Media and Mass Entertainment*. New York: Bloomsbury, 2015.

Hammersley, Ben. "Audible Revolution." *The Guardian*, February 12, 2004. https:// www.theguardian.com/media/2004/feb/12/broadcasting.digitalmedia.

Hanford, Paul. "Berlin's Love for Techno Has Turned It into a Music Setup Powerhouse." *Wired*, December 12, 2019. https://www.wired.co.uk/article/ber lin-music-tech.

Hanley, James. "Melody VR's Steven Hancock on How Virtual Reality Is Transforming the Music Biz." *Music Week*, September 26, 2018. https://ww w.musicweek.com/digital/read/melody-vr-s-steven-hancock-on-how-virtual-real ity-is-transforming-the-music-biz/073936.

Hansen, Kai Arne. "It's a Dark Philosophy: The Weeknd's Intermedial Aestheticization of Violence." In *On Popular Music and Its Unruly Entanglements*, edited by Nick Braae and Kai Arne Hansen, 235–56. Cham, Switzerland: Palgrave Macmillan, 2019.

Haraway, Donna. *A Cyborg Manifesto: Science, Technology, and Socialist-Feminism in the Late Twentieth Century*. Minneapolis: University of Minnesota Press, 2006.

Harper, Simon. "When in Rome." *The Clash*, June (2011): 72–81.

Harris, John. *The Last Party: Britpop, Blair and the Demise of English Rock*. London: Harper Perennial, 2004.

Harrison, Ann. *Music: The Business*. 7th ed. Croydon: Virgin Books, 2017.

Harvey, David. *The Condition of Postmodernity: An Enquiry into the Origins of Cultural Change*. Oxford: Blackwell, 1990.

Hawk, Bryon, David M. Rieder, and Ollie Oviedo, eds. *Small Tech: The Culture of Digital Tools*. Minnesota: University of Minnesota Press, 2008.

Hawkins, Stan. *Settling the Pop Score: Pop Texts and Identity Politics*. Aldershot: Ashgate, 2002.

Hawkins, Stan, ed. *Critical Musicological Reflections*. Aldershot: Ashgate, 2012.

Hawkins, Stan. *Queerness in Pop Music: Aesthetics, Gender Norms, and Temporality*. London and New York: Routledge, 2016.

Hawkins, Stan. "Introduction: David Bowie (1947–2016)." *Contemporary Music Review*, 37, no. 3 (2018): 189–92.

Hebdige, Dick. *Cut 'n' Mix: Culture, Identity and Caribbean Music*. London and New York: Comedia, 1987.

Hegarty, Stephanie. "Why I Married a Cartoon Character." *BBC News*, August 17, 2019. https://www.bbc.co.uk/news/stories-49343280.

Heilbrun, Adam. "An Interview with Jaron Lanier." *Whole World Review*, 64 (1989): 108–19.

Heidegger, Martin. *The Question Concerning Technology and Other Essays*. Translated by William Lovitt. New York and London: Garland Publishing Inc., 1977.

Hennion, Antoine. *The Passion for Music: A Sociology of Mediation*. Translated by Margaret Riguad and Peter Collier. Farnham: Ashgate, 2015.

Henriques, Julian. "Sonic Disapora, Vibrations and Rhythm: Thinking Through the Sounding of the Jamaican Dancehall Session," *African and Black Diaspora*, 1, no. 2 (2008): 215–36.

Henriques, Julian. *Sonic Bodies: Reggae Sound Systems, Performance Techniques and Ways of Knowing*. London: Continuum, 2011.

Henriques, Julian and Hillegonda Rietveld. "Echo." In *The Routledge Companion to Sound Studies*, edited by Michael Bull, 275–82. Routledge: Oxon and New York, 2019.

Henry, Pierre and Michel Colombier. "Psyché Rock." Recorded 1967. Philips 456 353–1, 1997. 12" Single.

Herman, Andrew and John M. Sloop. "The Politics of Authenticity in Postmodern Rock Culture: The Case of Negativland and the Letter 'U' and the Numeral '2.'" *Critical Studies in Mass Communication*, 15, no. 1 (1998): 1–20.

Hillis, Ken. "A Geography of the Eye: The Technologies of Virtual Reality." In *Culture of the Internet: Virtual Spaces, Real History, Living Bodies*, edited by Rob Shields, 70–98. Sage: London, 1996.

Holmes, Thomas B. *Electronic and Experimental Music: Foundations of New Music and New Listening*. New York and London: Routledge, 2002.

Homewood, Ben. "On the Radar: Lil Nas X." *Music Week*, May 6, 2019, 11.

Hope, Donna P., ed. *Reggae from Yaad: Traditional and Emerging Themes in Jamaican Popular Music*. Kingston, Jamaica: Ian Randle Publishers, 2015.

Horner, Jim. "The Case of DAT Technology: Industrial versus Pecuniary Function." *Journal of Economic Issues*, 25, no. 2 (June 1991): 449–57.

Hugill, Andrew. *The Digital Musician*. New York: Routledge, 2012.

Hunter, Andrea and Vincent Mosco. "Virtual Dystopia." In *The Oxford Handbook of Virtuality*, edited by Mark Grimshaw, 727–37. New York: Oxford University Press, 2013.

Hutchinson, Kate. "Hatsune Miku: Japan's Holographic Pop Star Might Be the Future of Music." *The Guardian*, December 5, 2014. https://www.theguardian.com/music/2014/dec/05/hatsune-miku-japan-hologram-pop-star#maincontent.

Idris Elba's How Clubbing Changed the World. Produced by Sam Bridger. Aired August 24, 2012, on Channel 4.

IFPI. *Recording Industry in Numbers 2008, the Definitive Source of Global Music Market Information*. United Kingdom: IFPI, 2008.

Ingham, Tim. "Marshmello Just Played a Live Set to 10 Million People in Video Game Fortnite – And That Wasn't the Most Interesting Move he Made This Weekend." *Music Business Worldwide*, February 3, 2019. https://www.musicbus inessworldwide.com/marshmello-just-played-a-live-set-to-10m-people-in-video -game-fortnite-and-that-wasnt-even-the-most-interesting-move-he-made-this-w eekend/.

Isbister, Katherine. *How Games Move Us: Emotions by Design*. Cambridge, MA: The MIT Press, 2017.

Jackson, Louise H. and Mike Dines. "Vocaloids and Japanese Virtual Vocal Performance: The Cultural Heritage and Technological Futures of Vocal Puppetry." In *The Oxford Handbook of Music and Virtuality*, edited by Sheila Whiteley and Shara Rambarran, 101–10. New York: Oxford University Press, 2016.

Jeffries, Stuart. "Music on a Roll." *The Guardian*, March 28, 2003. https://www.the guardian.com/music/2003/mar/28/classicalmusicandopera.artsfeatures.

Jenkins, Craig. "Damon Albarn Is Unfortunately Really Good at Predicting the Future." *Vulture*, November 8, 2017. https://www.vulture.com/2017/11/intervie w-damon-albarn.html.

Johansson, Sofia and Ann Werner. "Music, the Internet, Streaming: Ongoing Debates." In *Streaming Music: Practices, Media, Cultures*, edited by Sofia Johansson, Ann Werner, Patrik Åker, and Greg Goldenzwaig, 12–24. New York: Routledge, 2018.

Johansson, Sofia, Ann Werner, Patrik Åker, and Greg Goldenzwaig, eds. *Streaming Music: Practices, Media, Cultures*. New York: Routledge, 2018.

Johnson, Bobbie and Lee Glendinning. "Apple Proclaims Its Revolution: A Camera, an iPod . . . Oh, and a Phone." *The Guardian*, January 10, 2007. https://ww w.theguardian.com/technology/2007/jan/10/news.business.

Jones, Angie and Rebecca Jane Bennett, eds. *Digital Evolution of Live Music*. Oxford: Chandos Publishing, 2015.

Jones, Grace. *I'll Never Write My Memoirs*. London: Simon & Schuster, 2015.

Jordan, Ken and Paul D. Miller. "Freeze Frame: Audio, Aesthetics, Sampling and Contemporary Media." In *Sound Unbound: Digital Sampling, Digital Music and Culture*, edited by Paul D. Miller, 97–108. Cambridge, MA and London: MIT Press.

Kahney, Leander. "Inside Look at the Birth of the iPod." *Wired*, July 21, 2004. https ://www.wired.com/2004/07/inside-look-at-birth-of-the-ipod/.

Kane, Brian. *Pierre Schaeffer, Sound Unseen: Acousmatic Sound in Theory and Practice*. New York: Oxford University Press, 2014.

Kaplan, E. Ann. *Rocking Around the Clock: Music Television, Postmodernism, and Consumer Culture*. New York and London: Methuen, 1987.

Katz, Mark. *Capturing Sound: How Technology Has Changed Music*. Berkeley, CA: University of California Press, 2004.

Katz, Mark. "The Amateur in the Age of Mechanical Music." In *The Oxford Handbook of Sound Studies*, edited by Trevor Pinch and Karin Bijsterveld, 459–79. New York: Oxford University Press, 2014.

Kelly, Jem. "Pop Music, Multimedia and Live Performance." In *Music, Sound and Multimedia: From the Live to the Virtual*, edited by Jamie Sexton, 105–21. Edinburgh: Edinburgh University Press, 2007.

Kirkman, Stuart. "When in Rome: Danger Mouse and Daniele Luppi Interviewed." *The Quietus*, May 17, 2011. https://thequietus.com/articles/06268-danger-mouse-daniele-luppi-interview-rome.

Klosterman, Chris. "The DJ Auteur." *The New York Times*, June 18, 2006. http://www.nytimes.com/2006/06/18/magazine/18barkley.html?ei=5090&en=d69638926b798ed5&ex=.

Kollewe, Julia. "Google Timeline: A 10 Year Anniversary." *The Guardian*, September 5, 2008. https://www.theguardian.com/business/2008/sep/05/google.google.

Kraftwerk, *Kraftwerk*. Recorded 1970. Philips 6305058, 1970. LP.

Krautrock: The Rebirth of Germany. Produced by Ben Whalley. Aired October 23, 2009, on BBC Four.

Lacasse, Serge. "Intertextuality and Hypertextuality in Recorded Popular Music." In *The Musical Work: Reality or Invention?*, edited by Michael Talbot, 35–58. Liverpool: University of Liverpool, 2000.

Laing, Dave. "Record Sales in the 1980s." *Popular Music*, 9, no. 2 (April 1990): 235–6.

Lamont, Tom. "The Weeknd: Drugs Were a Crutch for Me." *The Guardian*, December 3, 2016. https://www.theguardian.com/music/2016/dec/03/the-weeknd-abel-tesfaye-interview-music-tom-lamont.

Latour, Brian. *Reassembling the Social: An Introduction to Actor Network Theory*. Oxford: Oxford University Press, 2005.

Left, Sarah. "Technology: Email Timeline." *The Guardian*, March 13, 2002. https://www.theguardian.com/technology/2002/mar/13/internetnews.

Leppert, Richard and Susan McClary, eds. *Music and Society: The Politics of Composition, Performance and Reception*. Cambridge: Cambridge University Press, 1987.

LeRoy, Dan. *Paul's Boutique*. London and New York: Continuum, 2006.

Les Paul Foundation. "Sound on Sound." Accessed May 8, 2018. http://www.les-paul.com/timeline/sound-on-sound/

Lessig, Lawrence. *Free Culture*. New York: Penguin, 2004.

Library of Congress. "2011 National Film Registry – More than a Box of Chocolates." Accessed May 21, 2018. https://www.loc.gov/item/prn-11-240/.

Lievrouw, Leah A. *Alternative and Activist New Media*. Cambridge: Polity, 2011.

Lim, Fredrich N. "Grey Tuesday Leads to Blue Monday?: Digital Sampling of Sound Recordings After The Grey Album." *Journal of Law, Technology and Policy* (2004): 369–80.

Lind, Stephanie. "Active Interfaces and Thematic Events in the Legend of Zelda: Ocarina of Time." In *Music Video Games: Performance, Politics and Play*, edited by Mark Austin, 83–106. New York and London: Bloomsbury, 2016.

Lloyd, Christian and Shara Rambarran. "'Brand New You're Retro': Tricky as Engpop Dissident." In *Mad Dogs and Englishness: Popular Music and English Identities*, edited by Lee Brooks, Mark Donnelly, and Richard Mills, 162–73. London: Bloomsbury, 2017.

Long, Tony. "YouTube and Your 15 Minutes of Fame." *Wired*, February 15, 2011. https://www.wired.com/2011/02/0215youtube-launched/.

Louvre, Alf and Jeffrey Walsh, eds. *Tell Me Lies About Vietnam*. Milton Keynes: Open University Press, 1988.

Lull, James, ed. *Popular Music and Communication*. Newbury Park, CA: Sage, 1992.

Lyotard, Jean-François. *The Postmodern Condition: A Report on Knowledge*. Translated by Geoff Bennington and Brian Massumi. Manchester: Manchester University Press, 1986.

Lysaker, John T. *Brian Eno's Ambient 1: Music for Airports*. New York: Oxford University Press, 2018.

M. H. "A Funny Business: The Relationship Between Musicians, Master Recordings and Record Labels." *The Economist*, July 8, 2019. https://www.economist.com/prospero/2019/07/08/the-relationship-between-musicians-master-recordings-and-record-labels.

MacDonald, John S. W. "Suzanne Vega Is the 'Mother of the MP3.'" *The Observer*, September 25, 2008. https://observer.com/2008/09/suzanne-vega-is-the-mother-of-the-mp3/.

MacNevin, Bob. "DAT as Storage Medium." *Computer Music Journal*, 20, no. 4 (Winter 1996): 5–6.

Madvillain. *Madvillainy*. Recorded 2004. Stone Throw Records STH2065. 2004. LP.

Malandro, Bri. "'One In Four Cowboys Are Black.' The YeeHaw Agenda's Founder on the Politics of Cowboy Style." *The Guardian*, February 21, 2020. https://www.theguardian.com/fashion/2020/feb/21/one-in-four-cowboys-were-black-the-yee-haw-agendas-founder-on-the-politics-of-cowboy-style.

Manghani, Sunil. "The Pleasures of (Music) Video." In *Music/Video: Histories, Aesthetics, Media*, edited by Gina Arnold, Daniel Cookney, Kirsty Fairclough, and Michael Goddard, 22–40. New York: Bloomsbury, 2017.

Mantie, Roger and Gareth Dylan Smith, eds. *The Oxford Handbook of Music Making and Leisure*. New York: Oxford University Press, 2017.

Markman, Kris M. "Everything Old Is New Again: Podcasting as Radio's Revival." *Journal of Radio and Audio Media*, 22, no. 2 (2015): 240–3.

Marshall, Lee. "'Let's Keep Music Special. F__K Spotify: On-Demand Streaming and Controversy over Artist Royalties." *Creative Industries Journal*, 8 (2015): 177–89.

Marshall, P. David, ed. *The Celebrity Culture Reader*. London: Routledge, 2006.

Mason, Andrew. "Madlib in Scratch Magazine." *Stones Throw*, May 8, 2005. https://www.stonesthrow.com/news/mad-skills/.

Massumi, Brian, *Parables for the Virtual: Movement, Affect, Sensation*, 21. Durham and London: Duke University Press, 2002.

Maxwell, Peter. "Line Boil on the Road to Hell." *Eye: The International Review of Graphic Design,* 24, no. 96 (Summer 2018): 101.

McAlpine, Kenneth B. *Bits and Pieces: A History of Chiptunes*. Oxford: Oxford University Press, 2018.

McGowan, Anthony. "Names and Terms." In *The Routledge Companion to Postmodernism*, edited by Stuart Sim, 244–5. London: Routledge, 2005.

McGowan, David. "*Cuphead*: Animation, the Public Domain, and Home Video Remediation." *J Pop*, 52 (February 2019): 10–34.

McGregor, Jock. "Madonna: Icon of Postmodernity." *Facing the Challenge* (1997). https://www.facingthechallenge.org/madonna.php.

McLean, Craig. "Caught in a Flash." *The Observer*, December 9, 2007. https://www.theguardian.com/music/2007/dec/09/popandrock.radiohead3.

McLeod, Kembrew. "How Copyright Law Changed Hip-Hop: An Interview with Public Enemy's Chuck D and Hank Shocklee." *Stay Free* (2002). http://www.ibiblio.org/pub/electronic-publications/stay-free/achieves/20/public_enemy.html

McLeod, Kembrew. "Confessions of an Intellectual (Property): Danger Mouse, Mickey Mouse, Sonny Bono, and My Long and Winding Path as a Copyright Activist-Academic." *Journal of Popular Music and Society*, 28, no. 1 (2005): 79–93.

McLeod, Kembrew. *Freedom of Expression: Resistance and Repression in the Age of Intellectual Property*. Minneapolis: University of Minnesota Press, 2007.

McLeod, Kembrew and Peter DiCola. *Creative License: The Law and Culture of Digital Sampling*. Durham, NC: Duke University Press, 2011.

McLuhan, Marshall. *Understanding the Media: The Extensions of Man*. New York: McGraw Hill Education, 1964.

Metz, Cade. "Larry Roberts Calls Himself the Founder of the Internet. Who Are You to Argue?" *Wired*, September 24, 2012. https://www.wired.com/2012/09/larry-roberts/.

Middleton, Richard and John Muncie. *Pop Culture, Pop Music, and Post-War Youth: Counter-Cultures*. Milton Keynes: Open University Press, 1981.

Miller, Paul D., ed. *Sound Unbound: Digital Sampling, Digital Music and Culture*. Cambridge, MA and London: MIT Press.

Miller, Kiri. *Playing Along*. Oxford and New York: Oxford University Press, 2012.

Miller, Kiri. "Virtual and Visceral Experience in Music-Oriented Video Game." In *The Oxford Handbook of Sound and Image in Digital Media*, edited by Carol Vernallis, Amy Herzog, and John Richardson, 517–33. New York: Oxford University Press, 2013.

Milner, Greg. *Perfecting Sound Forever: The Story of Recorded Music*. London: Granta, 2009.

Molesworth, Mike and Janice Denegri-Knott, eds. *Digital Virtual Consumption*. New York: Routledge, 2012.

Montgomery, James. "Wu-Tang Clan's First-Ever Cleared Beatles Sample Claim Is Incorrect." *Music Television*, October 3, 2007. http://www.mtv.com/news/articles/1571114/20071003/wu_tang_clan.jhtml.

Moore, Allan F. *Rock: The Primary Text – Developing a Musicology of Rock*. Oxon: Ashgate, 2001.

Moore, Allan F. "Authenticity as Authentication." *Popular Music*, 21, no. 2 (May 2002): 209–23.

Moore, Christopher. "2004 (Bowie vs Mashup)." In *Enchanting David Bowie*: *Space/Time/Body/Memory,* edited by Tolja Cinque, Christopher Moore, and Sean Redmond, 153–68. New York: Bloomsbury, 2015.

Mori, Masahiro. "The Uncanny Valley." *Energy*, 7 no. 4 (1970): 33–5.

Morley, Paul. *Words and Music: A History of Pop in the Shape of a City*. London: Bloomsbury, 2004.

Mumma, Gordon, Howard Rye, Bernard Kernfield, and Chris Sheridan. "Recording." Grove Music Online, 2003, https://doi.org/10.1093/gmo/9781561 592630.article.J371600

Murray-West, Rosie. "From 1876 to Today: How the UK Got Connected." *The Telegraph*, October 28, 2016. https://www.telegraph.co.uk/technology/connec ting-britain/timeline-how-uk-got-connected.

Nahon, Karine and Jeff Hemsley. *Going Viral*. Cambridge: Polity, 2013.

Navas, Eduardo. *Remix Theory*. Springer: Vienna, 2012.

Needleman, Sarah E. and Anne Steele, "Fortnite – Marshmello Mashup Showcases New Avenues for Games, Music." *The Wall Street Journal*, February 9, 2019. https://www.wsj.com/articles/a-glimpse-of-fortnites-future-music-and-dancin g-without-the-guns-11549720800.

Negus, Keith. *Producing Pop: Culture and Conflict in the Popular Music Industry*. London: Edward Arnold, 1992.

Nicholls, David. "Virtual Opera or Opera between the Ears." *Journal of the Royal Musical Association*, 129, no. 1 (2004): 100–142.

Nicholls, David. *John Cage*. Champaign, IL: University of Illinois, 2007.

Nielinger-Vakil, Carola. *Luigi Nono: A Composer in Context*. Cambridge: Cambridge University Press, 2015.

Noll, A. Michael. *Principles of Modern Communications Technology*. Boston and London: Artech House, 2001.

Nowak, Raphaël and Andrew Whelan. *Networked Music Cultures: Contemporary Approaches, Emerging Issues*. Hampshire and New York: Palgrave Macmillan, 2016.

O'Brien, Benjamin. "Sample Sharing: Virtual Laptop Ensemble Communities." In *The Oxford Handbook of Music and Virtuality*, edited by Sheila Whiteley and Shara Rambarran, 377–91. New York: Oxford University Press, 2016.

O'Connor, Brian. "M.A.S.H I.T U.P." *DJ Times Magazine* [online], August 17, 2004. http://www.djtimes.com/issues/2004/08/_features_index_08_2004.htm.

O'Donnell, Kevin. *Postmodernism*. Oxford: Lion Publishing, 2003.

O'Gorman, Daniel and Robert Eaglestone, eds. *The Routledge Companion to Twenty-First Century Literary Fiction*. Oxon: Routledge, 2019.

O'Malley Greenburg, Zack. "Forbes 30 Under 30: Cover Story: How Marshmello Became A $44 Million DJ." *Forbes*, November 7, 2018. https://www.forbes.c om/sites/zackomalleygreenburg/2018/11/07/forbes-30-under-30-cover-story-how -marshmello-became-a-44-million-dj/#6d5cb046618b.

Oliver, Rowan. "Bring the Beat Back: Sampling as Virtual Collaboration." In *The Oxford Handbook of Music and Virtuality*, edited by Sheila Whiteley and Shara Rambarran, 65–80. New York: Oxford University Press, 2016.

Ord-Hume, Arthur W. J. G. "Player Piano." Grove Music Online, November 2001. https://doi.org/10.1093/gmo/9781561592630.article.21928.

Osborne, Richard. *Vinyl: Analogue Record*. Farnham: Ashgate, 2012.

Partridge, Christopher. *Dub in Babylon: Understanding the Evolution and Significance of Dub Reggae in Jamaica and Britain*. London: Equinox Publishing, 2010.

Partridge, Christopher and Marcus Morberg, eds. *Bloomsbury Handbook for Religion and Popular Music*. London: Bloomsbury, 2017.

Patel Joseph. "Online Grey Tuesday Group Says 100,000 Downloaded Jay-Z/
    Beatles Mix." *Music Television*, April 3, 2004. http://www.mtv.com/news/articl
    es/1485593/20040305/story.jhtml
Paterson, Justin, Rob Toulson, and Russ Hepworth-Sawyer, "User-Influenced/
    Machine-Controlled Playback: The variPlay Music App Format for Interactive
    Recorded Music." *Arts*, 8, no. 3 (2019): 112.
Patterson, Thomas W. "Player Piano." *Oxford Handbooks Online*, November
    2014. https://doi.org/10.1093/oxfordhb/9780199935321.013.16.
Pattie, David. "Taking the Studio by Strategy." In *Brian Eno: Oblique Music*, edited
    Sean Albiez and David Pattie, 49–68. London: Bloomsbury, 2016.
Peirce, Charles S. "Virtual." In *Dictionary of Philosophy and Psychology*, edited by
    James Mark Baldwin, 763. New York: Macmillan, 1902.
Perone, James E. *The Words and Music of David Bowie*. Westport, CT: Praeger
    Publishers, 2007.
Peterson, Richard A. "Why 1955? Explaining the Advent of Rock Music." *Popular
    Music*, 9, no. 1 (January 1990): 97–116.
Peterson, Richard A. and Andy Bennett. "Introducing Music Scenes." In *Music
    Scenes: Local, Translocal, and Virtual*, edited by Richard A. Peterson and Andy
    Bennett, 1–15. Nashville: Vanderbilt University Press, 2004.
Pinch, Trevor and Karin Bijsterveld, eds. *The Oxford Handbook of Sound Studies*.
    New York: Oxford University Press, 2014.
Pirari, Elio. "Alessandro Alessandroni." *La Stampa*, July 9, 2007. http://acrhivio
    .lastampa.it/LaStampaArchivio/main/History/tmpl_viewObj.jsp?objid+7826191.
Poster, Mark. *The Mode of Information: Poststructuralism and Social Context*.
    Chicago: University of Chicago, 1990.
Prey, Robert. "Nothing Personal: Algorithmic Individuation on Music Streaming
    Platforms." *Media, Culture and Society*, 40, no. 7 (2018): 1086–100.
Prior, Nick. *Popular Music, Digital Technology and Society*. London: Sage, 2018.
Quantick, David. *Revolution: The Making of the Beatles' White Album*. London:
    Unanimous Ltd., 2002.
Rabinovitz, Lauren and Abraham Geil, eds. *Memory Bytes: History, Technology,
    and Digital Culture*. Durham, NC: Duke University Press, 2004.
Raby, Peter, ed. *The Cambridge Companion to Oscar Wilde*. Cambridge:
    Cambridge University Press, 1997.
Radio 1 and 1Xtra Stories. "The Beatles and Black Music." Presented by DJ
    Semtex. Aired February 28, 2011.
Rambarran, Shara. "Reality vs Hyperreality: Feel Good with the Gorillaz and
    Reject False Icons." Paper presented at Engaging Baudrillard: International
    Conference, University of Swansea, UK, September 5–7, 2006.
Rambarran, Shara. "'99 Problems' but Danger Mouse Ain't One: The Creative
    and Legal Difficulties of Brian Burton, 'Author' of the Grey Album." *Popular
    Musicology Online*. 2013. http://www.popular-musicology-online.com/issues/03
    /rambarran.html.
Rambarran, Shara. "'You've Got No Time for Me': Martin 'Sugar' Merchant,
    British Caribbean Musical Identity and the Media.'" In *Reggae from Yaad:
    Traditional and Emerging Themes in Jamaican Popular Music*, edited by Donna
    P. Hope, 64–82. Kingston, Jamaica: Ian Randle Publishers, 2015.

Rambarran, Shara. "99 Problems but Danger Mouse IS One: The Evolution of the Music Producer Brian Burton." Paper presented at The 10th Art of Record Production Conference, Drexel University, Philadelphia, USA, November 6–8, 2015. www.artofrecordproduction.com.

Rambarran, Shara. "'Feel Good' with Gorillaz and 'Reject False Icons': The Fantasy Worlds of the Virtual Group and Their Creators." In *The Oxford Handbook of Music and Virtuality*, edited by Sheila Whiteley and Shara Rambarran, 148–65. New York: Oxford University Press, 2016.

Rambarran, Shara. "'DJ Hit That Button': Amateur Laptop Musicians in Contemporary Music and Society." In *The Oxford Handbook of Music Making and Leisure*, edited by Roger Mantie and Gareth Dylan Smith, 585–600. New York: Oxford University Press, 2017.

Rambarran, Shara. "'Very' British: A Pop Musicological Approach to the Pet Shop Boys' 'Always on My Mind.'" In *Popular Musicology and Identity: Essays in Honor of Stan Hawkins*, edited by Eirik Askerøi, Kai Arne Hansen, and Freya Jarman, 148–59. New York: Routledge, 2020.

Rambarran, Shara. "'The Time Has Come, Exodus!': Congo Natty and the Jungle (R)evolution." In *Beatified Beats: Exploring the Spiritual in Popular Music*, edited by Mike Dines and Georgina Gregory. London: Bloomsbury, forthcoming.

Rambarran, Sharadai. "Innovations in Contemporary Popular Music and Digital Media, and Reconstructions of the Music Industry in the 21st Century." PhD diss., University of Salford, 2011.

Reynolds, Simon. "Versus: The Science of Remixology." *Pulse!* May, 1996.

Reynolds, Simon. "Krautrock. Kosmik Dance: Krautrock and Its Legacy." In *Modulations, A History of Electronic Music: Throbbing Words on Sound*, edited by Peter Shapiro, 24–37. New York, Caipirinha Productions, 2000.

Reynolds, Simon. *Retromania*: *Pop Culture*'s *Addiction to Its Own Past*. London: Faber and Faber, 2011.

Reynolds, Simon. *Shock and Awe: Glam Rock and Its Legacy*. London: Faber and Faber, 2016.

Rheingold, Howard. *Virtual Reality*. New York: Simon and Schuster, 1991.

Richardson, John. *An Eye for Music: Popular Music and the Audiovisual Surreal*. New York: Oxford University Press, 2012.

Richardson, John, Claudia Gorban, and Carol Vernallis, eds. *The Oxford Handbook of New Audiovisual Aesthetics*. New York: Oxford University Press, 2013.

Rietveld, Hillegonda C. *This Is Our House: House Music, Cultural Spaces, and Technologies*. London and New York: Routledge, 1998.

Rietveld, Hillegonda C. "The Residual Soul Sonic Force of the 12" Vinyl Dance Single." In *Residual Media*, edited by Charles R. Acland, 97–114. Minneapolis: University of Minnesota Press, 2007.

Rietveld, Hillegonda C. and Marco Benoît Carbone. "Introduction: Towards a Polyphonic Approach to Game and Music Studies." *Game: The Italian Journal of Game Studies*, 6 (2017): 5–12.

Rogers, Jude. "Total Rewind: 10 Key Moments in the Life of the Cassette." *The Guardian*, August 30, 2013. https://www.theguardian.com/music/2013/aug/30/cassette-store-day-music-tapes.

Royster, Francesca T. *Sounding Like a No-No: Queer Sounds and Eccentric Acts in the Post-Soul Era*. Ann Arbor: The University of Michigan Press, 2013.

Russell, Jeff. *The Beatles Album File and Complete Discography 1961–1982*. Dorset: Blandford Press, 1982.

Sanden, Paul. *Liveness in Modern Music: Musicians, Technology, and the Perception of Performance*. New York: Routledge, 2013.

Sanjek, David. "'Don't Have to DJ No More': Sampling and the 'Autonomous' Creator." *Cardozo Arts and Entertainment Law Journal*, 10 (1992): 607–24.

Santos, Natalia. "Chris Levine – Vulture Hound Interview." *Vulture Hound*, September 20, 2016. https://vulturehound.co.uk/2016/09/chris-levine-vulture-hound-interview/.

Satia, Priya. "War, Wireless, and Empire: Marconi and the British Warfare State, 1896–1903." *Technology and Culture*, 51, no. 4 (October 2010): 829–53.

Sawyer, Miranda. "State of Grace." *The Guardian*, October 11, 2008. https://www.theguardian.com/music/2008/oct/12/grace-jones-hurricane.

Schaeffer, Pierre. *La Musique Concrète*. Paris: Presses Universitaires de France, 1967.

Schaeffer, Pierre. *In Search of a Concrete Music*. Translated by Christine North and John Dack. Berkeley: University of Califonria Press, 2012.

Schloss, Joseph G. *Making Beats: The Art of Sample-Based Hip-Hop*. Middletown, CT: Wesleyan University Press, 2004.

Schroeder, Jonathan and Janet Borgerson. "How Stereo Was First Sold to a Skeptical Public." *The Conversation*, December 12, 2018. http://theconversation.com/how-stereo-was-first-sold-to-a-skeptical-public-103668

Scott, Derek B. "(What's the Copy?) The Beatles and Oasis." Beatlestudies 3: Proceedings of the Beatles 2000 Conference, 201–11. University of Jyväasklä, Finland.

Scott, Derek B. *Sounds of the Metropolis: The 19th Century Popular Music Revolution in London, New York, Paris, and Vienna*. New York: Oxford University Press, 2008.

Scott, Derek B. *The Ashgate Research Companion to Popular Musicology*. Hampshire: Ashgate, 2009.

Scott, Derek B. "Postmodernism and Music." In *The Routledge Companion to Postmodernism*, edited by Stuart Sim, 3rd ed., 182–93. London: Routledge, 2011.

Scratch. Directed by Doug Pray. Palm, 2001, DVD.

Second Life. "What Is Second Life?" Accessed March 16, 2018. http://secondlife.com/whatis/?lang=en-US.

Sexton, Jamie, ed. *Music, Sound and Multimedia: From the Live to the Virtual*. Edinburgh: Edinburgh University Press, 2007.

Shakhovskoy, Jonathan and Rob Toulson. "Future Music Formats: Evaluating the 'Album App.'" *Journal on the Art of Record Production*, 10 (July 2015). https://www.arpjournal.com/asarpwp/future-music-formats-evaluating-the-album-app/.

Shapiro, Peter, ed. *Modulations, A History of Electronic Music: Throbbing Words on Sound*. New York: Caipirinha Productions, 2000.

Shapiro, Peter. "Deck Wreckers, the Turntable as Instrument." In *Undercurrents: the Hidden Wiring of Modern Music*, edited by Rob Young, 163–76. London: Continuum, 2002.

Shaviro, Steven. *Post-Cinematic Effect*. Winchester, UK, and Washington, USA: O Books.

Shepherd, John. *Music as Social Text*. Cambridge: Polity, 1991.

Shields, Rob, ed. *Culture of the Internet: Virtual Spaces, Real History, Living Bodies*. Sage: London, 1996.

Shields, Rob. *The Virtual*. London: Routledge, 2003.

Sim, Stuart, ed. *The Routledge Companion to Postmodernism*. London: Routledge, 2005.

Sim, Stuart. *The Routledge Companion to Postmodernism*. 3rd ed. London: Routledge, 2011.

Sito, Tom. *Moving Innovation: A History of Computer Animation*. Cambridge, MA: The MIT Press, 2013.

Small, Christopher. *Musicking: The Meanings of Performing and Listening*. Middletown, CT: Wesleyan University Press, 1998.

Smith, Ethan. "Music Sales Decline for Seventh Time in Eight Years: Digital Downloads Can't Offset 20% Plunge in CD Sales." *Wall Street Journal*, January 2, 2009. https://www.wsj.com/articles/SB123075988836646491.

Sone, Yuji. *Japanese Robot Culture: Performance, Imagination, and Modernity*. New York: Palgrave Macmillan, 2017.

Spanos, Brittany. "How Lil Nas X and 'Old Town Road' Defy Categorization." *Smithsonian Magazine*, December 2019. https://www.smithsonianmag.com/arts -culture/lil-nas-x-old-town-road-american-ingenuity-180973492/.

Stahl, Matt. "The Synthespian'ss Animated Prehistory: The Monkees, the Archies, Don Kirshner, and the Politics of 'Virtual Labor.'" *Television and New Media*, 12, no. 1 (2010): 3–22.

Stanyek, Jason and Benjamin Piekut. "'Deadness' Technologies of the Intermundane." *TDR: The Drama Review*, 54, no. 1 (Spring 2010): 14–38.

Stavropoulos, Laura. "Massive Attack's App Lets Fans Remix Their Album 'Mezzanine.'" *U Discover Music*, December 7, 2018. https://www.udiscovermusic.com/news/massive-attacks-app-lets-fans-remix-their-album/.

Sterne, Jonathan. *The Audible Past: Cultural Origins of Sound Production*. Durham, NC: Duke University, 2003.

Straw, Will. "Dance Music." In *Cambridge Companion to Pop and Rock*, edited by Simon Frith, Will Straw, and John Street, 158–75. Cambridge: Cambridge University Press, 2001.

Storey, John. "Rockin' Hegemony: West Coast Rock and Amerika's War in Vietnam." In *Tell Me Lies About Vietnam*, edited by Alf Louvre and Jeffrey Walsh, 181–97. Milton Keynes: Open University Press, 1988.

Strinati, Dominic. *An Introduction to the Theories of Popular Culture*. London and New York: Routledge, 2004.

Stromer-Galley, Jennifer and Rosa Mikeal Martey. "Visual Spaces, Norm Governed Places: The Influence of Spatial Context Online." *New Media and Society*, 11, no. 6 (2009): 1041–60.

Summers, Tim. *Understanding Video Game Music*. Cambridge: Cambridge University Press, 2016.

Sutherland, Ivan. "Sketchpad: A Man-Machine Graphical Communication System." *AFIPS* Conference *Proceedings*, 28. Washington, DC: Thompson Book Co., 1963.

Tagg, Philip and Bob Clarida. *Ten Little Title Tunes: Towards a Musicology of the Mass Media*. New York and Montreal: The Mass Media Music Scholar Press, 2003.

Talbot, Michael, ed. *The Musical Work: Reality or Invention?* Liverpool: University of Liverpool, 2000.

Taylor, Timothy D. *Strange Sounds: Music, Technology and Culture*. New York and London: Routledge, 2001.

Thall, Peter M. *What They'll Never Tell You About the Music Business: The Myths, the Secrets, the Lies (and a Few Truths)*. New York: Billboard Books, 2006

Théberge, Paul. *Any Sound You Can Imagine: Making Music/Consuming Technology*. Hanover: Wesleyan University Press, 1997.

Théberge, Paul. "'Plugged In': Technology and Popular Music." In *Cambridge Companion to Pop and Rock*, edited by Simon Frith, Will Straw, and John Street, 3–25. Cambridge: Cambridge University Press, 2001.

Théberge, Paul. "The Network Studio: Historical and Technological Paths to a New Ideal in Music Making." *Social Studies of Science*, 34, no. 5 (October 2004): 759–81.

Thibaud, Jean-Paul. "The Sound Composition of the City." In *The Auditory Culture Reader*, edited by Michael Bull and Les Back, 329–42. New York: Berg, 2003.

Thompson, Bill. "The Rootkit of All Evil?" *BBC News*, November 4, 2005. http://news.bbc.co.uk/go/pr/fr/-/1/hi/technology/4406178.stm.

Till, Rupert. "Ambient Music." In *Bloomsbury Handbook for Religion and Popular Music*, edited by Christopher Partridge and Marcus Morberg, 27–37. London: Bloomsbury, 2017.

Toop, David. "Dub." *Mixmag*, 2, no. 19 (December 1992): 32–6.

Tough, David. "Virtual Bands: Recording Music under the Big Top." In *The Oxford Handbook of Music and Virtuality*, edited by Sheila Whiteley and Shara Rambarran, 306–34. New York: Oxford University Press, 2016.

Traub, David. "Art and Telecommunications Glossary." *Leonardo*, 24, no. 2 (1991): 253–8.

Trenholm, Richard. "Britain's First Mobile-Phone Call Was Made 30 Years Ago." *CNET*, December 27, 2014. https://www.cnet.com/news/britains-first-mobile-phone-call-was-made-30-years-ago/.

Tubby, King. *Father of Dub*. Delta. LC 3843. 2005. CD

United Press. "EMI Halts Beatles Remix Album." *United Press International*, February 16, 2004. http://web.lexis-nexis.com/executive/.

Vaidhyanathan, Siva. *Copyrights and Copywrongs: The Rise of Intellectual Property and How It Threatens Creativity*. New York: New York University Press, 2003.

Van den Bulck, Hilde and Anders Olof Larsson. "'There's a Starman Waiting in the Sky': Mourning David #Bowie on Twitter." *Convergence: The International Journal of Research into New Media Technologies*, 25, no. 2 (2019): 307–23.

Veal, Michael E. *Dub: Soundscapes and Shattered Songs in Jamaican Reggae*. Middletown: Wesleyan University Press, 2007.

Vernallis, Carol. *Experiencing Music Video: Aesthetics and Cultural Context*. New York: Columbia University Press, 2004.

Vernallis, Carol. *Unruly Media: YouTube, Music Video, and the New Digital Cinema*. Oxford: Oxford University Press, 2013.

Virilio, Paul. "Cyberwar, God and Television: Interview with Paul Virilio."
Interview by Louise Wilson, *CTHEORY*, December 1, 1994. Transcript. http://
www.ctheory.net.

Vorzick-Levinson, Simon. "Damon Albarn Is Living in the Now." *Rolling Stone*,
September 25, 2018. https://www.rollingstone.com/music/music-features/damon
-albarn-gorillaz-blur-tour-interview-727984/.

Warhol, Andy and André Leon Talley. "New Again." *The Interview*, 22 (October
1984): 54–61.

Warner, Timothy. *Pop Music – Technology and Creativity: Trevor Horn and the
Digital Revolution*. Aldershot: Ashgate, 2003.

Warner, Timothy. "The Song of the Hydra: Multiple Lead Vocals in Modern Pop
Recordings." In *Art of Record Production Conference Proceedings*. University
of Westmnster, London, 2005. http://www.artofrecordproduction.com/aorpjoom
/arp-conferences/arp-archive-conference-papers/17-arp-2005/82-warner-2005.

Webster, Andrew. "Chipzel Has Spent a Decade Making Incredible Music with
Gameboys." *The Verge*, April 2019. https://www.theverge.com/2019/4/19/18484
887/chipzel-game-boy-music-chiptune-interview.

Welch, Christopher. *David Bowie*. London: Carlton, 2018.

Werman, Marco. "Danger Mouse's 'Rome' Spaghetti Western." *Public Radio
International*, May 13, 2011. http:// www.pri.org/stories/2011-05-13/danger-mo
uses-rome-spaghetti-western.

"While My Guitar Gently Bleeps." Produced by Ben Cordrey. Aired March 25,
2017 on BBC Radio 4.

White, Paul. *Basic Sampling*. London: Sanctuary Publishing, 2003.

Whiteley, Sheila. "Progressive Rock and Psychedelic Coding in the Work of Jimi
Hendrix." *Popular Music*, 9 (1990): 37 –60.

Whiteley, Sheila. *The Space Between The Notes*. London: Routledge, 1992.

Whiteley, Sheila. *Women and Popular Music: Sexuality, Identity and Subjectivity*.
London and New York: Routledge, 2000.

Whiteley, Sheila. "Introduction." In *Music, Place and Space: Popular Music and
Cultural Identity*, edited by Sheila Whiteley, Andy Bennett, and Stan Hawkins,
1–24. Farnham: Ashgate, 2004.

Whiteley, Sheila. *The Oxford Handbook of Music and Virtuality*. New York:
Oxford University Press, 2016.

Whiteley, Sheila, Andy Bennett, and Stan Hawkins, ed. *Music, Place and Space:
Popular Music and Cultural Identity*. Farnham: Ashgate, 2004.

Wikstrom, Patrik. *The Music Industry: Music in the Cloud*. Cambridge: Polity
Press, 2009.

Wikström, Patrik and Robert DeFilippi, eds. *Business Innovation and Disruption in
the Music Industry*. Cheltenham: Elgar, 2016.

Wilentz, Sean. "The Birth of 33 1/3: How Columbia Records Won the Battle of
the Speeds." *Slate*, November 2, 2012. http://www.slate.com/articles/arts/books
/2012/11/birth_of_the_long_playing_record_plus_rare_photos_from_the_he
yday_of_columbia.html.

Williams, Justin A. and Ross Wilson's "Music and Crowdfunded Websites: Digital
Patronage and Artist-Fan Interactivity." In *The Oxford Handbook of Music
and Virtuality*, edited by Sheila Whiteley and Shara Rambarran, 593–612. New
York: Oxford University Press, 2016.

Wiseman-Trowse, Nathan. *Performing Class in British Popular Music*. Hampshire: Palgrave Macmillan, 2008.

Wolfson, Sam. "Madame X: Madonna's New Album Is Both Anonymous and Well-Trodden." *The Guardian*, April 15, 2019. https://www.theguardian.com/music/2019/apr/15/madame-x-madonna-new-album-alter-ego.

Wolmack, Jenny, ed. *Cybersexualities: A Reader on Feminist Theory, Cyborgs and Cyberspace*. Edinburgh: Edinburgh University Press, 1999.

Wonderland, "Virtual Adultery and Cyberspace Love." Produced by Fergus O'Brien. Aired January 30, 2008, on BBC Two.

Worby, Robert. "Stockhausen's Gesang de Jünglinge." BBC, October 17, 2013. https://www.bbc.co.uk/blogs/radio3/entries/9ddca641-f42b-3298-a657-57809377e0a5.

Yotka, Steff. "Go Viral, Post #Spon, Get #Canceled: How Social Media Transformed Fashion in the 2010s." *Vogue*, July 18, 2019. https://www.vogue.com/article/2010s-fashion-social-media-impact.

Youde, Kate. "Broadband: The First Decade." *The Independent*, March 28, 2010. https://www.independent.co.uk/life-style/gadgets-and-tech/news/broadband-the-first-decade-1929515.html.

Young, Rob, ed. *Undercurrents: the Hidden Wiring of Modern Music*. London: Continuum, 2002.

Zaborowski, Rafal. "Hatsune Miku and Japanese Virtual Idols." In *The Oxford Handbook of Music and Virtuality*, edited by Sheila Whiteley and Shara Rambarran, 111–28. New York: Oxford University Press, 2016.

Zagorski-Thomas, Simon. *The Musicology of Record Production*. Cambridge: Cambridge University Press, 2014.

Zak, Albin J. *The Poetics of Rock: Cutting Tracks, Making Records*. Berkeley: University of California Press, 2001.

Zurbrugg, Nicholas, ed. *Jean Baudrillard: Art and Artefact*. London: Sage, 1997.

INDEX